THEOLOGICAL
WORLDS

THEOLOGICAL WORLDS

W. PAUL JONES

Understanding the
Alternative Rhythms
of Christian Belief

Abingdon Press
Nashville

THEOLOGICAL WORLDS:
UNDERSTANDING THE ALTERNATIVE
RHYTHMS OF CHRISTIAN BELIEF

This book is printed on acid-free paper.

Library of Congress Cataloging-in-Publication Data

JONES, W. PAUL.
    Theological worlds: understanding the alternative rhythms of
Christian belief/W. Paul Jones.
    p.   cm.
    Bibliography: p.

ISBN 0-687-41470-9

    1. Theology—Methodology. I. Title.
    BR118.J63   1989   89-35389
    230'.01—dc20   CIP

Most Scripture quotations are from the Revised Standard Version of
the Bible, copyright 1946, 1952, 1971 by the Division of Christian
Education of the National Council of Churches of Christ in the USA.
Used by permission.
    Those noted KJV are from the King James Version of the Bible.

Lines on p. 104 from *Ani Maamin: A Song Lost and Found Again* by Elie
Wiesel, trans. Marion Wiesel, are Copyright © 1973 by Random
House, Inc. Used by permission of the publisher.
    Excerpt from "Immortal Autumn," p. 107, is from *New and
Collected Poems 1917-1982* by Archibald MacLeish. Copyright © 1985
by The Estate of Archibald MacLeish. Reprinted by permission of
Houghton Mifflin Co.
    "Epistle to Jose Coronel Urtecho," p. 192, is from Ernesto
Cardenal, *Zero Hour and Other Documentary Poems*. Copyright © 1980
by Ernesto Cardenal and Paul W. Borgeson, Jr. Reprinted by
permission of New Directions Publishing Corp.
    Quotations from Dietrich Bonhoeffer, *Letters and Papers from
Prison*, revised, enlarged edition, are Copyright © 1971 by SCM
Press, Ltd. Reprinted by permission of Macmillan Publishing Co.
and SCM Press.
    Excerpts on pp. 178-80 are from *Mass:* a theatre piece for singers,
players and dancers, text from the liturgy of the Roman mass;
additional texts by Stephen Schwartz and Leonard Bernstein. ©
Copyright 1971, 1972 by Leonard Bernstein and Stephen Schwartz.
Jalni Publications, Inc., Publisher. Boosey & Hawkes, Inc., Sole
Agent. Used by permission.

MANUFACTURED IN THE UNITED STATES OF AMERICA

To
Saint Paul School of Theology
and
Assumption Abbey

. . .

the two homes of my pilgrimage

We spend our years
as a tale that is told.
—*Psalm 90:9 KJV*

If you want to know a people
you must learn the songs they sing,
the stories they tell, the dreams they dream.
This is true of any people.
—Matthew Kelty,
Sermons in a Monastery

The Christian message is a proclamation
that strikes the ear of the world
with the force of a hint.
—Carl Michalson,
The Witness of Radical Faith

Yet to have:
—the soul of a Merton
—the fidelity of a Barth
—the tenacity of a Marx
—the compassion of a Claire
—the passion of a Zorba
—the ecstasy of a Teresa
—the vision of a King
—and the conscience-strickenness
of a Che . . .

CONTENTS

Chapter Three: *Anatomy of the Theological Answer—*
An Exercise in Epiphania

Chapter Four: *Anatomy of the Theological Dialectic—*
Atonement as Christology..................... 185

Chapter Five: *A Conclusion*

ACKNOWLEDGMENTS

This book reflects my teaching and research within the unique environment of Saint Paul School of Theology. Having previously taught at Yale and Princeton, I am convinced of the significance of the type of education we have created here. Its holistic understanding of formation, the action/reflection methodology concerned with praxis, the rigors of interdisciplinary team-teaching, and the importance of creating viable alternatives have provided the context out of which *Theological Worlds* has been created and tested. It is to this special place and to my unique colleagues here that I dedicate this volume.

Appreciation is due my students who, over the past five years, have been part of the Foundation Core in which research and experimentation have occurred regarding the approach to theologizing developed in this book. My doctoral students have provided further testing.

The Reverend Virginia Pych edited early versions and has long believed in the importance of this project. Acknowledgment goes to Robert Conn, whose interest in my writing provides rare support and a fine critical eye; and to Charles Cole, whose belief in me as a writer has been special.

I am grateful for cherished conversations with my five daughters, each of whom provides unrivaled accountability, asking in a variety of ways, "What really does a theologian do?" Attempts at answers have given shape to this book—in a subway at Washington, D. C.; on the northern face of Mount Sopris; in a sailboat at Pomme de Terre; at the birth of a grandson; and on a very special Christmas Eve.

Other faces include those of H. Richard Niebuhr and Reinhold Niebuhr, both of whom left their special marks on my thinking—one as teacher, the other as colleague. I am appreciative of dialogues with Peggy Rounseville in early English literature, with Cathy Burnett in sociology, and with Richard Shaull in liberation theology. My excitement with the church is fed by exchanges with Kathy Nickerson, Janice Granna, Susan Ruach, and Richard Burns.

There is also L. Vann Anderson, that special friend whose life keeps intersecting with mine at the important points. And I remember Ed Kozak, whom I have not seen for forty-one years. He started much by slipping a book of poetry by William Carlos Williams into my pocket, suggesting that I read the one about rainwater and a red wheelbarrow.

I acknowledge, too, special places such as Assumption Abbey, the Trappist monastery that has adopted me, providing a second home. This includes Abbot Cyprian and Father Robert, the saintly hermit who is my spiritual director. There is my own hermitage in the Ozark hills, in which I keep coming to believe again in the sacred. Finally there is South Fork, Pennsylvania, a coal-mining town on the side of a mountain, which proves that roots go deep.

In the preparation of this manuscript, special acknowledgments go to Greg Michael, Martha Fly, Betty Clinton, and Kathy Campbell.

In thinking of this rich diversity of persons, it is clear where the idea of "Theological Worlds" arose.

W. Paul Jones
Kansas City, Missouri

CHAPTER ONE

Functional Theology and Theological Worlds

The search for Atlantis is a search for ourselves. We are restless, and thus religious, for we are never satisfied with the apparent, or tamed by the known limits. Rather, like a spider trapped in a bottle, we push at the boundaries of life and death, puzzle over strategies of good and evil, while dropping from a string hung daringly over the edges of mystery. The religious in each of us is an impulse to journey, to quest, to seek—for self-identity, belonging, legitimacy, meaning. And in the end, it is a hope worth believing that the impulse within has its counterpart in a luring that is Without.

The Present Crisis

The crisis in the church today intersects the dilemma of contemporary theology in intriguing fashion. In each mainline Protestant denomination, there is a growing chasm. Liberals, on the one hand, advocate a broad relativism of options, encouraging openness as the mark of tolerance. The result in practice, however, is often an eroding of commitment through theological indifference. The result is a Christianity that provides little more than supplemental activities and religious support for the values generally implicit in modern culture.

On the other hand, conservative sectors have been

growing in number and appeal, in part because they exhibit faith as firm commitment and costly discipleship, providing a cultural alternative. Yet the result, in practice, is often allegiance to a historically conditioned dogmatism that fails to engage the majority of persons involved in the central sectors of contemporary life.

This convergence brings into crisis the function and nature of the church. We need the contributions of both factions, without their liabilities. The church of the future must be committed to a pluralism of alternatives, sufficiently viable to touch creatively the individual and social diversity operative in modern life. Yet these must be developed and offered not in an ethos of theological indifference, but as a call to profound commitment, leading to lively choice between alternative faith-styles.

As a result, the evangelistic thrust of such a church will focus upon identifying the meaning-world by which each person's living is already being defined, often unconsciously and thus unacknowledged. The church's pastoral task follows—to nurture and render accountable these unique "worlds" which characterize us. This requires the creation of alternative communities—communities which will emerge from common overlappings. Thus the church of the future will be variegated, a confederation of subcongregations that will provide alternative Worlds as variations on the common theme called Christianity. Their presence together will encourage not only a commitment to a World of unique particularity, but to its deepening as enrichment through profound sharing. Such interaction will be organic, based no longer on the indifference of finding a least common denominator or on the destructive hostility of aggressive competition. Thus the church's present struggle for survival is bringing us to a posture that is both postconservative and postliberal.

Paralleling this ecclesiological dynamic is the crisis within contemporary theology. Throughout history, theologians have been called to defend the content of Christianity against critique. Today the conflict is as new as it is basic—the establishment of the case for interest in religion at all; the truth-claim for Christianity is secondary. Now primary is the question, What can it mean even to make religious claims? Put bluntly, is there any activity left for which the term *theology* is appropriate?

These ecclesiastical and theological crises intersect in the issue of motivation. John Wesley spoke for most Christians in his day, as well as for many who preceded him, in identifying the required motivation for entering his groups: "a desire to flee from the wrath to come." While the conservative resurgence attempts to reactivate such concern, it is a fated holding operation against modernity. Yet if such fear is no longer a widespread concern, does any viable motivation remain for vital interest in religion in general, and for Christianity in particular?

This is the fundamental crisis within contemporary theology. And it is upon the emerging answer that the future of both theology and the church rests.

Functional Theology

The serious critique which religion has undergone since at least the Enlightenment is forcing a conclusion impossible to avoid. Theology can no longer be identified by a unique content. Correlatively, theological method can no longer claim to establish the objective existence of separate religious realities, such as a God. With this undercutting of theology no longer capable of being defined conceptually, a strong impetus for understanding theology *functionally* is emerging. Theologizing is the meaning-process necessarily involved in the human fact of existing, whatever content may emerge. Put another way, religion is a special kind of fundamental trusting, by which any content may be regarded. At this level, the key word *God* is not a proper term, but a generic one. God is a functional name for the who or what on which one wagers one's lived-meaning. The content, consequently, can range the spectrum—from country to promotion, to family, to mystic Power, to the One Israel called Yahweh. Thus God as *generic* cannot be avoided. The choice is involved in assigning a *proper* name, and this is done through a pilgrimage that is deeply auto-biographical. Theologizing is the task of awakening this necessity by impulsing its dynamic into self-consciousness, and thus into accountability.

Tillich distills these conclusions to which the past centuries have brought us by insisting that human beings are uniquely characterized by the inability to exist without meaning.[1] We are freaks, for while life all around us does unquestioningly what it seems structured to do, humans cannot quiet the question, Why? Such self-consciousness brings forth deep needs—to be meaningful, to be significant, to belong. These needs are not optional but appear to be essential to human existence as such. One's self-consciousness is the capacity to reflect on this ongoing process, making one aware of being alive. The term *bastard* means to be accidental, unplanned, and thus illegitimate. It is this state cosmically that humans find intolerable. The thought of it identifies one's life as trek—a search for whatever can grant proper belonging. Such a pilgrimage expresses both our plight and our uniqueness.

Peter Berger once observed that while dogs have an instinct for being dogs, humans alone are born into an unfinished world, one they must endeavor to complete in order to be able to call themselves human. Whatever functions as one's ultimate concern in this endeavor provides the content designatable as one's God. Such an understanding makes common cause with Augustine's insistence that by nature, each person must love. The theological issue is not *if*, but *who* or *what* functions as one's ultimate love. Theologizing, then, is concerned with ordering these loves *(ordo amoris)* in terms of primacy.

The Protestant Reformation was built upon this awareness. *Salvation* means "to render the self healthy and whole." Thus Christianity is not concerned basically with knowledge, but with healing. It follows that faith is not essentially belief *(assensus)*—accepting what cannot be proved. Faith is trust *(fiducia)*—truth determined by its capacity to effect healing.

This renders theology functional—concerned with identifying the magnetizing meaning-center from which the activities of a person or group impulse. The content emerges through this interaction of "why" with one's daily context. The religious issue is identified, then, not by a special content, but by the special quality of relation which one has with any content. As Henry N. Wieman once insisted, the issue is not, Does God exist? but, Which of the various realities one encounters functions as God? It is this orienting sensitivity which produces, universally and necessarily, the texture of the unique theological World which each individual inhabits. Selfhood is the process of owning, with conscious commitment, this World which functions as a construct of "convictions which one sees through like a pair of glasses."[2] These glasses are honed by root metaphors that function together as paradigm, so operating as to "author and authorize the way we think, the way we act, the way we communicate, and the way we judge."[3]

How, then, is the truth of one's theological World ascertained? It begins with the awareness that truth, defined functionally, is multiple, relative to the particularity of the subject and to one's defining context. Within that pluralism, what functions as God becomes that which one can trust without betrayal, and obey without idolatry.[4] This process of verification occurs by living as if one's World is true, expanding it to its broadest possibilities, intensifying it to its fullest self-consciousness. Thus a theological proposition is true, Gordan Kaufman insists, "if it somehow enhances human life, leading to its fuller realization."[5] Sallie McFague unpacks such *enhancement* further by identifying it as "internal consistency," citing "its capacity to comprehend the various dimensions of existence, its 'fit' with life as lived, its ability to deal with personal and public evil, and its fruitfulness for understanding the depths and heights of existence."[6]

Such conclusions expand the truth of H. R. Niebuhr's explorations of truth as progressive validation.[7] One can know theologically, he insists, only by beginning with the gaze of a believer. One looks, for example, with the eyes of Jesus, who looked with the eyes of the prophets, while they in turn peered through the eyes of Moses. This is what it means to begin with revelation, yet circularly, for it is known as revelation only when its consequences are rendered worthy of being so named in the living of them. Thereby revelation is disclosed as the unspoken presupposition from which one began, but now seen as that which claims one's life. So discovered, the risk, unconsciously involved, now becomes an imperative that insists upon decision. "As we begin with revelation only because we are forced to do so by our limited standpoint in history and faith, so we can proceed only by stating in simple, confessional form what has happened in our community, how we came to believe, how we reason about things, and what we see from our point of view."[8]

Such an understanding is the bedrock upon which modern theologizing must rest. This conclusion should not be greeted with alarm, as if in losing absolute truth or objective fact we have lost the heart of religion. It should be celebrated. Faith never should have been understood as belief, rendering religion a second-best way of knowing. Consequently, the modern dilemma is forcing us to recognize the uniqueness of theology—not as content, but as process, replete with all the risk, commitment, doubt, subjectivity, and rich pluralism characteristic of life as lived.[9] In so recognizing theology, we are rediscovering as well the nature and function of the church, and its necessity for contemporary life.

What is new is the discovery of theological Worlds as *pluralistic,* and thus the need of the church to be self-consciously *variegated.* Each theological World, emerging as dialectic between a unique self and a particular culture, is "relative to the speaker who gives [it] voice and the cultural milieu out of which he or she comes." Thus each person is alone with a unique version of reality, itself contexted by an ethos that emerges from "the spiritual needs and longings of particular people in particular times and in particular places."[10] This renders the theologizing process more complex than usually assumed, since it is thoroughly sociocultural and thoroughly autobiographical. Growth results from taking willed responsibility for one's ongoing theological World as it emerges and is furnished. Thus religion, functionally defined, is necessary to existence itself. Functional theology, as a self-conscious process, is the call into maturity through an accountability of depth and breadth.

The sociocultural context for this process functions in what Berger calls plausibility structures, which define as internalizing process the parameters of imbecility.[11] Thus what might be identified as insane behavior in one culture may be the mark of special calling in another. Understandably, the story that marks the advent of Christianity violated the parameters of both Greek and Hebraic Worlds, evoking tides of rejection as foolishness and folly. Christianity's persuasiveness rested in its capacity to withstand such parameters, generating contrasting theological Worlds with the power of alternative structures of plausibility. Each was rooted in the power of a common story to magnetize shared memories and collective anticipations, by, and into, a root event named Jesus as the Christ. This occurred in a cultural context in which existing root events were losing plausibility, their power functioning more externally than internally. Correlatively, Christianity's present crisis centers in the need to accomplish the same task—to establish its truth by the powerful living of alternative possibilities around a root event, in the midst of a culture whose stories are oriented by contrasting and confused parameters of "imbecility."

The strength of will necessary for the contemporary Christian to function creatively within a context of alternative plausibility structures makes clear the essential need of the church. One will succumb unless one's theological World sufficiently overlaps the Worlds of certain others in order for an alternative community of "ritual rehearsal" to emerge.

This means that seduction comes not only from secular options. Within the church itself, temptation comes from two directions. As the price for belonging, one may be pressured into believing uniform content, repressing one's own root metaphor as promise of unique selfhood. On the other hand, one may be lured into forfeiting the deep commitment demanded by one's uniquely personal World, to purchase belonging through a tolerance that borders on theological indifference. Thus we turn full circle, from the contemporary theological crisis to the urgent need for the church as variegated. Such an institution, which exhibits the richness of alternative Worlds within the plausibility structures of its plenary life, can bear witness to the profundity of *the* story—capable of magnetizing each member to a profound but unique allegiance.

A Social Typology of Theological Worlds

The central task of this book is to identify the family resemblances that emerge when, in practice, the myriad theological Worlds overlap with certain others, forming the contrasting but viable Worlds that compete for loyalty in the modern world. What we will present is the result of more than ten years' research, discovering five clusterings around which the multiple Worlds tend to coalesce functionally. Each of the five emerges from a contrasting feeling of existence which orients a fundamental life posture. Although these Worlds can be characterized by a host of images, they point toward five fundamental rhythms capable of being stated as themes. These are characterized by what we will develop as differing *obsessios* (dilemmas), attuned to contrasting *epiphanias* (resolutions). Each rhythm functions as an aperture through which one may perceive and, in turn, project, alternative meaning into common-day interaction. Since these Worlds are difficult to grasp conceptually without losing the magnetism of their wholeness, we will use nonconceptual expressions as well. It is central to be grasped by the primal feel that underlays and constitutes each of these as a pure type. Each is viable.

This typology first emerged as possibility through

research into the theologizing process of diverse theologians. Then, following five years of experimental work with more than two hundred Protestant seminary students and approximately one hundred pastors, the data gathered was explored further by one-on-one sessions with professional nonclergy types. After a fundamental typology began to emerge with sufficient clarity, it was tested and readapted, using other students and pastors. The next step was the development of a Theological World Inventory as an identifying tool. This was tested in helping individuals identify themselves as belonging to one or another of the types, in turn verifying its accuracy.

Each person was then individually interviewed, noting particular music, literature, and other image expressions each found important. After these were correlated, other persons, not instructed in theological Worlds, were exposed to more than two hundred paintings, and each chose those that best captured the feel of their living. A significant correlation was found between persons identified within a particular theological World and the paintings chosen. After a conceptual description of each World was drafted, these were critiqued by persons identified as belonging to each.

Ongoing research has continued by testing portions of this book with the persons it attempts to analyze and describe. While there is reason to believe that these types are comprehensive, this research has focused primarily on the Protestant context. Therefore we must be content with a more modest claim.

The rhythm of each theological World flows as interaction between the concrete poles of obsessio and epiphania. Expressed conceptually, and thus abstractly, these fundamental rhythms have been recognized as:

1. Separation and Reunion
2. Conflict and Vindication
3. Emptiness and Fulfillment
4. Condemnation and Forgiveness
5. Suffering and Endurance

Expressed in large strokes, the first World characterizes authenticity as questing in the face of an overwhelming cosmos. World Two is drawn to the dilemma of history as chaotic. The third World struggles with possibilities for the unfulfilled self. World Four knows one's path as passing through the valley of the shadow of guilt. The fifth World wrestles with an awareness that living means persisting on the edge of absurdity.

Such theological Worlds go far back into antiquity, preserved and rehearsed as mythology. Since, in one sense, to mythologize the world as one's own is the theological task, the dissolution of mythology in our time is at the heart of our anemia. Consider some epic works of our century: T. S. Eliot's "The Waste Land"; Hart Crane's "The Bridge"; Ezra Pound's *Cantos;* James Joyce's *Ulysses;* and more recently, Doris Lessing's *Four-Gated City*. Each has forged its own mythology as if in a desert, because this age has given none that could be readily and publicly accepted "as myth, religion, symbol."[12]

That is why our time is so deeply but painfully theological. We live in a famine of conscious and recognized mythology, capable of creating plausibility structures through narrative structuring, which would help to identify, evoke, expand, and deepen the rhythms in which each person can and does move.[13] Instead, our contemporary situation is characterized by a frightening morass of latent mythologies, competitively different from past periods of manifest myth. This may be why each of us feels terribly alone. Being deprived of explicit forms of public rehearsal, each of us is thrown back upon a self already congenitally isolated. The hope giving rise to this book is that by recognizing typologically the functioning of theological Worlds, we can begin to sense resources for alternative communities—not only within society, but as a renewal of the church, which has such a function as its reason for being.

These five latent theological Worlds can be given a manifest overview by the use of mythology, which once provided their roots. For each World, we will suggest a tragic form, which focuses the obsessio, and a comedic form, which focuses the potential transformation through epiphania:

World One: Separation and Reunion. In its tragic form, the obsessio appears in the Romeo and Juliet theme. The situation is that of agonized separation, longing for reunion, only to be so rebuffed by the inevitabilities of life that attempted reunion can lead only to the tragic loss of both. In this life, reunion seems possible only in death.

Likewise tragic is the myth of King Agamemnon, leader of the Greeks against Troy in punishment for its wrongs. After ten years, finally he is able to return home—only to be murdered by his wife, Clytemnestra, and Aegisthus, with whom she has been living in betrayal. A modern equivalent is K, the mythic center of Kafka's World. "Called" in one novel, "accused" in another, and "separated" in a host of short stories, K is no longer able to envisage his former World as home. An alien, he never succeeds in his search, for he can discover neither place nor figure that can sustain hope in any reunion.

Its comedic form is Odysseus, the traveler pushing for home who is tempted by the sirens, yet finally returns in joyous homecoming. As described by Homer, the ten years of wandering toward Ithaca present a classic epic of homesickness.

World Two: Conflict and Vindication. The tragic form is Beowulf, who helps a king defeat monsters, only to be defeated when his own pleas for help go unheeded.

Its comedic form emerges as Don Quixote. This knight-errant wages battles not even seen by others, with vindication of the conflict coming as much in the promise contained within the quality of the struggle as in the victory.

World Three: Emptiness and Fulfillment. The tragic form is Hamlet. Here the painfully sensitive person fails to act until the problem, originally external, becomes internalized. In the end, the tragedy comes to rest within Hamlet.

Parsifal distills the comedic version. Here is a hero epitomized by innocence, essentially uncorrupted by the world. Yet when sent on a quest, he seems unable to do anything right. Nevertheless, he is given a second chance and makes good his primal potential.

World Four: Condemnation and Forgiveness. The tragic form is Faustus, who, though rare in ability, loses his soul to arrogance and the craving for absolute power.

The comedic form is King Lear, whose pride comes close to destroying not only himself but those closest to him—until forgiveness comes through the undeserved love of the one he has betrayed most.

World Five: Suffering and Endurance. The tragic form is Oedipus, well-intentioned in doing all that is expected. Yet that very faithfulness creates such an inevitable and relentless suffering that he seeks termination in self-inflicted blindness. Or Sibyl, the prophetess who pleads to live for as many years as the grains of sand in her hand, forgetting the tragic aging of all things. Through suffering, her life is reduced to one plea—to die.

The comedic form is Sisyphus (as interpreted by Camus), condemned for his effort to remedy the way things are. Yet even in the face of a life devoted to pushing a rock up a mountain, only to have it roll down again, there is meaning in the defiant perseverance which, while changing nothing, enables a moral victory by enduring.[14]

Such mythological expressions suggest the potential power of these five theological Worlds as distillations of meaning within the contemporary secular scene. For the purposes of this book, our focus will be on these alternatives as variations within the whole called Christianity.

Our particular sensitivity will be with Protestant Christianity. It is our concern to clothe the pluralism of Christian alternatives with a richness that exhibits each as a vital contemporary option. In so doing, we hope that an imperative for understanding the mission of the church in a new way will emerge.

Theologizing and the Aesthetic Task

Before dealing with the content of these alternative theological Worlds, it is important to understand the process by which these Worlds are formed.

Functional theology, as we have indicated, is a reality not only for consciously religious persons and communities. It also points toward each person's human struggle for meaning.

So understood, we can recognize within this larger theological enterprise the crucial role played by the arts. The artist is one who participates with such sensitivity in one's times that she or he is plowed and harrowed by its underlying rhythms. The expressions that result create metaphorically a publicly available thematic universe, which, at its best, forms the outer edge of a paradigm struggling to be born.[15] Heidegger is right in identifying poetry as the foundation that supports history.

John Steinbeck came to recognize the theological nature of this creative process when, in creating *East of Eden*, he found himself drawn to discern the Cain and Abel story as a universal paradigm:

I think it is the symbol of the human soul. . . . The greatest terror a child can have is [to be] not loved, and rejection is the hell of fears. I think everyone in the world to a large extent has felt rejection. And with rejection comes anger, and with anger some kind of crime in revenge for the rejection, and with the crime guilt—and that is the story of [humankind].[16] *quite true*

The literary task, so understood, is concerned with discerning plot within life's material and exhibiting its parts as worthy of a viable World. As such, it is an intensification of the process of living that characterizes each person. In fact, the Christian understands this dynamic as true for God as well. God as Creator shapes material into form, imagining a plot worthy of being patterned into liturgical rhythms. This is the God who calls forth actors who share the same image as God, for a drama that invites each person to discern a part by which to wager that the whole is not a tale told by an idiot.

The aesthetic enterprise distills metaphors that promise a World. As these emerge through living, the task of theology, in turn, is to distill them into alternative plots, identifying them conceptually through a process of faceting. The result is disclosure of the anatomy of theological Worlds as they compete for loyalty in a particular epoch. Throughout this process, individual and sociocultural contexts interact in lively fashion. Thus what Steinbeck calls the story of humankind is actually a distillation of the rhythm that functionally defines his own autobiographical pilgrimage, proffered as inclusive by being so incarnated within recognizable flesh that it invites viability.

Thus the theological enterprise has two tasks. First, it helps to midwife into consciousness the theological World(s) that inform each person. Appropriately, literary critic Northrop Frye insists that each person "lives, not directly or nakedly in nature like the animals, but within a mythological universe, a body of assumptions and beliefs developed for [one's] existential concerns. Most of this is held unconsciously."[17] The second theological task is to discern where the heaviest concentration of overlap by these Worlds occurs. By standing within each such confessional vantage point, the theologian helps to discern, identify, and explicate the contours of these overlapping theological Worlds as pure types. In so doing, the theologian helps each person to confess, through common story with others, a purification of one's own. The content of faith is one's lived particularities within a common confession, translated functionally as that unique point of view which establishes one's way of life.

Such an understanding identifies theologizing as the most pervasive dimension of human interaction. This book leans toward the church side of that dynamic, to discern explicitly Christian variations of the five theological Worlds. These provide contrasting vantage points for engaging its common story. But we will draw upon secular expressions as well, placing the two in suggestive and inevitable interplay. Since the church is in the world and the world is in the church, the reader will find important analogies for each in the other.

The Emergence of Individual Theological Worlds

Theological method, or how one knows one's lived meaning as true, is at heart an autobiographical process. In each person is an *impulsing logic* which shapes and converges the raw ingredients of one's autobiography, energizing them into individualized quest. It is this impulsing logic that renders the classical ingredients of Scripture, tradition, reason, and experience into a "recipe," without which they are as useless for understanding one's approach to meaning as is a list of ingredients for baking a cake. Pushing the analogy, the manner (method) in which they fit together in each faith-quest resembles a good cook's use of such precise imprecisions as pinch, dash, a bit, and till done.[18] In contrast, what is usually identified by theologians as their method is, in fact, a rational defense of what each one already believes, operating in a manner quite foreign to both how they came to faith and why they continue to be affirmed by it.

The clue to faith's origination resides in this impulsing logic—which is similar, but unique in each self. Persons attempt to position themselves in the universe by selecting "certain happenings out of the chaotic flow of events they pass through, by which to understand their origins and destiny," thereby grounding persistence in hope.[19] This process is not as rational as one might expect or desire. In fact, the feel of faith in the end is less that of choosing than of being chosen. And what appears as conclusion is often a disclosure of the premise from which one has been operating unknowingly throughout. The theologizing process, consequently, is richly circular, because it is deeply autobiographic.

The writings of Annie Dillard are helpful in grasping the anatomy of this impulsing logic, fundamental to the emergence of a theological World. Her writings tend to be autobiographic, their ramblings held together by key images, which function with the power of symbol-episode. In searching for some unifying thread in her *Pilgrim at Tinker Creek*, I find two events emerging as crucial. In fact, they keep reemerging as variations on a theme. In each case, they have the power of an ache and the claim of a gestalt. The most powerful, and in that sense the most overarching, occurs as, flat on her stomach, she intently watches the surface of a pond. Her eye almost touches the water line—alert to any stirrings that might turn nature into an event. And there, no more than a foot or so from her eyes, arises out of the water the face of a frog. For a moment their eyes meet, locked together, clasped in sacred wonder. An eternal Now. But as she looks, the seeing turns into a stare, and the eyes cave in upon themselves from within. The frog's face is slowly sucked inside out, like a worn-out ball. It sinks slowly beneath the surface. But only for a moment. Rebreaking the surface, there emerges the head of a giant water bug. Almost with an evil grin, it stares at her, as it relentlessly crunches the life out of the frog—its "mouth a gash of terror." Horror! Paralyzed.

This moment has the makings of an instant replay—ongoing, for a lifetime. The Why? keeps replaying, as if a repetitive flashback from a poor drug experience. One tries to domesticate such an invading image by enfolding it into life-as-usual. But to no avail, for by now it has become an obsession. In fact, the more it replays, the deeper it bores. Thinking about it only intensifies its grasp. Finally, the obsession sinks its teeth in all the way, when she is forced to ask, "Would I eat a frog's leg if it were offered?" The answer is as clear as it is obsessive—*Yes!* And the image, once external, becomes deeply fastened internally.

However Dillard understands such matters conceptually,

viewed functionally, this image is the ground of an impulsing logic that cinches her work together as religious quest. The way this event functions as impulse is best identified as "obsessio." An obsessio is whatever functions deeply and pervasively in one's life as a defining quandary, a conundrum, a boggling of the mind, a hemorrhaging of the soul, a wound that bewilders healing, a mystification that renders one's living cryptic. Whatever inadequate words one might choose to describe it, an obsessio is that which so gets its teeth into a person that it establishes one's life as plot. It is a memory which, as resident image, becomes so congealed as Question that all else in one's experience is sifted in terms of its promise as Answer. Put another way, an obsessio is whatever threatens to deadlock the Yeses with No. It is one horn that establishes life as dilemma. It is the negative pole that functions within one's defining rhythm. The etymology of the word says it well: *obsessio* means "to be beseiged."

The possession of an obsessio is universal, involving one in the dynamic which shapes each person's existence. *Ex sistere* means standing outside oneself, pulled from one's self into self-consciousness by some graphic and grasping variation on the theme of Why? In fact, any "notion of an independent reality can emerge only when our drives, impulses, and desires encounter an obstacle."[20] This obstacle as obsessio marks the threshold of life as labyrinth, forging that driving impulse which serves both as motive and as test for meaning. While this dynamic is universal, its specificity in each individual illustrates functionally what theologians abstractly call the human condition. This functioning of obsessio becomes graphic in psychotherapy when the attempt is made to discern a patient's agonized life as variations on a theme. Therapy offers many techniques for uncovering such an obsessio, which in resisting identity becomes as immovable as it is insoluble. Whatever its content or intensity, we are dealing with that primal level of functioning in each of us with which one must make peace, for it will not go away.

This primal obsessio, which focuses lesser obsessios as

configuration, is the magnetizing force that drives and shapes one's consciousness as a defining rhythm of craving. For Dillard, it would seem, that obsessio means she must suffer, as the price for being, a horror that is knit into the fabric of her life. She is not to forget it—obsessio! And what is the impact of its pervasive weight? It gives the feel of exile—in her case, from nature, of which she is a part, and which is part of her. This means being a cosmic orphan, to be in and not of—or is it of but not in? Whichever, it is enough to serve as the impulsing logic of a lifetime.

But obsessio is only part of the logic. To be enwrapped in morose and moribund passivity within one's obsessio is to experience a state of spiritual abortion. *Depression* is the clinical term for this vicious circle. *Normality*, on the other hand, is the term for a lively dialectic between one's obsessio and that which functions as illumination, enabling a dynamic which entertains the possibility of wholeness. This second pole we identify as *epiphania*, etymologically meaning "to show upon," that which keeps the functioning of obsessio fluid, hopeful, searching, restless, energized, intriguing, as a question worth pursuing for a lifetime. It keeps one's obsessio from becoming a fatal conclusion that signals futility.

One's epiphania is as difficult to discern as one's obsessio. It too is most detectable functionally—in this case, by its evocative power. Reminiscent of the workings of an oyster, an epiphania is known by its capacity so to enfold an obsessio that the grating particle is made bearable. Indeed, quietly within its promise is the hope that the obsessio, while never lost, might become the center for a pearl of great price, flowing back to redeem the whole.

This is precisely what, one might be led to believe, happened to Dillard. At least once in reality, and far more often in memory, she is so claimed. It is a very special day. Nature, from which she has been exiled by violence, lays claim to her as epiphania. It comes as a morning moment when she sees a frost-covered cedar tree suddenly ablaze with light as three hundred red-winged blackbirds fill it to overflowing. If only for that one sacramental moment, the exiled Annie belongs—the prodigal is embraced on the road! But as the Gospel according to Luke alerts us, it "vanished out of their sight."

Yet the hint is sufficiently powerful that one can wager a meaning capable of enfolding the obsessio in epiphania. "Did not our hearts burn within us?" Emmaus. Resurrection. Epiphania! Thus the impulsing logic which renders each life a religious quest, whether consciously or otherwise, is this rhythm, slung between obsessio and epiphania, experienced or dreamed of. It is that which marks us as fugitives, vagabonds, clowns, or sojourners. Whatever, it drives us on to seek signs that the question wrapped in foil as one's obsessio is at least worthy. It is this impulsing logic that confirms us as theologians.

For Dillard, living concretely the rhythm that flows between her obsessio and epiphania means living the intersection between oceans of horror and oceans of beauty.[21] In *Teaching a Stone to Talk*, she echoes this same convoluting imagery. Here, again, it forms a rhythm that permits her to revel in a joyous absurdity. This irony that hyphens obsessio and epiphania appears in a true story of explorers who lost their lives in an expedition to the South Pole. They abandoned their sled in an attempt to walk out. And from all the provisions they could have taken with them in their effort to survive, what did they choose? Their frozen bodies revealed that they set out across the barren ice cap with food on their backs and beautiful silverware in their pockets.

What does such imagery capture about living? For Dillard, it identifies the human craving for gracious survival. She sees in it the passion to find, on a daily basis, a working compromise between the sublimity of beauty and the absurd and ruthless facticity of existence. Giant water bugs devour the innocent, while red-winged blackbirds decorate cedar trees as if for Christmas, even if no one sees. And what does the resulting impulsing logic look like? It incarnates itself in paradoxes which have the power of epiphania, paradoxes that feed—humans as gracious animals, nature as cultured cannibal.

Then, for a moment, she abandons the poetic, as if to discover any others "out there" with whom to overlap Worlds. "I alternate between thinking of the planet as home—dear and familiar stone hearth and garden—and as a hard land of exile in which we are all sojourners."[22] Here they are, set side by side. So hyphened, the image that emerges for me is that of Holy Saturday, marked by the creative tension of obsessio and epiphania, locked in deadly but exciting engagement.

I personally share Dillard's obsessio sufficiently to have one foot on the threshold that leads into her labyrinth. Yet I turn left and she turns right as we walk into theological Worlds that overlap but are different. Why? Because in light of her epiphania, she becomes intrigued by her obsessio. I, on the other hand, standing before a similar obsessio, can place her epiphania in my back pocket and still be appalled. Whatever might be epiphania for me can become so only by scratching a different itch. It must be one that acknowledges my feeling of exile in refusing frog legs.

The Bipolar Nature of Autobiography

The self wrestling for meaning is often a self unknown to itself. One becomes knowable as a theological self by distilling one's autobiography into a shape that identifies one's impulsing logic. This means identifying the configurations that function as obsessio(s) and epiphania(s). Dillard's suggestion for using Moses as a case study is illuminating.[23] It is possible to see his life congealed around two events. A primal encounter is the moment when, enraged over the beating of "one of his people," he is driven to kill the Egyptian and flee. How long does that take? He must bury the body in the sand. Is it twenty minutes—perhaps half an hour? But the real burial was of an obsessio, one that was to impulse the anatomy of soul. It will haunt him across the silent mountains of Midian. It will impulse him, against his stuttering will, into the face of his adopted father Pharaoh. It will obsess him with the driving passion of a cloud by day and a luring fire by night. It will not grow dim through desert cravings, though they last forty years. It grounds, as impulsing logic, a yearning for epiphania—one that for him, almost to the end, has the force of a hint and the foretaste of a guess.

Then comes the second event, when Moses is 120 years of age. This event, with the flavor of epiphania, occurs as he stands on the windswept peak of Mount Pisgah, looking out across the Jordan. The shadows of imminent death dim his tearful eyes. "This is the land of which I swore to Abraham, to Isaac, and to Jacob." Finally! But there is more: "I have let you see it with your eyes, but you shall not go over there." This is not at all what he had envisaged. Yet it is epiphania, nonetheless. Several glimpses, maybe some regrets? How long is he there on Pisgah? How long can one bear it? An hour? If so, we have the span of 120 years lived for the sake of 1½ hours! And all the rest of one's life? It is a matter of denial and longing, sprinkled with foretaste.

Poet T. S. Eliot refers to such epiphanias as the "unattended moments, in and out of time," which serve as "hints followed by guesses." All the rest, he insists, is "prayer, observance, discipline, thought, action."[24] Heidigger speaks of such epiphanias as divine lightnings, between which all else is a connecting valley, with or without trail. *Faithfulness* is the term the prophets preferred.

These intersecting moments are the poles that forge the impulsing logic around which one's entire life can be seen as explication. The most basic congealing, and thus the most difficult to discern, is the pole we are identifying as obsessio. This primal image-event of gnawing and longing impulses all else into Search. Its presence has the feel of wilderness moments, or the midnight moments of vulnerability. It is the shape of the horizon before which one stands, to identify which turf is one's own. In a sense, it is a sanctuary where one knows what must be true, or else. "What makes you tick?" points toward it. "What's gotten into you?" warns that one has been carelessly vulnerable about it. "If you really knew me you wouldn't like me" asks hesitantly if one might dare to share it. As the last thing to be shared, it is the primal thing in importance. And the degree to which it is shared is the measure of one's level of trust. It is the story one needs to tell if one is to be known.

Often one suspects the identity of one's obsessio best through the echo of multiple secondary obsessios. Anxiety is a reliable indication of proximity. Newspaper reporters are fascinated by the graphic extremes: a child molested, the Vietnam veteran bent on suicide, psychotic projections as foreign policy. And we are personally drawn by these because they offer a safe familiarity. Much harder to discern, and thus to confess, are the disclosures of those "childish" dramas rooted in our earliest days, which clutch us with talons. Such originations are reinforced by our living, often in direct proportion to their repression. This process becomes amplified by echoing and re-echoing down the corridors of one's autobiography. Understandably, Eriksen claims that "at their creative best, religions trace our earliest inner experience."

The agony of obsessios resides often in the fact that their re-remembrance threatens to evoke the deep precariousness of the first five years of life. Unless consciousness has quickly grasped and engaged these memories as clusters of direct and honest engagement, much of the rest of our years of theological questing will evidence aborted composites of denial, coping, reenactment, and self-doubt. Their fearful parameters will submerge some persons in the quiet anger of a life squandered, if even begun. Authentic self-consciousness, on the other hand, entails getting in touch with the feel of one's primal yearning, pushing and luring us toward that particularized epiphania which promises resolution. This process is called *salvation*, for *salveo* means "to render whole."

The career of the brilliant Russian Orthodox theologian Nicholas Berdyaev illustrates this dynamic well. The substance of his extensive theological writings is nestled in a five-sentence reflection in his autobiography, hinting at the interplay of obsessio and epiphania as impulsing logic in his own life:

From my youth onward, I have always felt myself a stranger in the world. Truly I have no abiding place in it, but I have ever sought for a city whose builder and maker is God. I have never felt at home in the universe. World harmony and an ordered cosmos do not exist for me: they still have to be created. Many delight in asserting that they are in love with life; I could never say that.[25]

To explicate this passage is, in effect, to write Berdyaev's theological volumes. On the other hand, to particularize it with implicit imagery is to enter the domain of deep autobiographical intimacy.

Our concern is to enter the storehouse of imagery, as Ezekiel calls it, out of which one's impulsing logic emerges as the interaction of obsessio and epiphania. This storehouse is most often unconscious, unrecognized, and unacknowledged. For this reason, one may best be known theologically through the contents of one's glove compartment.

Far more revealing than a twenty-page credo are the rhythms detected in one's ordinary environment and activity—one's furniture, paintings, record collection, favorite rooms; one's postures, the way one walks; one's driving habits, checkbook, wardrobe, food. Other fruitful theological discerners are dreams, fantasies, daydreams, doodles, word associations, Freudian slips. These are the instruments of disclosure for the informing images out of which behavior springs, often unknowingly. Just as doing emerges from being, theologizing involves discernment of being through doing.

This same process of discernment is appropriate for understanding each society. The theological groundings of contemporary culture find expression, for example, in advertising. Such expressions result from elaborate research into obsessios, in an attempt to identify that which shapes various target groups, in terms of what they want and why. So understood, an automobile is created as a theological statement, promising epiphania. Thus toy departments provide prophecies of future theological Worlds.

Thomas Groome, building upon Marx, explores education as this dialectic of reflection-upon-action, which leads
to increased self-consciousness for informed action.[26] This
process is one of thematization of the largely preconscious
and preconceptual limits which serve as needs to be
exercised—not only by the individual, but within subcultures and societies as well. All three interact in the forging of
a theological World. It follows, then, that a church's faith is
known not so much through creedal statement as through
its actions, especially in the interactive liturgy of individual
and community.[27]

There is no better way to grasp this theologizing process
in operation than to risk one's own vulnerability. As one
digs deeply into one's own obsessio(s), embarrassment
comes quickly. How unwise, even silly, how downright
insane, to let my life be twisted by its defining contours. Is it
possible that the concrete congealing of obsessio which
provides dynamic in my psychic cellar will turn out, in the
bright light of adult hindsight, to have been orchestrated—
as a friend once put it—not so much by demons as by mice
with megaphones? Yet even if so, that does not make the
impulsing logic less powerful. At midnight, even if mice,
they rattle chains that I hear as cosmic.

It is impossible to understand W. Paul Jones, either as
person or as theologian, without the obsessio gestalted one
night fifty-one years ago. It is the story of an only child, an
old creaking house, and a faraway upstairs bedroom with a
door to the attic. A nightly ritual, carried out a respectable
time after being tucked-in, was the arduous tiptoeing, in
attempted silence, down the length of the upstairs hall,
down three steps to the landing, and then a careful look
through the banisters to be sure . . . . I can finish the
sentence now—to be sure I was not abandoned. Histrionic?
Probably—until one special night. The ritual was the same,
up to the benediction. When I looked through the banisters,
that one glance confirmed what somehow I always had
known would happen. I was alone. Utterly.

This does not mean that in that night of paralysis what

was created was ex nihilo, or that it was an obsessio full-blown. Nor does it mean that after a three-second glance, the self-to-be was largely forged. It does mean that in that event, powerful congealing took place. Hints and signs and scattered episodes were, in that moment, gestalted, crystallized, fused into a pole of focused impulse. The obsessio had so little substance by which to be fed—only dis-ease, hints, inner doubts, suspicious configurations scattered along the way. In fact, when demythologized, it turned out that my parents were only down the street, playing cards with neighbors. Yet distilled in one glance was an indelible parabolic recognition—one powerful enough to push me into the attic that night, looking . . . .

An obsessio is never to be forgotten. It is always to be dealt with, even from afar, as one viscerally but invisibly weighs other questions and other actions into variations of risked alternatives for resolution. Epiphania? That came in remembering, years later, with a sudden primal understanding, that my Christian conversion occurred moments after singing "How Firm a Foundation," which ended with these lines:

> The soul that on Jesus still leans for repose,
> I will not, I will not desert to his foes;
> That soul, though all hell should endeavor to shake,
> I'll never, no, never, no, never forsake!

I have since been able to identify this obsessio of abandonment as based on the inner feeling that I was not worth remembering. I understand now my later captivation with Scripture. I found therein a connecting theme—that of Divine faithfulness in spite of broken human promises. My fascination with Barth came in hearing that all we have is Promise—that God will never abandon us. No matter what, God will remember, for God's self is wedded to us beyond the point of recall, sealing that Promise with death. Faith is trust in the faithfulness of the One who promises, the One alone to be trusted. Epiphania, in order to heal, must be

ongoing, as the primary congealing called obsessio encounters, again and again through liturgical rehearsal, the event
where, at least once, one came to know trust.

It fits. It connects. One's life makes organic sense when the
logic of impulse is discerned. I dared to share my story once,
when another person and I seemed to have intuitive rapport.
Amid the tears my story evoked, she shared that she had had
polio as a child: "When my mother left me in Sunday school, I
always asked to wear her locket. She thought I liked the
locket. That wasn't it at all. I knew I wasn't worth coming
back for, but I knew she would come back for her locket."
Obsessio! I understood. In that moment, there was a deep
overlapping of theological Worlds.

I pushed her about epiphania. She was less sure. Yet as
she talked, her stories had a haunting sense of variations on
the parable of the lost coin. And for both of us, the
wasteland between obsessio and epiphania has long been
that dynamic best identified as the Protestant work
ethic—for her, in order to become worth keeping; for me, to
make a mark impossible to forget.

Theologian H. R. Niebuhr is master at revealing story as
the inner art of the theologizing process. He contrasts
"inner history" with "outer history." The pronoun *my*, in
contrast to the pronoun *their*, marks appropriation by
participation in an impulsing logic. He is taken by the deep
contrast this entails—the creation of contrasting perspectives about supposedly identical events. Illustratively, "our
fathers," whom the Gettysburg Address heralded as
sacred, are not at all the same as "those rebellious colonists"
on whom the Cambridge history writers blame an
unfortunate situation. While Niebuhr did not take this
further, the truth is that "our fathers," powerful epiphania
for some Americans, becomes an obsessio for those for
whom the image has been corroded by the erosive qualifiers
of white and male. Epiphanias do not change information;
they effect import. They do not remove obsessios; they
incorporate them into themselves, thereby reconstituting a
history once outer into a history that informs from within.
This is redemption.[28] One becomes a Christian, says

Bonhoeffer, when one begins to read Scripture as one's own autobiography.

If an epiphania for one person fails for another, it is either because the two have contrasting obsessios, or because one person's particular obsessio preserves its veto power, neutralizing the epiphania by incorporating it into its own webb. Teachers can recall times when they tried to compliment a promising but self-deprecating student. No matter how strong the praise, the student would qualify it, reducing performance to the power of exception rather than disclosure. Affirmation thereby has the effect of water filling a sieve. Until an epiphania occurs, the obsessio remains insatiable.

This theologizing process we are describing gives content to what Pascal calls "the reasons of the heart." It clarifies as well the strange statement attributed to both Tertullian and Augustine: "I believe because it is absurd" *(Credo quia absurdum est).* The absurdity of good news is not so much logical or conceptual as spiritual. It is rooted in the discontinuity of obsessio and epiphania, for there is no rational connection between the two. While one may yearn for an epiphania, the irony is that such desire renders easy answers unavailable. The deeper the obsessio, the more its insatiability, and the less likely that simple projection can ever feed it.

The transition from the yearning, "Let it be so," to the unbelievable confession, "It is so!" is marked by the word *grace*—that is, gift. Epiphania is epiphany precisely because its absurdity resides in being too good to be true: "I can't believe it!" For the Christian, the miracle of being able to believe that the yearned-for impossibility is true has the causal name of Holy Spirit. Whatever the content of an epiphania, its generic shape is recognizable in Plato's cry that marked his birth as philosopher-theologian: "Being must prevail over meaninglessness and death!"[29]

Poet W. H. Auden once suggested an analogy for this engagement of epiphania which the church calls revelation. We respond to the second-rate poetry of a Kipling by saying, "That is just how I feel." But in encountering great

poetry, one exclaims: "I never realized before what I
felt . . . and from now on I shall feel differently." What a
self or culture regards as great is that by which one is so
reprieved that one can start again, a moment outside the
sequestered, obsessed self. Emmaus is classic. Obsessio as
crucifixion is the abortion of promise: "We had hoped
. . ." (Luke 24:21). Through this loss, such "foolish men,
and slow of heart" have their eyes opened as epiphania—
"in the breaking of bread" (24:25, 35). Conversion occurs at
this intersection of obsessio and epiphania. Such a
happening for the self is so crucial that Christians confess it
for history—dividing quest into before and after.

Thereby religious practices become variations on the
liturgy of rehearsal—a dual re-remembering (anamnesis).
With eyes so honed, life can become ongoing discovery of
epiphania as presence (epiclesis), capable of wrestling the
powers of obsessio into submission.

Conversion

Two final issues remain before we turn to the content of
the five theological Worlds. First, how is conversion
possible between theological Worlds?

Such a process has two factors—one of "push," one of
"pull." The power that impulses conversion comes not so
much from choice of a more desirable option, as from an
inability to continue in one's present World. Kierkegaard
identified this process as a "leaping from."[30] Afterward,
seen from the other side, it appears as a "leaping toward."
To tamper with, let alone abandon, the only World one has
is a terrifying affair. Thus it is the suffocating sense of
trappedness that is most likely to provide the impetus for
significant growth within one's World or the dynamic for
seriously entertaining the viability of an alternative World.
Faith and doubt are inherent. Put another way, such
dynamic emerges through the eroding power of an
unresolved obsessio.

Yet this push is never without an accompanying pull

from an alternative epiphania, luring with possibility. This function is best understood in terms of the human capacity for aesthetic engagement. Through significant poetry, for example, one can participate intransitively in the reality of the poem's "object." As long as this relationship remains aesthetic, the question of truth or falsity never arises. Such experience is called pure dramatic immediacy, unmitigated and direct, to the point of absorption.[31] Poetry, consequently, is evaluated qualitatively not by its "truth" but by its power to effect participation.

This capacity for aesthetic participation serves as hermeneutic, making it possible to experience an alternative theological World from within. Externally, such engagement is evoked by the creative expressions which function "liturgically" for participants within that World. Internally, one may be impelled by one's own disposition. Cassirer insists that "concentration always depends upon the direction of the subject's interest, and is determined not so much by the content of the experience as by the teleological perspective from which it is viewed."[32] Here the power of unfulfilled obsessio passes beyond superficial curiosity to an existential passion for serious participation—even anticipation.

This experience of participation can itself be the truth. Job's resolution is not an answer that can be disengaged from the poetic form in and through which his new World is evoked and shaped. That World comes into existence for a Job who now, with eyes specially opened, looks out as if for the first time. Thus a theological World is never reducible to a conceptual paraphrase. It is deeply intertwined in those creations which emerge from and as that World. Consequently, T. S. Eliot can declare that through theology, one can learn what a Christian believes, while through drama, one experiences what it means to be a Christian. Relatedly, faith for the Christian is inseparable from Scripture as heard and sacraments as practiced.

Aesthetic experience, then, involves "fascinated concentration" in which "the mind submits itself to its object and finds that the object is no stranger, but akin."[33] For the duration of that event, one can participate in what previously was the external history of another World, but now is experienced as the inner history of one's own functioning. Even though one might be vehemently opposed, for example, to Sartre's philosophy of existence, through his drama *No Exit* one can become an atheistic existentialist for two hours, living and moving and experiencing one's being from within that World. In fact, I was once so caught by that play that my comment to a companion was a plea: "Let's go have coffee—I need to talk myself out of this." Had our conversation not accomplished disengagement, that aesthetic participation would have continued to hold such claim that I never could have returned to what, just that morning, I had fondly called home. In Christian circles, such transition from aesthetic knowing to existential commitment is identified as the work of the Holy Spirit.

The process of furnishing one's World, new or old, is an ongoing one. One's World remains true only as long as one cannot claim to know otherwise. If growth flounders, doubt feeds the obsessio. Or if one tires of the life entailed by such transaction, weariness marks the presence of image dissonance. Either way, conversion is born out of hemorrhaging—of caughtness or of boredom.

Bultmann defined hermeneutics as understanding the great forms of human existence.[34] He did not recognize that they were multiple. Thus these great forms emerge as contrasting theological Worlds, through the interplay of obsessio and epiphania within the defining sociocultural context in which one finds oneself.

Temperaments

There is one more factor to be identified in the emergence of a theological World—the role played by what we will call *temperament* ("proper mixing"). While the dynamic of obsessio and epiphania is universal, for some individuals, the emphasis falls heaviest on obsessio; for others, on epiphania. Expressed functionally, the dynamic for some is more characterized by absence and drivenness; for others, by pull and lure. For some the obsessio has the feel of entrapment or boredom; for others, it exudes the energy of passion. There is reason to believe that such temperaments become established at an early age.

Of the two overarching temperaments, Type A most often characterizes a person born into an environment in which the child is anticipated, wanted, named, accepted, nurtured, and loved. In a word, she or he belongs. The resulting temperament shapes, as expectancy, a universe lively and immanent with epiphania. To use Chesterton's image, the earth is like a woodcutter's cottage, to which one returns at evening to have wine with friends before an open fire. As expressed by a representative of this temperament, "I have never known myself as unloved or not belonging."

Others, Type B by temperament, enter existence as being or feeling unwanted—nameless and alone. Consequently, this temperament is shaped by a universe heavy with obsessio. Epiphania is most likely to be promise, rather than a present reality; such moments may break in, rather than being illuminations of a more constant presence. Here the earth is like an ogre's castle, to be taken by storm. A representative of this temperament put it this way: "My father wanted a boy, and I am a girl. He refused to name me for three months. Finally, under pressure, he gave the local boys a quarter if they came up with a name. They named me for the stray dog in the back alley."

While these temperaments may favor one or another of the five theological Worlds, they provide significant contrasts within each World. Type A sees the defining rhythm from the vantage of the epiphania. Type B tends to look at the whole from within the shadow of the obsessio. The danger of the first is an indigestion of indifference, the tendency to take life and its mysteries for granted. The temptation of the second is an apathy bred of hunger, the inclination to qualify to death each potential epiphania. Since the author belongs to this second temperament, it is

THEOLOGICAL WORLDS

Essential Rhythm	Issue	Feel	Obsessio (human condition)	State	Atonement	Christology	Epiphania (salvation)
1 Separation and Reunion	Cosmos	Longing	Isolation experienced as abandonment (mystery, obtuseness, thrownness, opaqueness)	Alien/ Orphan	Experiential (substantive, humanistic, revelational) "To mediate" Love as tearing the veil	Revealer/ Evoker (to lead me home)	Coming home/ Being home (harmony)
2 Conflict and Vindication	History (evil)	Anger (rage)	Normlessness experienced as chaos (enigma, wrenched, invaded, oppressed, opposed)	Warrior	Constitutive (classical, ransom, dualistic) "To combat" Love as taking our part	Messiah/ Liberator	New Earth (consum- mation)

3 Emptiness and Fulfillment	Self	Ache (void)	Self-estrangement experienced as impotence (insignificance, self-alienation, not belonging, lost potential, invisibility)	Outcast	Enabling (subjective, representative, incorporative) "To model forth" Love as filling to overflowing	Example/ Model	Wholeness (enriched belonging)
4 Condemnation and Forgiveness	Demonic	Guilt	Powerlessness experienced as idolatry (diseased, condemned, falling short, fearful)	Fugitive	Compensatory (objective, forensic, exchange) "To take away" Love as forgiving the unworthy	Savior/ Redeemer	Adoption (reprieve)
5 Suffering and Endurance	Life	Over-whelmed	Meaninglessness experienced as engulfment (plagued, flooded, controlled, manipulated, wronged)	Victim/ Refugee	Assumptive (subjective, reversal, cancel, annealment) "To write off" Love as outlasting with long-suffering	Suffering Servant/ Companion	Survival (integrity)

possible that the five Worlds as described in this book may unknowingly reflect such weighting.

We turn now to the five theological Worlds themselves. In order to gain an interior feel for these Worlds, we will return to each several times, looking through the kaleidoscope of different questions. The first exercise in faceting consists in sketching contrasting obsessios. Such redrawing is for the sake of reenforcement, ongoing comparison, and multiple invitation. The method resembles a fugue, permitting little tolerance for a cheap pluralism of easy choices. Such an invitation is to play in *counterpoint*. Those for whom such a fugal style is difficult will have found here a chart which portrays in abbreviated, linear fashion the anatomy of each theological World, indicating the ingredients to be developed. Throughout, the intent is to portray each World from within, establishing all five as alternatives, insisting upon each as a viable and legitimate place in which to set up housekeeping.

CHAPTER TWO

Anatomy of the Theological Question—An Exercise in Obsessio

World One: Separation and the Cosmos—The Alien

Theological World One, characterized by the overarching rhythm of separation and reunion, has as its focus the cosmos. As one stands under the dome of its vastness, there emerges the sense of being an alien.

In becoming awakened in this World, one experiences life as having a fundamental arbitrariness. Everything that is could just as well not have been. What's more, everything could just as well have been radically different. If Australia had had more explorers, the world map as we now draw it would be totally reversed—up would be down and down would be up. One's own name is accidental and incidental, as arbitrary as the names of streets, cities, countries, stars, galaxies. Folks act as if to name is to identify, but this only hides the pall of an unknown "x-ness" that falls over everything. So often, relationships feel like fragile passings in the night, or the slight wave of a hand glimpsed through the gap in roaring semis on a freeway. And even the rare intimacies that occur have the strangeness of shared strangeness. We are separated. We are aliens.

Awareness of the tenuous fiber of this world can begin with a glance. As we stare up and out, the infinite largeness of our solar system comes to be only a mite in a galaxy of staggering size, which itself forms but a dot among numberless galaxies. Science demythologizes the initial romance of such glitter into a frigid vacuum of the outer remoteness of space. Even in this morning's paper, just before the comics, come reports of 6 new galaxies—the energy of 5 trillion suns, a collection of 2 billion stars 600,000 trillion miles across, located 18 trillion billion miles away from us.[1] Isn't whether the yoke of my egg is done enough to worry about?

Evidently not. This space/time, which soars infinitely outward, plummets back toward us. Sometimes life feels like one is descending rapidly on an elevator from a restaurant on top of a glass cylinder, through the roof into the atrium, and through the floor into a parking garage cluttered with empty beer cans. So our glance toward the infinitely large can pass through the appearance of our flesh to the staggeringly small. Deep inside, our own very modest composition is lost in a mystery of countless photons scattered randomly as the indeterminancy of energy. Caught arbitrarily between two besetting realms, we are *in* but not *of* either.

Life on such an in-between plane is a lonely affair. We live on a planet where we alone are self-conscious, and thus are blessed by being damned to watch, wonder, ponder, ask. Even this odd feature called consciousness is late, very late indeed in our planetary history. Time is characterized above all as billions of years of nonconscious, immaterial aloneness, squirming into subconsciousness through a holocaust of staggering waste and squishing to monstrous dead ends. Standing on its far end, we look back at an evolution of frayed and nibbled survivors that lived because they devoured before being devoured.

Yet before one can focus hostility externally on this Pac-Man called cosmos, we begin to sense that such nonbeing from without is the same as that which works quietly from within. Cancer was diagnosed yesterday for a friend. This evening, familiar names appeared in the obituary. This morning, an aging face peered back as I shaved. All this is sufficient to justify resigning from this cold-water flat called Earth, this alien parody of Job's dung heap. But just as I think I am approaching a firm conclusion, it is uprooted before I reach the office. During the waiting—the waiting for nothing more than the bus—someone unthinkingly whistling a Bach Aire catches me broadside. Or the sunrise on the freeway reflects the flash of a hawk in flight. These are the simple moments that shroud my head with mystery—and I am doomed to be a grounded angel with muddy feet, mumbling poetry over coffee in a deserted hanger.

Perhaps we are sketching this World with strokes too large, too clumsy. Many do not ponder deeply over the great and the small. Yet whatever the circumference of their version, it centers in the feel of longing. Somehow separation should not be, for one cannot be content in lonely unconnectedness. In fact, to be a stranger in a strange land is not strong enough. One's state is that of an alien—a streetwalker of the Spirit. One simply does not belong—that's it. And yet, deeply within, one senses beyond sensing that one was "made" to belong, somewhere, to "something."

Dostoevsky's Dmitri knew this. Standing before the Virgin Mary, he lusted for Sodom; and in the pits of Sodom, it was the Virgin for whom he longed. God, "you have made us too broad."[2] We do not belong on either end, and there is a wistful sadness within the restless limits of the center. Ecclesiastes captures that feeling: "[God] has put eternity into man's mind, yet so that he cannot find out what God has done from the beginning to the end" (3:11).

Looking at all this with a slightly different glance, two issues appear. The longing is such that one might seek solace in friendships or in the perfect marriage—but *it is never enough*. And yet even if it were enough, a second issue would become pervasive—*it will not last*. Thus not only are we thrown into life, but that which is thrown is very fragile. Our tissue-paper thinness—in fact, the contingency of everything—hints that nothing was intended, or at least not as much more than a whim. Here a focus is beginning. *The enigma is not of our doing, but of our nature*. Enigma invades us, making us not only a stranger in a strange cosmos, but a foreigner as well to each of its parts. Desultory, fitful, erratic, aimless, rangling, disconnected, we find ourselves in a context best fitted for a life of absent-minded digression.

Some citizens of this World make frequent use of the word *nightmare*. All seems to be moving along efficiently, no apparent breakdown in its proper workings. In fact, the wages may be good, and a promotion is rumored to be forthcoming. But during a strange moment, one seems pushed to ask, Why are we doing this? and from that moment on, nothing makes sense. Yet other people keep right on, some persevering, some becoming heralded for the way they do their task. But few seem to know to what end, and fewer still dare to ask. So the temptation is to go on living as if someone knows—though in the dark hours, the question quietly persists: Is it "a tale told by an idiot"? The most graphic nightmares appear as circles—of struggle, work, agony, running, only in the end to find oneself precisely at the lost intersection where one began.

Such hauntings can take graphic expression not only in the separation of self and cosmos. They come far closer—in the separation experienced in relationships—family, subcultures, and beyond. Whatever form they take, there is a feeling that is hard to capture. What is evoked is not anger (as in World Two), for that would somehow imply that things could be otherwise, and thus must be changed. Rather, one is invaded by plaintiveness: This is the way things are, and will be, no matter what we do—so much so that the more one struggles with such arbitrariness, the more it tends to take on the feeling of abandonment. Unlike World Five, however, this World does not permit resignation. To resign is to say Yes to this strange state of affairs. In fact, it would mean awarding an undeserved "oughtness" to the whole.[3] But in this World One, the way things are *should not be*. This is the paradox that renders the situation so absurd. We are coerced into asking questions of a universe that is perversely silent. We are born with a gregarious aching, into a universe that abandons her children. This is absurd.

This same absurd polarity finds abundant expression in our relation with nature. Here, as we saw in Dillard, we experience two sides—the obsessively arbitrary *and* the deliciously lyrical. The earth is indeed intoxicating. There is the incessant ocean, the majesty of the Matterhorn, the winged rhythm of a great blue heron, the gentle spring sun on virgin skin. Yet behind the spangled screen, the shadow taunts—of simply being seduced by a harsh nothingness, of indifference, of happenstance, of "nothing more." Archibald MacLeish's parable points toward the obsessio of this World. We are spectators watching within a circus tent, until "quite unexpectedly the top blew off." And then? Everywhere, before the "dazed eyes" of "thousands of white faces," there was simply "the black pall of nothing, nothing, nothing—nothing at all."[4]

Such separation haunts one with a sense of dualism. Since life seems to have the respectability of an arranged marriage, it also is shadowed daily by the threat of inevitable divorce. Tillich knew this world well, having almost died on the day of his birth. Franz Kafka's novels model this obsessio of World One. It is a world haunted, for it is a society in which others act as if it all makes sense. But while they assume that the pieces interlock with a margin that defines, "K" himself is an extra piece, from another puzzle. Some of the illustrations for his novels are formed by dotted lines, for nothing has a clear outline, an established place, a stable or definable feature. In *The Trial*, he is awakened on his birthday to be arrested, in effect, by the question, Who are you? He has a bicycle license as his only identity. And in *The Castle*, he is called to a job he can never find, ostensibly by the dilemma, What am I to do?[5] This is the obsessio of World One—arrested without real charge or Judge, called without a known or knowable Caller, made misfit by being awakened to walk to a drummer others seem not to hear. In a way, what renders one alone is the persistence of the one word, Why? When it intrudes, one becomes separated from a cosmos that might otherwise be home.

Yet can the question ever be quieted, once raised? To *exist* means "to stand outside of." Precisely. We are damned to look back or forward, inside or out, to watch, to see, to wonder. In being no longer able simply to participate, we are driven to question. While everything else seems to belong, self-consciousness renders the cosmos into "object," and in so doing, the self is rendered "object" for the cosmos. One becomes a freak. Elsie is able to be the contented cow *precisely because she cannot know that she does not know*. In fact, she belongs because she is blessed by being unable to know. Know what? She cannot know that her destiny is to be stew meat, awaiting her with packaged inevitability. If ever she were awakened, the daisies would never taste the same.

And so we are envious of her. At moments it seems that just to quiet the question would be enough. Yet we are born into the question, bred by the birth experience itself. As one student put it: "We're safe in the womb, and Pow! Our heads are twisted into a narrow and painful passage, we fall into a blinding light, and we are literally cut off from the one who gave us birth. From then on, one is always trying to go home." The issue is, in which direction—back to the womb, or toward a home not of this order?

Facing the full power of this obsessio is overpowering. What is strange is that because the cosmos so experienced is too harsh to admit, we end by intensifying the enigma. To be helplessly alone and abandoned is an unthinkable thought. It means to be totally out of control. And as we tremble before unthinkable thoughts, we are tempted to pull the cosmos down around us, clutching for control. But it is to no avail. We are the ones, Alves claims, who are *obsessed by the presence of the absence*.[6] Here the obsessio is nudged by something quietly slinking, sometimes dozing, in an unsweepable corner. It has the feel of an unasked but unquietable question, with something egging it on. For some it is triggered by the facticity of death, haunting the cosmos as if by law: "We must all die, we are like water spilt on the ground, which cannot be gathered up again" (II Sam. 14:14). It is horrendous that knowledge of this as our final destiny is the price extracted for our cosmic "specialness."[7]

Then comes the root of the question: What if that specialness could mean *being special to someone*—to belong. That is all that matters, really. From the side of the obsessio, that specialness bequeaths our damnation—separation. Yet in that separation, are we not blessed?—for we can *smell* the very flower that, in fading, damns us into knowing our destiny. And so our question: Can it be that behind it all, capable of a relation not possible through the separation of subject and object, is a *Who?*

We are the only animals, Marcuse observed, destined to hold up a mirror to ourselves. In a sense, the real mirror comes in staring at the cosmos, craving to catch, through a glass darkly, the shape of a face. Is there no presence of "otherness"? Simone Weil captures the hope that "we have been thrown out of eternity; and we are indeed obliged to journey painfully through time, minute in, minute out." It is the image of eternity that can make a point of contact in World One, for any God who could emerge as answer must be one not caught within our dilemma. God cannot be temporal, for to be *in* time is inevitably to experience abandonment *to* time. The poet Edwin Muir knew this, for it has been said that he was "obsessed with God, time, and his sense of dislocation."

The rhythm of each World, as we have indicated, is formed by the two poles of obsessio and epiphania. While we will develop the epiphania in a subsequent chapter, let us watch for a moment as the two poles illumine each other in this first World. It is this bipolar nature of the dilemma itself, ironically, that provides the hint of epiphania. We find ourselves at the intersection of that which repels, yet attracts; which horrifies, but still mesmerizes. Put most pointedly, we are the stepchildren of both abandonment and mystery, in a cosmos contoured by both void and fecundity.

Since for World One the dilemma is grounded in the structures of existence, any resolution is likewise structured there, but not so that the structures are changed. If there is to be an epiphania, *it will be one's perspective that will be changed.* This would enable experiential participation in a

presently unrecognized whole. For some persons, such
otherness focuses in the vantage point of an elsewhere
(e.g., heaven). For others, the focus is a unifying experience
that transcends all separation, if only in foretaste (e.g.,
mysticism). In either case, resolution emphasizes "re":
re-union, re-solution, re-conciliation. The positive image of
circle is daily engrained in this posture by epiphania. Our
present state is apogee, in an unseen rhythm known
through the experience of perigee.

This status of separation, seen from the perspective of an
epiphania, is often brought out by such images as "fall,"
"estrangement," "illusion," "unreality," "appearance."
The "why separation" must reflect the feel that it should not
be, with the hope that, *essentially*, it is not so. What appears
to be depends upon whether one sees from the narthex of
the father's house, or from the pigsty of "a far country."
Paul Tillich, an inhabitant of this World, states the bipolar
feel well. It is a yearning for the "reunion of the separated."
"We know that we are estranged from something to which
we really belong, and with which we should be united."[8]
Here the impulsing logic is given its defining rhythm.

Any resolution that befits the obsessio of World One is a
variation on the theme of final Harmony, but it cannot occur
here, other than by foretaste. Thus epiphania is a variation
on the theme of Going Home. Consequently, the here is, in
some sense, appearance rather than ultimately real. But as
residents in Plato's cave, we can come to know the "other
world" wistfully through recognizing passing shadows as
shadows. Whatever expression the obsessio takes, there is
about it a melancholy yearning for that which is other.

Richard Rubenstein remains close to the obsessio side of
this World. Gone is any possibility of World Two, for "if
there is a God of history, he is the ultimate author of
Auschwitz." Thus the only viable image is evoked by
nature's cyclical repetition and necessity. But the price is the
conclusion that evil is not only in us but in God. The sadness
experienced beneath every joy is the Ground of that "Holy
Nothingness known to mystics in all ages, out of which we

have come and to which we shall ultimately return"—in a "mystical nihilism."[9]

Examples of residents in World One are legion. In cinema, the movie fantasy *E.T.* is a near-parody of this World, distilled when the hero finally is able to shape his yearnings with the words, "E.T. phone home." It is the rhythm that defines *The Wizard of Oz* in what has become almost a folk liturgy. Of Dorothy we are told: "That little girl wishes to cross the desert. But no one has ever done it before." The good witch prophesies the route: "It is a long journey, through a country sometimes pleasant, and sometimes dark and terrible." And the goal—to return home, and to know it for the first time. In Bergman's *Seventh Seal*, the obsessio emerges in the intersection of a Knight (as tormented seeker) and a Squire (as cynical but compassionate disbeliever). Frustrated by the futility of the intent of the Crusades to change things, they seek to return home—only to discover it rendered nightmare by the plague of death.

In poetry, T. S. Eliot is major resident. His "waste land" is characterized by our separation from images which have "roots that clutch." In the absence of linear meaning, his expressions of epiphania take on the image of a circle. Obsessio comes in encountering the futility of death's circle, in which "my beginning is my end." Epiphania comes through a reversed circle: "In my end is my beginning." The issue is whether one is experiencing from the meaningless motion of the circumference, or from the still point of the unmoved center. The latter is a moment of reunion, enfolding all in wholeness. Then one knows that "the end of all our exploring will be to arrive where we started, and know the place for the first time."[10]

In fiction the obsessio of World One is captured in the novels of Herman Hesse. The hero of *Steppenwolf* is "a wolf of the Steppes that had lost its way and strayed into the towns and life of the herd." He is characterized by "his shy loneliness . . . his restlessness, his homesickness, his homelessness." Wandering the lonely streets, he discovers a door in the wall. It is an entrance to the "magic theatre,"

seen only by those who are madmen, coming as "a greeting
from another world." It is lit with a blaze, a "golden trail,"
where one is "reminded of the eternal, and of Mozart, and
the stars. For an hour I could breathe once more and live and
face existence, without the need to suffer torment, fear, or
shame." In attempting to describe such an encounter, images
of epiphania flood the pages: "To attain the cosmic," "the
unconditional," "the distant calls from another world,"
"seeking the essence," "to be extinguished in God," to "leap
into the unknown," life as a "perilous bridge," "greatness
through the loneliness of Gethsemane."[11] Finally Hesse blurts
it out as a confession:

All births mean separation from the All, the confinement within
limitation, the separation from God, the pangs of being born ever
anew. The return into the All, the dissolution of painful
individuation, the reunion with God means the expansion of soul
until it is able once more to embrace the All.[12]

The titles of two novels by Thomas Wolfe capture the
bipolar rhythm of World One's obsessio: *Look Homeward,
Angel* and *You Can't Go Home Again.*

Naked and alone we come into exile . . . into the unspeakable and
uncommunicable prison of this earth. . . . Which of us has not
remained forever prison-pent? Which of us is not forever a
stranger and alone? . . . O waste of loss . . . . Remembering
speechlessly we seek the great forgotten language, the lost
lane-end into heaven. . . . Where? When?[13]

Wolfe's World occurs as the hemorrhaging of "time and
the river," for "everything is going. Everything changes
and passes away." The promise of vindication, characteristic of World Two, is not possible here, for he cannot find
anything abiding in history. His hope is signaled by
nature—in the changeless pattern of change.[14] "Amid the
fumbling march of races to extinction, the giant rhythms of
the earth remained . . . germinal spring returned forever
on the land . . . and then the voyages, the search for the

happy land. . . . I believe in harbors in the end."[15] But there is no believing in these without the moments of foretaste along the way. While "the minute-winning days, like flies, buzz home to death," still "each moment is a window of all time." The "little things," as sacramental pointers, are sufficient—just "a stone, a leaf, an unfound door."[16]

In painting, this World is grasped in the longing of El Greco's twisting figures. Each is a flame barely anchored, stretching contortedly toward that which defies earthly containment. In their reaching, objects are stretched nearly into translucence, as if stained-glass emblems, harbingers of pure spirit, desperately in but persistently not of this world. They are aliens, yet bathed in a light whereby they know where to reach for home.

The same feel is present in the secular paintings of Botticelli. Berdyaev interpreted him well in indicating that his Venuses have left the earth and his Madonnas have left heaven.[17] It is in the touch of their meeting that our existence transpires. Here we know ourselves as world-weary and heaven lost—wistful, waiting, maybe.

Chirico's paintings provide a modern version. Seen in *The Disquieting Muses* are a Greek statue, a medieval castle, a factory, and a tower of the future. In their coexistence, time becomes centripetal in an extended Now. In such a moment, space becomes ominously empty, as objects recede along lines of multiple vanishing points. Yet there is a pregnant emptiness, with open doors and abandoned arcades of glimpsed shadows. Forlorn walls keep us in; or keep us out? Solitude is primary, yet with presences hinted by absences. And over it all is mystery, as the unspeakable. To what end? We do not know. And there is little hope that the question can be quieted.

Modern music has a special capacity for distilling the obsessio of World One. Unlike traditional classical music in which movement occurs in ordered, linear, and predictable patterns for the sake of closure, atonal music is characterized by continuous flux. Without a single tonal center as "home," tone becomes the notes' relativity to one another at any moment, devoid of any absolute. Resolution in any usual sense is impossible. The result is a prophetic hauntedness, reflective of an age of separation.

The spell of World One is resident in the plaintiveness of Gregorian chant. Its dynamic is a cautious moving from a bass note, always to return, in a mournful wholeness that gives each note a rightness. Yet in contrast with the emphatic downbeat of much current music, each rhythmic group begins with an upbeat that aspires. The rhythmic energy occurs at "the moment of take off, not at the moment of return to earth after flight." It is this "vaulted pattern of rise, rest, and fall" that captures the rhythm.[18] It is an obsessio of restless yearning, fed particularly in the final notes of each grouping. The return to the cadence is not direct, with a determined rigor. It is indecisive, tentative, hinting. What one experiences in a "waivering unpredict-ability" is a wistful and homesick wandering to mount again, after the unknown. This is the music of separation *seeking* reunion.

One of the most brilliant musical distillations of this rhythm that characterizes World One is Beethoven's string quartet Opus 132. While most of his music forms the defiance character of World Two, this piece was written after an illness near the end of his life. In the third movement, "Holy Song of Thanksgiving of a Convalescent to a Deity," World Two melts into World One. Drawing upon the Lydian mode, characteristic of the church's more mystic expressions, it begins slowly, sadly, quietly. There is a simple but hesitant ascending, haunted by backward steps, as if to gather momentum for the next step. The mood is that of hesitation following upon repetition. Finally there is a breakthrough, the violin section soaring, almost as solo instrument, drawing the other instruments to its level. And yet, even here, the violins break, sink, causing the other instruments to flutter with them, much as a fall breeze plays a requiem with the final leaves. The movement then brings a full return to where it began. There are occasional risings to a more comfortable height, only to be drawn down further, as if sampling the deep. The process takes place twice, the second time opened by a D-major brilliance with increased tempo. High and low counterplay, first violin and cello separated by a huge spread, yet drawn increasingly together by a descending harmony. Hauntingly, they approach each other, touch in order to separate, teased into soaring almost beyond range, until even the cello is in the treble octave. Then defiant strokes, reminiscent of the earlier Beethoven. But the final notes merge beyond harmony, in a quiet, almost breathless sadness. Separation and reunion pass beyond any challenge that could promise vindication, into a yearning melody of another order. The end is slow, almost to the point of gasping—outreaching and outreached.

Whatever content World One assumes, there is a longing for reunion. The world will not change. Hope is an experience whereby wholeness is known through a rival aperture. The master hymn of the obsessio of World One is:

"Precious Lord, Take My Hand."[19]

World Two: Conflict and History—The Warrior

As we have seen, the obsessio of World One, the theological World of separation and reunion, is the cosmos as a whole, and nature in particular. World Two, characterized by the rhythm of conflict and vindication, wraps its obsessio in the dilemma of history as a whole, and evil in particular. It emerged personally for me when a required college text for "Modern Social Problems" was Thucydides' *History of the Peloponnesian War*. There I encountered not only one of the first histories, but a paradigm of World War II—a war being waged as I read. The question inevitably arose: Have we learned nothing? Only an escalation in the means of destruction seemed different.

The obsessio began to focus. The world seems to thrive on conflict, in which no balance of power stays balanced.

The grin behind foreign policy is the thirst for domination. Survival of the fittest is a law of nature, while the "fittest" in history is a euphemism for exploitation. Reinhold Niebuhr traces the way the early biological necessity of being center becomes an obsession. The drive to be convolutes, at least for most males, into the craving to be *the* one. In the urban ghetto where I live, to leave one's mark is a deadly preoccupation. In suburbia it is called a vocation. The night streets are jungles, and the marketplace by day is hauntingly similar. This World is one of competition, in which winners determine the rules.

Yet it is more complex. Achievement gives no stability, not even for winners. There may be an extended stable moment, but it always ends too soon. In embarrassed silence, each life rounds out, as one begins down the slope marked "golden years." And all the while, others with younger energies are rushing up your down staircase, eager to fill the void of your demise. Water will be water when the finger is removed. But human life is slower. A gold watch and a lukewarm memory will mark the entropy of a lifetime struggle.

Such a portrait is too pure. Ours is a time that has lost innocence in peering beneath the sophistication. We have heard tapes made in oval offices and know of bishops being "called of God" in the politics of nonsmoke-filled motel rooms. One does not need to live long to see how human is evil's face. Conflict begins as a dilemma of the heart. Freud marks us as standing at an intersection, where death wish and life wish entwine in a living self-contradiction. Not only is the self pitted against other selves. Pitted even against me, my own self is in conflict—as traitor.

Yet even this does not bring us to the deepest level. The issue is not simply evil folk against good folk. Nor is it simply the individual, as pawn of one's own deep "within." To push these dimensions is to move into the obsessios of other Worlds. *The deepest agony is that all of us seem caught.* It is as though we are products of a vast extendedness that interlaces us with nothing less than "powers and principalities." *Violence is within because it is thoroughout the without.* In our time, we know this best as the Holocaust—eight million lives intentionally destroyed, yet no one to blame. It simply happened. No, it was worse. Eichman was simply following "rationally" (even creatively) the logic of orders given to him—given not by barbarians, but by the offspring of Bach, Beethoven, and Brahms. It is as if each participant served a system none had created and for which none would be responsible.

Will such massive conflicts ever change? One hopes that in knowing, there will be no repetition. But what is one to do with the fact that only one generation later, Israelis permitted the holocaust on a defenseless Lebanese "concentration" encampment. Scandalized? It is as though there is no longer the luxury of that possibility. We recognize such "anomalies" as a disclosure of the "normal." The very fabric of society is structured by conflict, where values are the pall for interests, coercion is the motive for "moral" action, and exploitation of the powerless is the measure of success. *Structured inequality* is the pleasant sociological term for this obsessio. It all fits, holding together, in a tragic whole, both winners and losers—in the illusion that each individual can win. To be a warrior, then, goes with the territory. And what is to be decided? The question of conflict is: Against whom? With whom? and For what end?

Some psalmists felt this obsessio deeply. They struggled to believe in a Creator in whose image all were created—created to till a garden designed by God's moral wisdom. Yet they were forced to agonize over the way things actually are: "Even my bosom friend in whom I trusted, who ate of my bread, has lifted his heel against me" (Ps. 41:9). Such events are not exceptions. Betrayal is the way things are:

> One dies in full prosperity,
> being wholly at ease and secure,
> his body full of fat
> and the marrow of his bones moist.

> Another dies in bitterness of soul,
>   never having tasted of good.
> They lie down alike in the dust,
>   and the worms cover them. *Job 21:23-26*

Why dost thou stand afar off, O Lord?
Why dost thou hide thyself in times of trouble?
In arrogance the wicked hotly pursue the poor. *Psalm 10:1-2a*

The cry for epiphania in World Two follows directly:

> May [God] defend the cause of the poor of the people,
>   give deliverance to the needy,
>   and crush the oppressor! *Psalm 72:4*

While World Four is drawn to focus on the duplicity that lurks in the individual heart, World Two has as its obsessio a different question: To what avail is the struggle of a lifetime, or of an epoch—indeed, of history itself? The haunting spectre is of history full of sound and fury, in its violence signifying less than nothing. Shall one become resigned to it, as an Aquinas in his later years, when in mystic moments characteristic of World One, he discerns in joy that the works of his hands were only "idle straw," hardly fit for burning? For inhabitants of World Two, the response is clear: *Never.*

It would be the cruelest of jokes if the Kingdom "yet to be" turns out to be the Garden of Eden that "once was." While citizens of World One find solace in *re*-storation, imaged by circle, World Two sees circularity as absurdity. History is a nightmare if it is only a frantic struggle to return us to square one. Such a preposterous rhythm would render history a mistake, an unfortunate product of sin. In so doing, time becomes illusion, for our efforts cannot be more than tragic deception. *The only hope is that the future will be significantly different.* Therefore, if the future is not future because it is already a present tense for God, there can be no vindication of history's conflict—none at all. History is rendered unreal, and thus so are we.

Consequently, any epiphania that could captivate World

One as hope is a *foe* of World Two. Death is illustrative. While in World One, death can express the obsessio, it often becomes threshold into eternity—or short of that, a metaphorical instrument of reunion. In World Two, on the contrary, the facticity of death is overbearing. Death is not enigma—it is crime. The grim reaper is Foe. In no sense can death be accepted as essential to life—as part of God's inexplicably wise design. Death is Invader, the symbol of all that should not be. *It must be fought!* This is why, unlike World One, nature is no solace. Arising from nature, self-consciousness renders those rhythms terrifying—into obsessio. If there is to be vindication, nature's circle of repetition must be turned into history as meaningful linearity—moving toward consummation.

For World Two, the condition is not that of illusion, as if the self is myopic. Thus the answer is not to see death in a new way. The cry is for the death of death. The finite is not a transparency for otherness, but exists for its own sake. Thus the language of epiphania will be that of incarnation rather than immanence. It must render the fleshly joyous. This is why Bonhoeffer can insist that "it is only when one loves life and the earth so much that without them everything seems to be over that one may believe in the resurrection and a new world."[20] The obsessio is concerned for this world, so that any epiphania that pulls attention to another world is treasonous.

Miguez de Unamuno is illustrative. His characters crave an "eternal carnality," a desire so clear that even God, to be God, must have created the world in a fleshly struggle for eternal glory. Personhood is a restlessness born of conflict with death. Even if it turns out that there is no epiphania, one must create it by a double obsessio: "Let us act so that Nothing becomes an injustice. Let us battle against destiny even if there is no hope of victory. Let us battle against it quixotically."[21]

A friend captured the feel of this obsessio by contrasting the way each of us responds. "While things make me cry," he stated, "they make you angry." His sadness, expressed best at a piano, reflects his residency in World Five. My anger, rooted in the ways things are, is a rebellion. And so, characteristic of World Two, there will be change, or, short of that, protest as long as one lives. And still I am attracted to monastaries, where the anger is slaked into an ache, and for a while, I can let myself act as if World One is home.

Albert Camus shares this ambiguity. He yearns for the epiphania of World One, for otherwise, existence is "absurd." Without it, his options are suicide, murder, or rebellion. Yet since the first two mean saying Yes to cosmic silence and death, which are what make life absurd, rebellion is the only way to say No as a Yes. If a loveless universe is wrong, I shall love the unloved until my last breath. If death is insane, I shall so cherish life that death must do battle at every step. An absurd response to absurdity is a moral victory over history—as ironic vindication. So seen, there are two types of responses in each World: One can be grasped by an epiphania, or one can so live the obsessio as to make it a protest over the absence of epiphania.

The latter approach in World Two appears as parable in Camus's *Plague*. Each day Death saps the power from an asthma victim, yet day after day he passes peas from one pan to another, giving tortured defiance as the only vindication there can be. Each effort is a protest against the contest itself.

Unlike World One, what is needed in World Two is not new experience or an awakening to a hidden aperture through which to perceive everything as Whole. The dilemma is factual. It resides not in me but in the world itself. Actual change, not new awareness, can be the only epiphania.

This obsessio, particularly intertwined with death, as it is in this World, receives classic expression in Dylan Thomas's plea to his dying father:

> Do not go gentle into that good night . . .
> Rage, rage against the dying of the light.[22]

His shout of epiphania is clear: "Death shall have no dominion."[23] Obsessed with birth as the beginning of death, Thomas's life (and poetry) illustrate the passionate refusal to accept this terror, this threat to life. Ernest Becker identifies all history precisely that way—as a frantic convolution with death.

And the options? The most common is the denial of death, for which civilization is the screen. But for refusal to succumb to the obsessio, with epiphania at best a hint, Becker insists that heroes are demanded. Such insurrectionists carve out their mark against nature, whether in creating a cathedral, a totem pole, or a family that spans three generations. The obsessio of World Two births a yearning for an earth on which "the things that [humankind] creates in society are of lasting worth and meaning, that they outlive and outshine death and decay, that [we and our] products count."[24] Vindication, then, is not in "otherness," but in "future."

Becker's frantic grappling for meaning, rendered graphic in his own futile battle against cancer, gambles that behind the chaos is a driving force, a cosmic heroism, that draws us to "heroic transcendence." Such faith frees us to "fashion something—an object or ourselves—and drop it into the confusion, make an offering of it."[25] While such a "mite offering" has affinity with the endurance theme of World Five, it is the heroic quality that keeps pulling Becker centrally into the rhythm of conflict and vindication. Culmination must be *of* history, *in* history.

Bonhoeffer proffers the Christian epiphania for World Two by asking, "Does the question about saving one's soul appear in the Old Testament at all? Aren't righteousness and the Kingdom of God on earth the focus of everything?" His distillation of Scripture places it squarely within this World: "The redemptions referred to here are *historical*, i.e. on *this* side of death." So stated, he points to a bridge over which many liberation theologians have chosen to pass.[26]

Representatively, liberationist Miguez-Bonino distills the epiphania necessary to engage the obsessio: "In this tradition, the eschatological kingdom is experienced and understood as constantly pressing to manifest itself in history, inviting people to enter obediently into the sphere of God's sovereignty on earth."[27]

The question that follows is whether one's rage is *at* God or *with* God. If World One is true, inhabitants of World Two seem justified in anger against a God for whom history lacks reality. For our rage to be together *with* God, the epiphania must disclose God as taking sides within history. The image of God's wrath is central, but not as judgment against individuals (as in World Four). God's judgment is upon the shenanigans of history. It is because the powers and principalities are presently threatening this earth with extinction, that "never have we been so plainly conscious of the wrath of God."[28]

Here the impact falls less upon individual sin and more upon evil. In World Four, the focus is upon the fallen self, blinded by pride and obsessed, in arrogant glee, with aggrandizement. But in World Two, the self appears less as vicious and more as pitiful. Behind the masks of power is hidden the bravado of frightened children. Crowded by conflicting and manipulative societal powers and structures, the self cringes, donning an assigned costume in order to belong. Whatever the names of the games, the rules all sound like those of Blind Man's Bluff. Attack is defense; pretense is control against vulnerability.

In such a conflictive atmosphere, one learns quickly. One is squeezed into a contorted shape, as being and nonbeing conflict within and without—until one is unclear who one is. This is why Marx can judge the capitalist system so harshly, yet harbor no anger at individual capitalists. They too are pawns of that over which they have no control.

We are only too willing, for at the edges of life's hemorrhaging we are terrorized into false consciousness. In staring at death, eyeball to eyeball, one clutches for anything as if it were an absolute. "Eat of this tree," says the satanic, and "you will not die" (Gen. 3). And so I eat—and clutch. It's all I have. I'm white—white is best; I'm American—the Third World is ungrateful; I'm Protestant—Roman Catholics are superstitious. The dynamic goes on, clutching at superiority—I'm schooled, heterosexual, male, middle-class, ad nauseum, ad infinitum. Such idolatry piled upon idolatry, regarding whatever I am as normative, is not the expression of viciousness, but of fright—a shaping and being shaped by the collective sanctuary of class or culture or nation, against my inevitable demise.

Looking through the back window, we see not monsters of evil but bloated structures of pretense. And with such support, the individual dead ends can become the silly but elevated prance called Playing God. For most persons, such bravado is more vicarious than active. One so loses one's self in the processes of the collective whole that self-consciousness is minimized. Obsessio is dealt with negatively by not feeling, not knowing, and thus not questioning. The temptations, then, are to control or to be controlled—in human systems, rendered demonic.[29] But they can be changed, for they rest not in humans as diseased (World Four), but as deceived. "Father, forgive them, for they know not what they do."

Whatever form epiphania takes, God must take sides. God must be *within the conflict itself.* I remember my own painful encounter with this issue. My mother had died three months earlier, and my father had just lost to cancer. As only child, I stood alone by the coffin. Christian after Christian clutched my hand, ministering to me with variations on a common theme: "You can't understand, but it is God's will." "God called him home."

These words, meant to comfort, were spoken most likely out of World One. They were sentiments by fine and gentle people. How can one not be touched by the graphic power of a Socrates, who long before them had acclaimed the swan's song as rejoicing—for death as a welcomed lintel into eternity.[30] But that day, by that coffin, I learned how solidly I live within World Two. I had to excuse myself. Stepping out to the solace of tears in a dark parking lot, I trembled, knowing deeply that the God they offered was my enemy.

Soon afterward, a friend died in the midst of opening

Christmas gifts. At the funeral, the priest said, "This Christmas God gave Lil the finest present of her life." For me, these are treasonous statements. They betray not only me, but my father, Lil, and God. For residents of World Two, death cannot be God's idea or design. If there is a God, that God must be railing against it—and suffering death's onslaughts with even greater sensitivity than we. Dostoevsky's Ivan spoke deeply as he burned with this obsessio: If violence against just one innocent child is the price woven into the fabric of God's great design, "I shall turn back the ticket."[31] Were my friends wrong? That is not the question. Their obsessio is elsewhere.

Death is more than literal for World Two. It is symbol of *loss*, whatever its form. Thus epiphania entails a God who clearly prefers the loser. This God knows, with special care, the orphan, the widow, the poor, for these are the expendable. Barth expanded this conflict into metaphysical dimensions. God's foe is the *Nihil*, that active nothingness which gnaws relentlessly to undo God's creativity. Thus the obsessio of being conflicted is true even for God. This, in fact, must be especially true for God, for we are powerless before the Nihil. Thus epiphania is in knowing that our foe is likewise God's foe.

Harvard theologian Arthur C. McGill struggled personally and intellectually from within World Two, focusing on the demonic. Demonism, he claims, is the dominant religious experience today, and thus suffering is the central theological problem. The demonic is the unseen faceless energy of destruction, which causes dread, whether through violence, disease, or death.

The demonic is not the wound itself, but that power, present in the wound, which generates the infection and eventually devours the entire life of the body [or] the dynamic of hate that magnifies the hostility into inhuman proportions until it becomes an insatiable rage. . . . Its essence is to twist and break apart the forms of things, to stunt human growth, to disrupt the social order, to misshape animals and trees, to obstruct the fruitfulness of the earth. The demonic is known only by the destruction it causes.[32]

In resisting any reduction of evil to sin, McGill insists that vindication over evil requires a divine transfiguration of creation with us on our behalf. Thus resolution tends to appear as variations on the theme of vision. For World One, vision refers to a transfiguring gaze into timeless transcendence. Vision here in World Two, clearly different, means prolepsis of a future that will, in time, vindicate the struggle which is history itself. The heart of prayer for this World is "Thy Kingdom come, *on earth* as it is in heaven": "Behold, the dwelling of God is with [humankind. God] will be with them . . . will wipe away every tear from their eyes, and death shall be no more, neither shall there be mourning nor crying nor pain any more, for the former things have passed away" (Rev. 21:3-4).

While a wide sweep of political loyalties is clustered under this umbrella, for the radical, the "eschatological banquet" will have Che Guevara and Sojourner Truth as co-celebrants in the Holy City. Here such atheists as Camus and Marx can make common cause with the Christian. On the one hand, we have the "absurd protest" against such a God for not existing. On the other, we find a commitment to preferential treatment for society's losers because the structures of history are on their side. Either way means living "as if"—gambling on a vision worthy of a struggle that alone can vindicate the interfaces of history.

In summary, the converging images that fashion the obsessio of World Two are rooted in a basic feeling of anger, emerging as a passion for justice. As Beverly Harrison insists, "The power of anger is the work of love. . . . All serious moral activity, especially action for social change, takes its bearings from the rising power of human anger."[33] The enigma is born midst the nameless faces forgotten and used in the apparently purposeless struggle called history. Lost are not only simple random individuals, but the collective victims endlessly caught in the cycle of empires in their rise and fall. Such wars and rumors of wars are the backdrop writ large for whatever one touches, for life and death are in an ongoing pitched battle.

The yearning is not for escape, but for consummation.

"There are no ways around crucifixions, given the power of evil in the world. . . . The aim of love is not to perpetuate crucifixions, but to bring an end to them in a world where they go on and on and on!"[34]

Epiphania is a vision of sabbatical shalom, giving joy to tragedy turned comedy, even for blades of grass. Ours is a struggle in behalf of the last act, of a script titled, like Luigi Pirandello's play, *Characters in Search of an Author*. Therefore its residents feel especially the pathos of a joke in which the punch line is forgotten—or a mystery novel from which the last page has been torn—or the five-thousand-piece puzzle from which the last piece is missing. No one can be Christ for World Two without being able to say, "It is finished."

The theological task, then, is not so much to *know* reality as to *change* it. If resolution for World One is beneath, behind, above, or surrounding that which appears to be, for World Two it can be only *through* the conflict—a conflict declared to be real because of what shall be. Since the Nihil, however understood, is real and not a projection of our sinful doings, history's conflict tends to take on cosmic proportions. Thus Incarnation becomes a *bridgehead*, interpreted by Webster as "an advanced position seized in hostile territory as a foothold for further advance."

In literature, this obsessio is well imaged in Herman Melville's *Moby Dick*. The inscrutible white whale focuses that which leaves one without a leg and with half a lung. It drives the Ahabs to set sail—not in flight but in pursuit, though with a hunch that they may be the pursued. Dostoevsky's literary battlefield is shaped by this dual agony. On the one hand, "Can we live with God?" given the pervasiveness of evil. This is the obsessio of World Two. On the other hand, "Can we live without God?" given the demonry of humans playing God in the vacuum. This is the obsessio of World Four.

In poetry, Edna St. Vincent Millay is clear. Of death she declares, "I know. But I do not approve. And I am not resigned." Her conclusion follows: "I shall die, but that is all that I shall do for Death."[35]

In painting, one is drawn to Van Gogh. His cypresses

swirl upward, catching the rhythms of the earth itself. But the feel is not the otherworldly mystical foreshadowing characteristic of El Greco. The aura is deeply of struggle, capturing a frenzied longing *of* as well as *for* the earth. His own suicide appeared to be an acting out of R. D. Laing's insistence that the real sickness is adjustment to the way things are. Therefore purple cows and green hair are emblems of vindication. Van Gogh's fanatical insistence upon working from direct observation of the earth functions as obsessio, with the epiphania of art as transubstantiation. His was the calling to midwife the inner will of life as Spirit, seething and vigorously teeming forth. He lived as he painted, with a pungent, restless rippling, as if splashes of sunlight were erupting into rude and fearless combinations of visibility. An unmailed letter found after his death functions almost as eucharistic prayer over his paintings, and over this World: "My own work, I am risking my life for it."

Beethoven's Symphony No. 5 is easily recognizable as a paradigm of World Two. The theme is one of costly but impending resolution. Even the verbose endings of many of his symphonies reiterate this determination for final vindication. Symphony No. 3, the Eroica, expresses particularly well this heroic mode, which he himself called "moral purpose and steadfast resolve." The brilliance of many of his later works is understandable as magnificent defiance in the face of final deafness. It is no surprise, then, when we are told that on his death bed, as a loud thunderclap roused him, Beethoven sat up, shook his fist, and died.

An alternative version of World Two is orchestrated by J. S. Bach. During his last years, he realized that the contrapuntal World of conflict and resolution, which characterized his life and music, was being replaced by a contrasting World, expressed by increasingly homophonic music. In a supreme effort, he created *The Art of the Fugue*. It was his struggle for final vindication, not only of his work, but of his religious vision. In an enormous cycle of fugues, all in the same key and derived from a single motif, he displayed the full range of conflict capable of resolution. When he sensed the approaching defeat in death, he stopped, wrote the choral prelude "Before Thy Throne I Stand," and offered up his incomplete fugues for vindication.

World Three: Emptiness and the Self—The Outcast

World Three is shaped by the rhythm of emptiness and fulfillment. While the obsessio for World One is the cosmos, and for World Two it is history, for this World the obsessio is the self. It is birthed by an absence, standing where what was once called an "I" has dissipated. For many it begins as an aching void. What seemed to make sense is collapsing in parody. The weight of this obsessio is a lack of self-confidence, which emerges from an inability to believe in one's self. The only certainty is the truth that if anyone really knew me, they wouldn't like me. Perhaps this is too mild; they would simply choose to have nothing to do with me. This is not like World Four, in which the issue centers in guilt, as if I were shielding a bedroom closet full of skeletons. It is more that I am hiding my nothingness. My secret is that there is simply vacuum behind the facade of what I appear to be. Here Adam and Eve experience not so much guilt as nakedness.

Playwright Eugene O'Neill portrayed this obsessio with masks. Normality in relationships rests in appearance. But there are moments when a certain affability lures me into carelessness. The mask slips, and the whitewashed sepulcher of "me" peers out. The other person pulls back, embarrassed at best, horror-struck at worse. Vulnerability risked is vulnerability made lethal. "Sorry about that." The mask—the pleasant one with the slight smile—is adjusted. Then, with restored propriety, life regains its feigned respect.[36]

Sartre's *No Exit* portrays life as convincing others that I am who I would like them to believe I am, hoping that if they believe the facade, the lie might be lived as true. He likens this to hell, for it never works. In the loneliness, I so crave to be accepted that in the game of trying to be who they want me to be, I no longer know the me with whom the "I" and "they" are playing. To quiet the obsessio, the game becomes mutual blackmail.

So one acts out the daily rhythms as if they are a meaningful whole, at least for others. But when the day is over, the tedious routines are quieted, the family is in bed, and the cat is put out, then sleeplessness at the kitchen table takes on a persistent ache. It seems bottomless, for it has no apparent reason, aimed at nothing in particular. It is not boredom rooted in inactivity, but often activity born of boredom. One is P.T.A. president, youth sponsor, entertainer, chauffeur—it's a "zoo." It's just that more and more are increasingly adding up to less and less. No one tells me this. They don't need to. No one is accusing me of anything, other than that I don't "look myself." In what goes on, I am simply an afterthought.

The dilemma, at bottom level, is not external. If I could continue to function the way I always have, all apparently would be well. They would never know. But I do—that's the problem. The problem is within me. "I" can no longer deceive "me" by living in the vacuum. There is nothing there. No matter how pleasing others may find my appearance, or my performance, or my anything, I know that zero and zero and zero, infinitely listed, still add up to one fat zero. No, not even fat—but maybe so. It is time to diet.

For some, this obsessio has a sudden birthing—an unexpected divorce, a missed promotion. For others there is forced time alone, as in a fragile recuperation. There is little to do but think—and think. And in thinking, one is forced beyond the immediate Now. For the first time, one can see with graphic inevitability the one hour of "glory" twenty-five years in the future. There is an engraved watch, followed by a respectful sadness, marking transition into forgottenness. After a massive coronary, my cousin's life was torn into two realizations. As the beer commercials say, You only go around once. And his once was dedicated to talking people into smoking one brand of cigarettes. For the dutiful wife, even the accolades of the retirement banquet are vicarious.

There can be shadows of World One around the edges, but the weight here is not on the cosmos. It falls full blown on me. I am an outcast—not because I have been cast out, but because there is nothing there to begin with. "Hollow men," T. S. Eliot called us, the ones who are "quiet and meaningless as wind in dry grass." Such "paralyzed force" seems to contrast graphically with Dostoevsky's characters—the vigorously passionate, even bloody ones, those more at home in World Two. No, in World Three the end will be not a bang but a whimper. It has the feel of a personal "Waste Land." As Eliot watched the treadmill of morning traffic over London Bridge, returning at night to the same everything, he cried, "I had not thought death had undone so many."[37] The high point of the workday is a peanut-butter-and-jelly sandwich with those who, like me, would choose not to be there.

For some, the obsessio arises as an underemployed self. It assumes many faces: women with IQs of 130, socialized to find fulfillment as authorities in detergent effectiveness; black youths of fine ability, washing cars until a drugged oblivion is preferable. These are symbols of the ache that signals vacuum at the core. We see not the tragedy of human nature *depraved,* as in World Four, but *the pathos of human nature deprived.* It is psychological asphyxiation, rooted in anorexia of the spirit. We become desperate and alone because that which seems sufficient for others leaves us gasping. For these walking dead, the nothingness of suicide can take on the appeal of a definitive tranquilizer. Members of World One are afraid of losing the address of home; in World Three, I am afraid of losing me.

Others describe this obsessio as "being by-passed." Life goes on, but in such a way that I am treated as if I were not. Ralph Ellison identifies this as the obsessio pressed upon black people in this country—the "invisible ones":

[handwritten marginalia:] or of never knowing me

I am invisible, understand, simply because people refuse to see me. Like the bodiless heads you see sometimes in circus sideshows, it is as though I have been surrounded by mirrors of hard, distorting glass. When they approach me they see only my surroundings, themselves, or figments of their imagination—indeed, everything and anything except me.[38] *This why we need friends, I can't complain if I accept this dating*

Invisibility begins early. Children should be seen but not heard. Others are to be heard but not seen. Either way, one is rendered transparent. Invisibility is made the social rule of "feminine graciousness." The goal of entertaining is that all goes so well that it seems to happen without a happener. Nineteenth-century mansions call for secret panels, out of which black servants glide—providing invisible service. As a result, one is forced to live vicariously rather than directly—the derivative of belonging to another, whether owner, husband, corporation, class, or nation. World One has the feeling of looking in from the outside. In World Three, I am in the room, but no one notices. So it may be better to remain invisible than to open my mouth and be rejected. At least I'm in the room; they might put me out.

At some distance from the situation, the obsessio seems obvious—and advice from other Worlds is always available. But the real truth is that the obsessio can be made bearable, sometimes for a lifetime, by the seductive rewards for not changing. The payoff can be variations on the themes of security, advantage, access, propriety, possessions. I may not *be*, but I certainly do *have*. There may not be much inside, but the outside can look just fine. Yet Eleanor Rigby remains the symbol of paucity in the midst of all recompense: "I knew too much, but I can't forget."

In fact, it is when one knows, that the real pain begins. It takes up residence without rent somewhere near the solar plexis. And the drugs prescribed for depression only lock a badly fitting cellar door. Erikson's bald-faced description of a woman's defining social context clarifies why many feminists live in World Three: "She holds her identity in obeisance as she prepares to attract the man by whose name she will be known, by whose status she will be defined, the

man who will rescue her from emptiness and loneliness by
filling 'the inner space.' "[39]

When such a game-plan for filling emptiness is stripped
of its pink bows, one is awakened to rage. Only then is the
carefully groomed passivity invaded, to reveal, behind
aborted assertiveness, a true self. Individuals ripe for such
rage today are legion—women, ethnics, native Americans,
poor whites, gays, the Third World, the aged. These are the
expendables, outcasts even to themselves. Once exposed,
this obsessio broadens. Even the religion once so support-
ive becomes exposed as one of the most subtle instruments
of oppression. One begins to view with suspicion such
simple virtues as patience. And what was once the heart of
piety seems the road map for Death Row: "Let one deny
oneself and follow me." One's experience does not warrant
the promise that to lose oneself is to find it—at least not a
self that is "me." And the waiting lines to cash in the
coupons are very long. The self—*my* self—always seems to
be last, an afterthought, *even by me.*

Perhaps one could live this expected way if it were not for
double standards. To struggle with this obsessio in World
Three is to find oneself not far from the shadow of guilt.
When I begin to think of me, I am made to feel selfish. Yet
this morality of self-denial is being taught by the self-af-
firming! What does one do with a Christianity that
condones the behavior of slaveowners, while converting
the slaves to inner docility? Epiphania can begin with the
recognition of psychological slavery as a patronizing
subversion of those who already have so little by those who
have so much. And the virtue of patience, well internalized,
is a masochism of self-crucifixion.

Kierkegaard distilled this World Three presence powerfully around an idea that marked the emergence of
existentialism. To become who I am—that is a task worthy
of a lifetime. Knowing the truth is what World One is about.
Changing the truth is what World Two is about. In World
Three, the pilgrimage is to *become* the truth—not to know or
to do, but to *be.* The task is to embody the truth, known as
true only in the fullness of self, nurtured in the living of it.

This centrality of self is a special cause for cleavage between Worlds Three and Four, focusing on the contrast between love as agape and love as eros. Anders Nygren defines *agape* as love of the other for the other's sake. *Eros* is love of something for one's own sake. With World Four, he claims the former as the Christian ideal, the latter as the heart of sin.[40] The dilemma of World Four is the self's arrogant insistence on being central. An alternate tradition is the one that receives expression in World Three. For Plato, eros is the upward movement for wholeness. Augustine recognized love as an immanental seeking of each thing for its own measure. This impulse for fulfillment receives various names—*entelechy* (Aristotle), *conatus* (Spinoza), *libido* (Freud). Thus the passion emitting from the obsessio of World Three is the passion to be. Peter Homans, clearly of World Three, insists that theology since Freud must entail shifting the idea of self from self-limitation to self-completion. Foundational must be the impulse of the self "to complicate, to expand, to enrich, to double back and look again and again."[41]

This World permits wide diversity in understanding the nature of the self. Since there is no God for Sartre, authenticity means the reconciliation of one's existence and essence through the self-consistency of willing, in each moment, an essence which one gives to one's self. By contrast, the theistic perspective of a Kierkegaard insists that each self has a unique nature given by God. One's task, then, is discernment, for the gnawing ache of the obsessio is the feel of the self's alienation from itself, the crying out of a deprived human nature for its essence. One becomes outcast by being an outcast to oneself and thus to the Creator. Or the nature of the self may be identified as creativity, as in Whitehead—one chooses, in each new moment, the optimum possibility of each new "initial aim" to become a unique event.

Whatever the description, the greater the stress on an innate essence, the more the weight falls upon self-discovery through some form of suffering. The more open-ended the issue of essence, the more the tendency

toward a lyric quality. Sam Keen captures this in his title
Beginnings Without End. "I prefer passion, folly, and
interesting mistakes," he states, as over against "calm,
harmony, and wisdom."[42] Norman O. Brown develops this
perspective by rejecting commitment, promise, or will
power, for the sake of spontaneity. Central for him is not
the ego but the id. The self is creative by nature. The
problem is that society contaminates the self through
repression, blocking its libidinous expansiveness. In strong
contrast with World Two, he insists that acceptance of
death, as the natural conclusion to a full life, can free us for
total eroticism.[43] Therefore resurrection—a resurrection
alight with poetic imagination—is from the death imposed
by culture.

In such expressions, epiphania entails being set free. This
might be understood as freedom from predetermined
limits, from hierarchical roles from patriarchal patterns, or
from those subtle interdictions rendered internal as guilt.
The passion for fullness must be unlocked, whereby
genuine living becomes life in love with itself. If Christianity
is to be other than foe, it means taking seriously the Jesus of
John's Gospel: "I am come that they might have life, and
that they might have it more abundantly" (10:10 KJV). Since
"the kingdom of God is within you," faith brings wholeness
in which one can believe in oneself. One cannot love others
if one cannot love oneself. "Wilt thou be made whole?" (5:6
KJV). Then "take up your pallet, and walk. . . . Your faith
has made you whole."

What, then, of evil? It is the squandering of life's
potential. Thus shadowing World Three can be a sadness of
paths not taken, of relations neglected or refused, of
opportunities deprived or dissipated. To be awakened is to
recognize the heaviness of being conditioned, controlled,
socialized, or misborn—until often too little, too late.
Things have been on hold for so long that I feel at least one
tentative step behind. Even more, there is that inbred
hesitation to assert myself, or they'll put me back in the box.

In World One, the void is in the mysterious heart of the
cosmos. In World Two, it appears as entropy at the center of

history. In World Three, the void is within, at stomach height. Unlike the first World, in which one never belongs, here one does, but so submerged that the self is hardly distinguishable from its environment. It is unclear where it stops and one's self begins. Thus belonging actually intensifies solipsism. One is trapped in the self, nicely boxed from without, a bolt on the lid from within—afraid, vacant, not even for rent.

For many, the first board may be pried loose from the outside. Though fascinated, one is seized by anxiety— inveigled into looking, frightened to see, paralyzed to step. Sometimes the beginning is in seeing those more blessed, who from childhood have known outreached hands that invite new steps. Either way—whether awakened to the new or lured toward novel breadth—one is exposed to the anxious excitement of a sprouting terrain. Paralleling the cosmos itself, the Big Bang of self-discovery results in an expanding universe of eager energy, pushing, exploring, ceaselessly falling in love. One is awakened to a world uncovered, as in springtime one discovers everywhere the magic continuity of gentle unfolding. Being lured forth is never without risk, especially for those driven to make up for unused life. But as the song says, "The heart afraid of dying can never learn to dance."

The shape of epiphania can be suggested by contrasting the spirituality of the first three Worlds. For World One, spirituality tends to take on the marks of contemplation, with variations moving toward the sacramental or mystic-like participation in mystery. Spirituality in World Two tends to focus upon prayer (*preiere*, "to ask"), characterized by intercessions. Central is the dialogical companionship of co-creators, in faithfulness to promise. Spirituality in World Three tends toward meditation. In Ignatian meditation, one is invited to move inside the feelings of biblical participants: How did Ruth feel? What would it be like if you were Peter? Particularly helpful is open-ended fantasy: You are going down a road and you come to a fork. Spirituality has the flavor of invitation, with evocation directed toward the imagination. The consideration of possibility is the invitation to be. Mary Travers sings it well: "I wish I knew how it feels to be free."

Once awakened, one sees differently. Camus's imprisoned "stranger," peering through a crack in the prison wall, sees the blue of sky and the sounds of earth. It is then that he realizes that he can live, in the fullness of one moment, more than most persons do in a lifetime. Risking overstatement, World One is recognizable as fantasy. World Two moves toward comedy (meaningful ending). World Four has the marks of tragedy or a morality play. World Five drinks of pathos.

And what of World Three? It savors deeply of lyric poetry, which e. e. cummings captures as life-style: "We can never be born enough. We are human beings, for whom birth is a supremely welcome mystery, the mystery of growing: the mystery which happens only and whenever we are faithful to ourselves. . . . Life, for most people, simply isn't."[44]

How does such a World appear visually? With El Greco as master for World One and Van Gogh for World Two, Rubens and Renoir serve well as heralds for World Three. Even in Rubens' crucifixions, epiphania is suggested neither as a power that comes in upon the event, nor as a transparency that points to a realm beyond the event. An intrinsic quality exists within the figure itself—a vitality that is fulfillment in its own immanent and expansive strength. Renoir's significance for World Three can be seen in juxtaposition with Rembrandt's World Five. In Rembrandt, one senses an internal depth, where the soul is annealed through the lonely buffeting of the external world. In contrast, Renoir's fleshly surface of soft and gentle fecundity emits an intrinsic beauty as its potential nature. The radiance of the female figure takes on such vitality as to be a portent of divine immanence. Paintings of World One are characterized by transparency and kenosis, the cosmos functioning as medium that points through and beyond. Particularity tends to be sacrificed for the sake of symbolic participation in an eternal and universal Whole. World Three, in contrast, is characterized by incarnation—in the sense of fleshly and healthy embodiment. Meaning is less referential and more intrinsic, as if life clearly seen is self-authenticating. Thus in Michelangelo's Sistine Chapel, robust figures on the ceiling strain eagerly to test the contours of their powers.

In literature, Tolstoy grasps the obsessio that characterizes World Three. In *Death of Ivan Ilych*, Ivan is not born an outcast. He becomes one in being awakened through emptiness to a self he had never been. The story, in Tolstoy's words, is about the "ordinary death of an ordinary man . . . most simple and most ordinary and therefore most terrible." Ivan, disappointed in failing to receive a promotion, falls into "intolerable depression." He regains his previous "character of pleasant lightheartedness and decorum," only to receive his second "failure." He is incurably ill. Everything changes. He recognizes that "his social pleasures were those of vanity." He bewilders his friends, for even a grand slam in bridge no longer has appeal. He knows that it "is not a question of appendix, or kidney, but of life and . . . death," and this meant living "all alone on the brink of an abyss, with no one who understood or pitied him." Such emptiness is the mark of an outcast. A life aborted brings the question, What is it all for?[45]

For the first time, Ivan weeps, because of "his helplessness, his terrible loneliness, the cruelty of men, the cruelty of God, and the absence of God . . . why?" In one huge grief, he tries all the Worlds, but "there was no answer and could be none." It is then that the irony of the obsessio sets in, but that which forces Ivan's awakening tempts others into deception. Unable to "accept the fact of his dying," "they reduced it [and life] to the commonplace."[46] His utter aloneness arrives in the banality of invisibility.

The irony turns out to be a double one. The darkness of nothingness, born "in inverse ratio to the square of the distance from death," sequesters the power of an epiphania. The deception Ivan experiences in others is simply the universal condition rooted in himself. His life rehearsal sounds like a litany with the feeling of a *Dies Irae*— "I did everything properly." Suddenly the impossible possibility is born: "What if my whole life has really been wrong?" No longer are we talking of what he did, but of who he is. The epiphania begins as the underbelly of the obsessio rendered deadly. Out tumbles the self-awareness. His whole life has been "a terrible and huge deception which had hidden both life and death."[47]

There follow three days of suffering, as if in a tomb. Then comes the moment called resurrection. Two hours before Ivan's death, the son captures his flailing hand with a kiss. It "could still be rectified." We are not in World Four, where the issue is expiation. The issue here is *self-awareness*. There is no debt to be paid, but there is a waste to be acknowledged. It is not a matter of undoing what has been done, but of discovering a quality of fulfillment that never has been lived. In a word, the feeling is not guilt, but sorrow. "He was sorry for them, he must act so as not to hurt them: release them and free himself from these sufferings." He yearns to be free to be, if only for an hour, in the midst of terrible pain. It is sufficient. *To see* is the light that replaces even death, so that "it is no more."[48]

"He who loses his life will gain it"—World Four stresses the first half; Tolstoy, of World Three, stresses the second half, the life that is found. The issue is bankruptcy, but not of an account overdrawn. It results from living on drafts from petty cash rather than on annuity income. For Tolstoy, the kingdom of God is within, a matter of each self living to a perfection inbred by love and compassion. It is by so following the teachings of Jesus that our natures may be progressively nurtured into wholeness.

While Tolstoy focuses this obsessio through hindsight, James Joyce's *Portrait of the Artist as a Young Man* captures the lyric fascination of youthful anticipation. The hero is caught between two images. First, the Jesuit principal, "his back to the light . . . slowly dangling and looping the cord" of the window blind, symbolizes the repressive noose-like soul/body dualism of Christian priesthood. The second is the image of a girl standing in the sea, the "wild angel" who

[handwritten marginalia: I am in good company. Joyce is cool]

calls his soul to the imaginative re-creation of reality. She is the spirit's cry to "express itself in unfettered freedom," to lure forth "the loveliness which has not yet come into the world." His awakening to this World is a "crying to greet the advent of the life that had cried to him."[49]

Epiphania is the call "to live, to err, to fall, to triumph, to create life out of life . . . on and on and on and on!"[50] Epiphania lures into fullness. The *chronos* of World Two, in World Three is emptied into *kairos*. Although the later Joyce moved toward the sacramental dimensions more characteristic of World One, he continued to defy World Two. The courage to live has no need of a conclusion. The freedom to be needs only the consummate present.

To summarize, the obsessio of World Three is rooted in self-alienation. Despite the socialized limits and structured expectations that press heavily upon the self, the power of such parameters resides finally in one's willingness to be controlled or identified by them. Whatever the epiphania, its vision is that of being one's own person—of exploring, dreaming, experiencing, failing, trying. Regrets focus on time being short, and one life being not enough. Time is not the future, but the pregnant Now, drunk deeply. The disposition is Dionysian. Its preference is for the creation spirituality of a Matthew Fox, suspicious about the Lenten flavor of World Four's redemption spirituality.[51] It has as its litany a favorite refrain: "Behold, it is very good." Incarnation is the insistence that "grace is carnal, [for] healing comes through the flesh."[52] What is craved is a "God" to touch, smell, see, taste—and only then, hear. For some, it is sufficient that the self become united with the earth in its organic rhythm of birth, growth, and death. For others, as we shall see, no epiphania is sufficient that does not render eternal the richness of life as increase.

World Four: Condemnation and the Demonic—The Fugitive

World Four is captured by the rhythm of condemnation and forgiveness. Its obsessio centers in the power of the demonic upon one's will. Job belongs to World One; his friends attempt to bring him back into World Four. In the end, Job repents, as they insist, but he does so in a manner that continues to keep the two Worlds almost beyond communication. He repents in a paroxysm of mystery, animated by awareness of ignorance. In World Four, one encounters "oughtness," animated by feelings of guilt. Focus is upon sin, but not so much as missing the mark (World Three) or as impotence (World Two). Here sin is willful, intentional, and chosen—relished at least in part because it is forbidden.

Augustine stands at the end of the ancient world and the beginning of the Christian.[53] The threshold is marked by a new understanding of the human condition, the understanding that characterizes World Four. For Greek thinkers such as Aristotle, reflective of World Three, knowledge of the good is the key for doing the good. This locates failure in the reason, either through error in detecting what is proper for well being, or through weakness in guiding the passions to their proper goal. But for Augustine, following Paul, the human dilemma is rooted in the will itself. Rarely before in history was it seriously entertained that one could know the wrong and deliberately will it.

Augustine may have gone beyond Paul. Paul cries out in anguish, "I do not understand my own actions. For I do not do what I want, but I do the very thing I hate" (Rom. 7:15). This anomaly tempts him to find a source that is exterior: "It is no longer I that do it" (7:20). In fact, though he admits he "cannot do it," he insists that he "can will what is right" (7:18). He tips the issue more toward performance than intent. Reinhold Niebuhr, struggling precisely at this fulcrum, drives deep the dislocation. We are not "totally depraved." It is far worse. We rarely consciously will the evil for its own sake. Yet rather than having a modifying effect, this renders our sinning more devious. Sin is cloaked in "self-deception."[54] I hide my motives even from myself. In fact, I may be the last to know who I am, even though all around me are those who suffer from my willfulness.

Milton's *Paradise Lost* captures this dynamic. Eve eats the apple eagerly, arrogance deep within her will. But as the possibility of her death haunts her, she decides to share the apple with Adam. Why? Because she cannot bear the thought that he will live if she doesn't. So off she goes in search of him. And by the time he appears, she has convinced herself that her plan of calculated, premeditated murder is, in truth, an act of rare love. She is sharing with Adam for Adam's own good.[55] This has nothing to do with male or female but with human nature.

There is no act not tainted by pride, claims Niebuhr, for our natural will to survive quickly becomes chosen as a way of life. Thus deep within the self is the will to dominate, aggrandize, and vanquish. *We are driven out of the garden, then, by a diseased soul.* And finding ourselves east of Eden, we are condemned to run, even from self-knowledge. *Fugitive* is the name. "We all have our Jews," said Arthur Miller. "And the Jews have their Jews."[56]

Although William Saroyan's romanticism is not reflective of this World, his play *The Time of Your Life* focuses the obsessio. The theme is simple: "In the time of your life, live—so that in that wondrous time you shall not add to the misery and sorrow of the world, but shall smile to the infinite delight and mystery of it."[57] This is an affirmation worthy of World Three. Yet it appears that the sinlessness of this negative Golden Rule is not possible for the hero, even living it passively and reactively. As a murder occurs, it is clear that even such minimal integrity is impossible—not even to live as if you had not lived, leaving no tracks. One's muddy tracks seem inevitable.

One interpretation of Kierkegaard's stages along life's way is useful here.[58] The first stage (the aesthetic) comes to a dead end in boredom. One then leaps into the moral stage, which in turn is aborted in impotence. Consequently, the leap into the religious stage is the attempt to be empowered through belief in God. But awareness of God only heightens the dilemma. This is the intersection that marks the obsessio of World Four. To "be the truth" requires a decision each moment, without which there is no ongoing self. But each decision is in the face of the infinite qualitative difference between one and God. Consequently, before God, one is always in the wrong. "If thou, O Lord, shouldst mark iniquities, Lord, who could stand?" (Ps. 130:3). The leap into Christianity, then, is forced by the drive that emerges from the obsessio World Four knows well—guilt. Faith means wagering on a paradox—that the Eternal entered time. This is absurd, since it entails the declaration that all that is sinful is forgiven. Just as it was the discovery of his father's immoral act that pushed Kierkegaard into a debilitating depression, it was only his father's confession that was able to unlock what he called "the great awakening."

The consequence that can awaken one to the nightmare of self-deception is condemnation. For Paul, the instrument was Law. For Calvin, the Beatitudes. For Niebuhr, the figure of Jesus as the "impossible possibility" that punctures arrogance. Scripture quotes are legion: "Be ye therefore perfect, even as your Father in heaven is perfect" (Matt. 5:48). "For the gate is narrow and the way is hard, that leads to life, and those who find it are few" (Matt. 7:14). The "good news" must first be heard as "bad news"—for every effort to obey God, even in intent, lasts about as long as some New Year's resolutions.

The urban ghetto is a powerful illustration. The informing image is that of a jungle. Standard fare are triple locks, night watches through torn window shades, the spectre of rape. It is a world to be walked only by daylight. Even then, the games simply become more visible. They are identified by signs everywhere: Easy Credit; We Buy Anything—No Questions; Good as New! Everyone wants something; no one is neutral. The dynamic is take or be taken. In this World, every tour guide has a hidden agenda.

Behind the shiny signs life is hardly better. Empty promises render girls pregnant at age eleven. Six-packs for adolescents are available at triple-price. Escalated costs exploit nonmobile elders. Vacant buildings promise ecstasy—arson for money, drugs for pleasure. The ghetto is a distillation of the world of winning and losing, weighted heavily toward variations on the theme of losing. There is an indelible saunter characteristic of losers. External "order" is preserved by police with the working assumption that "violence is all they understand." And internally? The sign on a liquor store—We accept food stamps! Today's Lottery—Chance of a Lifetime. The golden rule of the street is a maxim for the obsessio of World Four: "Treat everybody as if each is a used-car salesman."

Stories from the suburbs, once scandalous in *Peyton Place*, are now boringly commonplace. However sophisticated the distinction between "dirty collar" behavior and "white collar" indiscretions, the rhythm is the same. It centers in the ego—which insists upon being central. "All our righteousness," cried Luther, "is as filthy rags." Do we never do anything helpful? Perhaps, but the issue is motive. No matter how outwardly moral an act, the haunting question is Why?—to be seen, to receive, to win, to feel better, to gain respectability, or even to earn my salvation. No matter what I do, in the end, it is a means to *my* ends. Scripture knows:

Help, Lord; for there is no longer any that is godly. . . .
Every one utters lies to his neighbor;
  with flattering lips and a double heart they speak. *Psalm 12:1a-2*

And me too.

We are parasites—eat before we are eaten. Yet in a way, we have no choice. This is the way evolution operates. We are no different from other animals. But if that is so, where is the problem? It is a problem because we are damned to be more. Conscience is its name. No matter how much it is relativized by culture or one's own autobiography, Kant understood well its unavoidableness. The nature of the mind is such that it operates on the logic of noncontradiction—that is, consistency.[59] In spite of ourselves, 2 plus 2 equals 4, and will do so even on Tuesdays. In like manner, if we do what we prohibit others from doing, this violates

ourselves, even on Wednesdays. If we do to others what
angers us if done to us, we are living self-contradictions.
Such actions turn us against our natures in spite of
ourselves. Thus self-consciousness itself brings the rum-
blings of obsessio, for the capacity to make an object of
oneself establishes the Golden Rule as part of the basement
plumbing.

This guilt that congeals as container for the soul is
masterfully portrayed in Dostoevsky's *Crime and Punishment*. Raskolnikov tests the theory that since there is no
God, all things are lawful. He kills a contemptible
pawnbroker, planning to use the money for his education.
Yet this sets in motion a relentless interior dynamic which
brings him finally to confess: "I murdered myself, not
her!"[60] Ironically, the persistence of guilt is the edge of
epiphania. There is no hope without confession of the need
for atonement. Only through suffering is guilt propitiat-
ed—expiation, catharsis, undoing. Without it, sin is
rendered "mistake" and guilt is buried—to arise another
time, in other places, with mammoth proportions and
disastrous timing. "When I declared not my sin, my
body wasted away through my groaning all day long"
(Ps. 32:3).

Job knew Catch 22. If I am innocent, why do I suffer? If I
defend my innocence, I am arrogant. If I am silent, I
approve the penalty as just. So we reach the deadly
dynamic Luther knew at soul-depth: We cannot will the
change needed, for the will can will only what it deems to be
in its own self-interest. Even choosing to be selfless can be
done only for selfish reasons. Thus sin is embedded within
the lining of the heart.

But there are overtones of something more. Even as we
covet something because it is not ours, deep inside there is a
haunting—an almost lost memory. At moments it appears
to be a yearning for integrity. It is a taste for purity, a
longing to be innocent, washed—to try Eden one more
time. It is the unshakable image of the virgin, even in
Sodom. There is a penchant for the ethical, even when
someone sees a wino drop a dollar unnoticed, right there on

the sidewalk of Twelfth Street. Even if one calls them
stupid, one still quietly admires people who do what is
right, not because of consequences or because of what they
will gain. They do it simply because it is right—no matter if
no one knows. Such moments do erupt, apparently from
nowhere. And they only make things worse. This is the
paradox at the heart of the obsessio World Four knows.
Even the atheist can share with the Christian the alienation
that this strange pull creates. Camus's Tarrou feels it:

> "It comes to this. . . . What interests me is learning how to
> become a saint."
> "But you don't believe in God."
> "Exactly. Can one be a saint without God?—That's the
> problem."[61]

As all around him T. S. Eliot discerns society "falling
down," still the question persists: "Shall I at least set my
lands in order?"[62] There is a restlessness for morality in the
immoral residents of an immoral world. Even the Mafia
does not easily betray family. Yet these acts that flirt with
integrity never seem to make headway against the back-
log of guilt. So fugitives we remain—but haunted ones.

There seems to be a conspiracy against integrity. Ours is a
post-Vietnam era. World War I, the "war to make the world
safe for democracy," has, in half a century, become an
imperialism of desperate skirmishes to preserve supremacy
at all costs. Such "national interest" cloaks with acceptability a whole code book of double standards, double
language, doublethink—freedom fighters versus terrorists,
foreign troops versus military advisors, puppet states
versus allies. Watergates and Contragates are standard
newspaper fare, until the domains of "trusted authority"
have been demythologized into facades of intrigue and
manipulation. We now have an automatic suspicion of
authority, for we have walked behind too many cardboard
sets. We know too much about the private lives of
evangelists. We cry out to forget.

We yearn to believe otherwise—to hear anyone who,

with parental sounds, makes it sound proper. But Calvin is the prompter, just beyond the footlights. The line we forget is that the perversity of the will renders reason into a pawn for rationalization. We reason not *to* our choice, but *from* it—to justify what we already want to do. The problem is not that the world gives little witness to God's existence. The problem is that we reject all such evidence because *we want to be God*. The obsessio is a way of life. Celia, in Eliot's *Cocktail Party*, is pointed: She feels guilty—not for anything she has "ever done," but for "failure," and she feels she must "atone." The dynamic has a dual cause: One is "unloving and unlovable."[63]

The mark of sin is not so much in "doings." It is the quality of one's life itself that is in need of atonement. Simply "to be" means living at the expense of others. Whatever the diameters of one's version of World Four, whether it expands into the social, the ecclesiastic, or the political, its nucleus is constant—the self's secret soul. It may be embellished by images of hell, of graphic penalty, of purgatory, or even of the demonic personified. But whatever form the external impact upon the self might take, the bottom line is the fact that wrong is wrong, and I revel in it.

"Perhaps I could decide not to do this anymore, and stop," said one counselee. "But the truth of the matter is that I just don't want to, I really don't!"

World Four understands this so well that some residents claim that only the threat of hellish torments can provide sufficient pressure for repentance—again and again. The secret soul is that touched by the effective advice of the marriage counselor to the impotent husband: "Fantasize that you are with someone else."

No wonder this World tends to focus upon sexuality to understand the workings of sin. What others see as an antisexual posture in World Four is a recognition of the sexual as paradigmatic of the self's inner dilemma. The will seems unable to will itself, as the tormented teenager is swept by fantasy into every imagined perception of illicit possibility. The situation resembles a storm that can overtake even the most determined sailor.

Even Saint Anthony, as disciplined a Christian as one could imagine, alone in a desert hermitage for sixty-six years, insisted to his death that "there is only one conflict, and that is with fornication." These are not imaginative wonderings about the beauty of love. They are X-rated fantasies. Nor is the issue restricted to the momentarily overpowered will. What overtakes one at the outer wall at evening is the temptation that parallels that for which the soul has been secretly longing since dawn.

Nor is the issue the simple desire for sex. Recent studies of pornography show that sex becomes more exciting for males if laced with images of violence. The fantasies that arouse have to do with using, forcing, overpowering, humiliating, exploiting. While motion pictures, to arouse, once needed only to suggest the naked body, they now need not only vulgarity, but even the blatantly bloody. Dirty language achieves the same physiological effect at less expense. The elements which render words into curses are blasphemy and sexual violence. It should come as no surprise, then, either for them or for us, that so many TV evangelists (firm citizens of World Four) should have difficulty with the obsessio which plagues this World.

For those with less lurid tastes, the obsessio works in the lure of carnival offers: Take a sledgehammer to this car—$1.00 a swing. For a price, one can throw a baseball which, if well thrown, will drop someone into a tub of water. There is unfailing delight from a custard pie pressed into a person's face. It extends to children and butterfly wings. It issues in delight over wrecking sand castles. Teenagers know it in throwing stones through the windows of abandoned buildings. Adults are attracted by ambulances and watch with fascination as fires burn out of control. There are even the strange feelings of destruction some of us have upon hearing the weak and helpless sounds of a kitten.

The psalmist projects backward from such propensities: "In sin did my mother conceive me" (Ps. 51:5*b*). From the womb came I, clutching, craving to leave my mark. From the deepest level, a confession vomits forth unsolicited:

> Have mercy on me, O God . . .
>   blot out my transgressions.
> Wash me thoroughly from my iniquity,
>   and cleanse me from my sin! *Psalm 51:1a,2*

The beginning of epiphania is as clear as the obsessio:

> The sacrifice acceptable to God is a broken spirit;
>   a broken and contrite heart. *Psalm 51:17*

To be broken means to recognize and confess myself as Fugitive. Yet if I do, that simply alienates me all the more from the world. And what of the animals? Should they confess, too, and do penance by becoming vegetarian? But if their God-given chore is to eat one another, why should I be consumed with guilt for being like the rest of creation? Yet I am. *A primal recognition in World Four is that just to be born is to experience indebtedness.* The Protestant work ethic is both born in and fed with this guilt. It is the drive to "do," in order to justify oneself—as if one must atone for being alive.[64] Guilt is given astride the womb, bidding one to expiate with life the debt that comes with one's name. "The human race," Barth concluded, "is insolvent."[65]

Nonresidents of this World often misunderstand it by romanticizing the obsessio. The truth is that sin, in practice, is not exciting. Sin, in Graham Greene's novels, rather than being heroic, is the commonplace boredom of flesh conflicting with spirit. Life copes with the tiresome foibles of tiresome characters, so ordinary as to rise neither to great heights nor to grand sinning. World Four is a World shaped by original sin, for we have lost even the capacity to sin with originality. Depravity, truly experienced, has no primal coloring; it is neither black nor white, but smudged gray. Its music sounds with a sterile inbetweenness, an incurious sadness. There is neither the strength to will the good nor the capacity to lose self-transcendence sufficiently to live happily with capitulated copulation.

I played such a dynamic daily for more than ten years. The rule of the game was to buy cigarettes one pack at a time, though buying them by the carton was far less expensive. Each pack purchased was to be my last. The Marlboro man had a will made of noodles.

While World Four focuses on the hidden caverns of the human soul, an anatomy fit best for a portrait brush, the context for sin is often painted with a broom. The magnitude of the wreckage caused by our sin brings some residents to admonish that while the self is liable, the "credit" belongs elsewhere. Viewed from the human side, one must confess that accountability, liability, default, and insolvency are all ours. Characteristic of us is an aborted power, a will diseased, a vision with an appetite for parochial smut.

The image of an ant playing elephant has the makings of street humor. So what provokes humans to such absurd behavior? The power needed for such undoing is hardly the kind that belongs to an ant. Therefore we can better understand what is really happening if, at the outer perimeters of the human scene, we think of God and the demonic in lethal interaction. We are horses, Luther insisted, ridden either by God or by Satan. Dostoevsky, as we have mentioned, images their work in the soul as Madonna and Sodom, as two kinds of "beauty"—the mysterious and the terrible. "God and the devil are fighting there, and the battlefield is the heart of man."[66]

Even for a Christian hermit as liberal and worldly as contemporary Matthew Kelty, such dramatic dimensions of the soul-struggle are central:

A monk must reckon with the powers of darkness. You cannot just pretend that they are not there. The reason I have such a profound faith in angels and their good influences in our behalf is that I have a far more profound belief in evil spirits. . . . If I had no other reason, there is my own heart, where there are shadows enough and dark times and dark influences that frighten me.[67]

And Reinhold Niebuhr, after he has analyzed the sources of human sin, is driven to identify our temptation into fallenness as "suggested [to the self] by a force of evil which precedes [humankind's] own sin."⁶⁸ Joseph Conrad's Kurtz, in *The Heart of Darkness*, captures that feel of malevolent groping in the murky depths which drives one to suspect a living Viciousness incarnating the heart. It is not even blunted, and certainly not repented for, at the time of death. Kurtz died with his mouth wide, "as though he had wanted to swallow all the air, all the earth, all the [people] before him."⁶⁹

With such power given to the obsessio, it is no wonder that in World Four transition to epiphania takes place more from behind than in front. One is neither lured nor nurtured into change; one is *broken*. Only when one can no longer reach, can one be reached. Only when one knows oneself as unlovable, can love break in as gift. This is so true that for some in this World, the persistence of obsessio threatens to keep eating away at any epiphania. Such seriousness brought Luther to declare that while as Christians we are forgiven sinners, nonetheless, sinners we remain. Thus our righteousness is an ascribed one—what Paul calls an alien righteousness.

This condition appears powerfully in Georges Bernanos' *Diary of a Country Priest*. The parish is a World so "eaten up by boredom" that the motivation in the people is a "yearning for the void." Ironically, the only hope rests in the fact that such self-death is impossible—for such darkness is, in truth, the providential work of God. Because of such restlessness, we will "never be able to give up the search." The world of sin confronts the world of grace like a reflected landscape in the blackness of still, deep waters. It is through these waters that we are driven by loneliness, passing from lust through sterility and illusion, to spiritual starvation as self-hatred. "Hell is not to love anymore," thereby uncovering the guilt that exposes our life as rebellion against a Love not of our invention.⁷⁰

Through the valley of the shadow, one must pass into this "dark night." "God will break you," shouts the priest. His prayer follows: "God grant that you may despise yourself." Nothing less can strip us to the "horrible undeveloped monsters" we are. To "think of oneself as one dead" is to offer oneself in resignation, in the cruciformed posture of self-abandonment. Whatever epiphania may mean, it is the "miracle of the empty hands." Only brokenness can bring forgiveness as "joyous resignation." New life is not being given as a clean slate. It means having no slate at all. Faith is childlike trust, the simple wonder of a restored child. Acceptance, in spite of unacceptability, is the joy of forgiveness as pure gift, so that one can behold, with awe, that "grace is everywhere."[71] Such moments, of being broken and forgiven, form a lifelong dynamic. Epiphania is always gift, never possession. The seriousness of obsessio dare not be undercut, as in World Three, by regarding redemption as awakening the locked potential within the self.

Seen from its epic proportions, World Four is assailed by forces profoundly intent upon undoing God's crowning accomplishment in humankind. The souls created little less than the angels are now only slightly higher than the demons. We are both Sodom and the Madonna—but not either alone. Only seduced for and by such "greatness" are we unworthy of so great a redeemer. World Two sees humanity caught unwillingly in the macrosystems of history. In World Four, the macrocosm *is* the microcosm—the self writ large, sinfully so. While some persons today see this perspective as dated, those within this World see such an attitude as an indictment against our times. Modern life is lost as an arena for greatness, precisely because the heights of majesty and the depths of depravity which define the parameters of World Four are leveled out in mediocrity. Loss of guilt is loss of a context fit for the human venture.

Literature is the central artistic vehicle of this World, which suggests how inward the obsessio is. In fact, World Four reflects the defining context for much of the significant literature of this country. Birthed in Puritanism, Nathaniel Hawthorne provides the foundation. His works focus on human depravity experienced as guilt, while the secret harboring of pride relentlessly reduces the self to numbing isolation. In contrast with such World Three writers as

Whittier, Emerson, and Thoreau, Hawthorne knows of that which tugs at the will with such power that the self is no match.

In his *Alice Doane's Appeal*, Leonard kills a man who has made love to the sister to whom he himself is inordinately attached, only to see himself in the victim. In *Rappacini's Daughter*, Hawthorne exposes a character's "self-reliance" as the false pride on which "inevitable progress" is impaled. Individualism uncovered is the immorality of instinct. Humanity stands helplessly at the intersection of "ingenuity and thwarted nature, and of the fatality that attends all such efforts of perverted wisdom."[72]

And in *Ethan Brand*, the "unpardonable sin" is acted out as a literal fall—"the sin of an intellect that triumphed over the sense of [community] . . . and reverence for God, and sacrificed everything to its own mighty claims."[73] Against every epiphania that World Two might offer, Hawthorne insists that human nature is incurably marred. The contours of the skull are never hidden by the thin covering of flesh. And unlike World Three, evil in World Four is not the absence of good, or even misdirected good. It is malevolent power. Haunted, wild, plagued, we are caught in a maelstrom of forces that pull us beyond both understanding and grasp. Thus entrance into any epiphania must be the reverse of arrogance. It must be the acceptance of dependence upon that Being who alone is worthy of pride.

Such a perspective is not restricted to Protestant eyes. Roman Catholic novelist Francois Mauriac concurs. The human is "a creature condemned to death and who lives under a stay of execution for an unknown length of time. Anguish is consubstantial to the human condition." Yet the Spirit ruminates in the desperate ashes of thwarted passion, driving self-will to arid dead ends, whereby it might be overtaken by grace, as a harsh "nevertheless." Obsessed with money, property, and flesh, people shadow-dance in bored slow motion through a monstrous parody of life, helplessly feeling "the slow and noiseless approach of ineluctable dissolution."[74] Doomed by the "wages of sin," they are not hopeless, however, for they are haunted.

Epiphania will be the revelation of One "who, unknown to them, had drawn and summoned from the depths of their beings this burning bitter tide."[75]

Convolutions upon the obsessio of guilt characteristic of World Four are traced brilliantly in the novels of William Faulkner. His mythical Yoknapatawpha County in *The Sound and the Fury* is a haunted county, robbed from the native Americans, "civilized" by whites, carved from the virgin earth by blacks as they were robbed of their selfhood. While white mansions persist, the porches rot and the inhabitants decay, lost in the lies of arrogant tradition. With illusion, they continue to deny the guilt that gnaws the joints and curses the land.

Here we meet Benjie, the last of the guilt-strewn clan, the result of the judgment on the parents, upon the children unto the third and fourth generations. Judgment has been laid upon judgment, until the once proud family is held together only by the free associations of this mentally three-year-old adult. And Jason, final bearer of the "fleeced" golden fleece, clutches on helplessly, doomed as if by birth, as "his invisible life raveled out about him like a worn out sock." As Greek chorus, Benjie wails in fright: "He smells the rot," the "sins [of] your high and mighty people." He pays, vicariously and unknowingly, with an extravagance of suffering shamelessly extracted by, and now upon, the custodians of pride. It is Dilsey, the servant, who prophesies against this "moral elite." She says she saw the first and the last; she saw the beginning, and now she sees the ending.[76] Condemnation.

Faulkner's World is populated by biblical characters who incarnate the theme that the price shall be paid. Either the guilt will be owned and atoned, or the guilty shall be no more. One way or another, only blood can extricate the deadly workings of guilt. In *Light in August*, a name distills the theme: Joanna Burden. And into the deadly vortex comes a Christ-figure—Joe Christmas. He is half-black, half-white, the creation of multiple scapegoating. As witness to guilt, he has been sent away time after time—not to atone, but so that guilt may be pretended away. Yet he keeps coming back, as illegitimate offspring are wont to do, as innocent reoccurrence of impeccable judgment. "A race doomed and cursed to be forever and ever a part of the white race's doom and curse for its sins. Remember that. His doom and his curse. Forever and ever."[77] To confess, or to exterminate the judge—these are the harsh options. And so, with near-inevitability, Christmas festers the viciousness of the judged into performing bloody crucifixion.

It is here, in this "sense of the terribleness of history," that Faulkner is drawn "to reach for a patience beyond hope or despair."[78] But the last word in this novel is with the crucifixion—the horror of an event so profound that it is burned as judgment into the souls of the actors, never to be lost, but "to rise soaring into their memories forever and ever . . . of itself alone triuimphant."[79]

Faulkner's obsessio is of World Four: "Thou art the one!" His epiphania, as we shall see, tends more toward World Five—the stance of endurance. His is a dual World, populated by two "races." And whatever epiphania he holds out for those annealed by innocent suffering, the destiny is bleak for those of this nation who broke treaties for every advantage, pillaged the earth for gain, and bought and sold souls as the unspoken medium of exchange. And all of this was done by the self-proclaimed covenant people on a "divine mission" to midwife the kingdom of God. These are the ones now duty bound to "bless" the earth with their hegemony.[80] But guilt is the mark of a God and a people and an earth that does not forget.

In painting, powerful expression appears in the paintings of Georges Rouault. *Two Nudes* portrays the sad dissipation of prostitutes eaten away from within, ugliness permitted not even the solace of pathos. Most objects in his paintings are imprisoned with bar-like outlines, either/ors of somber tonalities—harsh, violent, sad, repulsive, broken, exposed, as if the pieces are tarred together by arrogance from the inside. In Grant Wood's *American Gothic*, pathos is permitted the promise of the tragic. From the two figures we sense a stern but resolute binding tension—forgiven, thus obedient—with frugality as rectitude.

In music, the hymnology of evangelical Protestantism has most profoundly nurtured this World: "Come every soul with sin oppressed . . . "; "Heavy laden, bruised and mangled by the fall . . . "; "In true repentance bow . . . "; "Sinners, turn: Why will ye die?"; "Just as I am! Thou wilt receive, wilt welcome, pardon, cleanse, relieve." Such expressions are endless.

World Five: Suffering and Life—The Victim/Refugee

At first glance, Worlds Four and Five might seem to overlap in terms of the agony that colors their landscapes. But the feel is different. In World Four, focused by guilt, the dynamic moves from the inside outward to infect the whole. The self is central, as diseased agent. In World Five, characterized by suffering, the dynamic comes from the outside and moves inward. Here the self is not so much agent as *victim*. The cause of such victimization can fluctuate considerably—self upon self, class upon class, or from a burden seemingly metaphysical. But what World Five people have in common is an obsessio characterized by a feeling of being overwhelmed. The middle section of Job (without the beginning and ending sections, which reflect a different World) focuses on this theme:

> Surely now God has worn me out (16:7).
> He has shriveled me up (16:8).
> My face is red with weeping (16:16).
> My spirit is broken, my days are extinct,
>   the grave is ready for me (17:1).
> I am hemmed in by darkness (23:17).

Overwhelmed is the basic feel. But the Job of the full canonical book knows too much to be a permanent inhabitant of World Five. His insistence upon his innocence and upon fulfillment through action are variations upon World Three. He has an unflagging belief that there is a God and that in knowing life's ordered ways, he knows himself.

When it turns out that he is right in appraising his behavior, and thus that the "rules" after all are not ultimate, the conversion into the mystery characteristic of World One then occurs. But in World Five, neither of these possibilities exist. Certainty is not even rumored. The density from all sides is such that the World remains opaque, where causes and amplitude, by definition, seem cryptic. The only certain knowledge available is distilled by Ecclesiastes: "As he came from his mother's womb he shall go again, naked as he came, and shall take nothing for his toil, which he may carry away in his hand" (5:15).

The only primary unknown is, When? Job gambled his life on the fact that he was different. Others suffered too, but his suffering was a mistake. But in World Five, Job isn't different—he is "everyone." Suffering is morally indiscriminate.

As an analogy, think of walking very slowly on tiptoe across a river, a few possessions held over your head. The slightest slip will throttle you. Or living by breathing softly, with gritted teeth, as if the noise of breathing will place you in jeopardy. Or crossing a dark vacant lot covered with broken glass, to avoid detection by those with questionable motives on the street corner. Or counting out pennies on the counter before a suspicious clerk.

Life is like an ocean grabbing at an island. To presume there is a God only exacerbates the sense of being overwhelmed:

> My God, my God, why hast thou [too] forsaken me?
> Why art thou so far from helping me? *Psalm 22:1*
> O Lord—how long? *Psalm 6:3b*

Ivan Mestrovic's sculpture *Job* incarnates this agony of emaciation and desperate spirit:

> Thou has fed them with the bread of tears,
>   and given them tears to drink in full measure. *Psalm 80:5*

Since a quarter of the people in this country are below the poverty level, and two-thirds of the earth's people go hungry to bed (if they have a bed), the recruits for World

Five are legion. But the obsessio is not restricted to economics. The ticket to enter can have three words: "You have cancer." It is then that the words *expendable* and *terminal* take on tender meaning.

The feel here is not of a World cloaked in mystery, waiting to be recognized and trusted (World One). There is no victory to be won (World Two). Nor is there some fulfillment yet to be realized (World Three). And most fundamental, the obsessio is not one for which guilt, either active or defining, is an ingredient (World Four). On the contrary, this World is an amalgam of psychological, social, and metaphysical dimensions, experienced with the impact of a conclusion: "That's the way things are." Everything has the weight of fact. Thus citizens of World Five are transfixed by sheer givenness, for which nothing can be done. Put bluntly, it is to recognize life as Predator—so much so that even epiphania brings no radical reversal. It is a matter of "keep on keeping on" in such a way that living takes on an aura of authenticity beyond pathos.

Central to this World is suffering. In Bernanos and Dostoevsky (World Four), the positive function of suffering is to puncture pride. Suffering is a cathartic for guilt, enabling the redemptive process. Not so for World Five. Suffering is a tempering, as in a refining fire. Paul lists his "works" which count as "naught"—shipwrecks, scourging, imprisonment. Yet these are the "naughts" that establish the quality of his life—the tempered, determined strength of "pushing on." But Paul knows too much. In World Five there is no prize to lure us forward—other than the quality of life so tempered. From the side of the obsessio, one forges on, persistence its own waggish prize. The epiphania seems destined to echo the obsessio itself: One is resolute because that's just the way one is.

I was raised in this World, never recognizing it until much later. My home was in Appalachia, shafts protruding from hillsides, houses huddled in gray clusters. I remember the quiet miners on the slow walk home, blackened beyond recognition except for huge white eyes—and yellow teeth. One learned through apprenticeship, linked to the third and fourth generations, in an endless line of sameness. One didn't look back, or really forward. One took it as it came. One day was enough—sometimes too much. We had just enough to make it, unless something happened. There was hardly margin for error—or respite. Life was living near the edge, often with the feel of a game of "catch up," with the rules those of diminishing returns.

I remember especially the shrill scream of the siren. As a child, I knew terror. At 4:15A.M., "Number 5, Argyle mine," someone yelled as the siren paused for breath. It was a cave-in. Somehow you knew. You ran hard. You waited even harder. Waiting was like life. Dark vigils were parabolic.

"Have some coffee."

"Any survivors?"

"The Lord gives and the Lord takes . . . ."

Every one of my relatives has been scarred by the mines. Matt died of black lung. Dad's ear was ruptured. John was blinded. You just take it. You don't talk about it. But you never forget—down deep. Never.

Purged of romanticism, this is a hard World—never willed and rarely desired.[81] That's why a corrosive danger of brittleness can sometimes cake around it: a mixture of vulgarity, hardness, insulated sensitivity, inversion in quiet self-aversion, and a subtle clumsiness. Continuous disappointment can lead to no expectation. Blessed are those who expect nothing, for they shall not be disappointed. It is hard to talk about this with language that is proper, not battle-scarred by conveying "the sounds and smells of the action."

But there is something else—something important. It emerges not in spite of, but because. I remember it in the eyes of women—patient, softly hard, annealed, a determination as enduring as the hillsides. I've read about mountain folk. These are mine folk. You could feel something when couples said good-bye—a last ritual before starting up the hill to work. It had an unspoken touch of "farewell." There was little they hadn't been through. These were the quiet ones—except when drunk. Janis

Joplin sang about it: "Freedom's just another name for nothing left to lose."

The most philosophizing I can remember came from a neighbor whose son never came out: "When you've been close to death so often, it can't get you. You can live okay if you're not afraid of dying."

One senses it in faces. Daumier's painting *Third-class Carriage* captures the quality. At first glance, we see only tired women, old far beyond their years. At second glance, they are strong, with qualities for outlasting and enduring—with integrity.

"Don't be sorry for the elderly," said my doctor. "They are the strong ones, the survivors."

Native Americans understand that this wisdom belongs with aging. This World moves beyond words in the Edward Curtis portraits of native Americans.[82] The faces of the elders are invincible—ploughed and furrowed until there is an earthy belonging beyond question. It isn't that they have answers. Life is not a problem to be solved. What is present is an aura. It is in endurance itself that one touches wisdom—a wisdom that knows better than to attempt articulation. So *to be* is its own strange answer.

The image of a co-worker on an early job at Bethlehem Steel Company is indelible. A huge Polish immigrant, he worked in the open hearth. Everyone made fun of him; he couldn't speak English, so that made him a "dumb Pollack." He didn't talk—but he knew. He endured it all quietly and kept shoveling coke in the ovens when the heat had stopped everyone else. Only when the job was done did he go back to his corner. He used to drink a gallon of water with half a lemon in it. The lemon rarely changed— neither did he. I remember that he was steady, immovable, dependable. I didn't know where he went at the whistle, or what he did. I just knew that the next morning he would be in his corner. Then one morning they said that yesterday had been his last day.

This World finds scriptural foundation. It echoes around the theme of barrenness as the condition native to God's working. Israel emerged from the barrenness of Sarai (Gen.

11:30), was saved from extinction through Rebekah's barrenness (25:21), as through Rachel's (29:31), and was brought its final forerunner in the barrenness of Elizabeth (Luke 1:7). So prepared, the author of Hebrews summarizes *hope* as living in the face of all evidence to the contrary that renders us "strangers and exiles." This is the absurd hope which confesses that from one person who was "as good as dead, were born descendants as many as the stars of heaven and as the innumerable grains of sand by the seashore" (11:12). This is not the kind of hope that belongs to World Two, as a present action to be consummated in future result. Instead, the future stands as miracle in the face of the present, so absurd that for Sarah in her sterile aging, the very thought deserved only laughter.

World Five requires special talents of discernment, if one is to sense in such unpropitious images strange hints of epiphania. At the steel mill, there was always a special moment—tapping the furnace. Everyone watched, even the old-timers. It was pure liquid gold. You would not turn your back on an event so deserving of awed respect. If it was your tap, you knew—not one mistake could be made. Salt tablets, a warm orange, and a sweaty commonality—that was what it was about. We were in it together.

In front of the mine-company houses, old cars sat on blocks. You could exchange parts, do anything with a coat hanger, and take pride in grease under your nails. It was called making do. Its symbol was only one 40-watt bulb on at a time. There was a common drinking pail, common bath water, common everything. But best of all, there were the times together on a country road in the old pickup—determined, proud, with a shared beer. This was a World apart.

The nuances of World Five emerge clearly in the portraits of those who tried but could not sustain the effort—the Janis Joplins, the Billie Holidays, the Lenny Bruces, the Sylvia Plaths, the Jimi Hendrixes. Few can escape touching this obsessio when it is offered yearly on television as *The Wizard of Oz*. Obsessio is what one feels as Judy-Dorothy sings, "Birds fly over the rainbow. Why, O why can't I?"—and knowing what was to happen in real life.

One does not soon forget a slow dying. I remember some folks drawn together to help a friend with leukemia. Such an experience changes people. In preparing another for death, one lives life as dying. It was a year lived in World Five. Paul knew when he quoted Psalm 44: "We are being killed all the day long; we are regarded as sheep to be slaughtered" (Rom. 8:36).

Whatever epiphania may occur, it cannot center in another time or another place. It must be now, in the midst of life purged of romanticism, either as foundation or as hint, and from which any dream of a changed future has been properly evicted. Bonhoeffer, in the concentration camp, knew this: "As to the boundaries, it seems to me better to be silent and leave the insoluble unsolved. . . . God is beyond in the midst of our life."[83]

Residents of World Five understand Rubenstein: "If one penetrates beneath the surface of the joys of the flesh, one finds sadness even in our most precious moments." The only change possible is one of perspective, but not one that renders the whole different, as in World One. All things stay as they are, except the way we "take it." Carved into the obsessio is a foreboding not only that the Messiah is dead, but that the "Messiah is death." Then one knows that "the promise of radical novelty in the human condition was a pathetic, though altogether understandable, illusion. . . . The old world goes on today as it did yesterday and as it will tomorrow."[84]

Does this result in passive individualism? It need not. Reinhold Niebuhr, hardly one to be charged with inactivity, grounds his social view on the obsessio of World Five: "The history of [humanity] is a perennial tragedy, for the highest ideals which the individual may project are ideals which [one] can never realize in social and collective terms."[85] Thus "the Cross clarifies the possibilities and limits of history and perennially refutes the pathetic illusions," declaring for the realm of ethics that "the revelation of Christ is foolishness." Consequently, the pattern of all historical reality is a "rise and fall," and "the end of an individual life is, for [that person], the end of history." Thus one can be a "new self" only by "intention rather than an actual achievement," and so always require "the divine mercy."[86]

Niebuhr's two conclusions serve well as parameters for the obsessio of World Five: (1) The self "does not have the power to extricate [itself] from flux and finiteness"; (2) "It is equally obvious that history does not solve the basic problems of human existence." Thus he ends as a grudging but faithful citizen of World Five, straining for "confidence in an eternal ground of existence which is, nevertheless, involved in [our] historical striving to the very point of suffering with and for [us]. . . . It is tragic. . . . Faith completes our ignorance."[87]

These bold outlines of obsessio that inform World Five are stroked well by the theological struggles of Elie Wiesel. *Holocaust* is the indelible given for existence, before which even prayer becomes ironic. The one to whom one needs to pray is "that God in which I no longer believe."[88] The agony of Wiesel's World is born by knowing the impossibility of resolution, in either the theism of a Fackenheim or the atheism of a Rubenstein. Rather, any epiphania will rest in the tension of a *fatigued center*, recognizing God as presupposition of the very question of God. The condition of being plagued into asking could turn out, itself, to be the gift of the Unknowable. Suffering is at the center, for it drives us into this "endless quarrel with God."[89]

> Pray to God
> Against God,
> For God,
> Ani Maamin ("I believe").[90]

Such paradoxical behavior convinces us that an answer does exist, in spite of its unknowability.[91] Yet we continue to be plagued. In this "universe as brothel," is God executioner, or victim?[92] That is the question. Our hope being that God too is victim, we must stand steadfast in silence, finding therein the power to endure. Here we might discover that "the silence of God is God."[93] In faith, may we conclude that the affirmation of God shall be the passionate commitment to endurance together.[94] If every blasphemy ends as "a prayer in spite of me," then "the essence of the question is to be without an answer."[95]

The obsessios of the first four Worlds center, in turn, on the cosmos, history, self, and the demonic. In World Five the focus is on Life itself. What is plague? The pea-passer in Camus's *Plague* knew: "Just life, no more than that."[96] To live is to be plagued, engulfed, controlled, powerless, wronged—victim. This does not mean that the self is innocent—but that is not the issue. One is so positioned by "life" that it must be defined reactively. Thus the issue is not the situation, but one's response to it. Even though imprisoned, one's inner attitude is free. Epiphania will require variations on the theme: of resoluteness, of steadfast will, of integrity as tenacity. "Purity of heart," said Kierkegaard, "is to will one thing."[97] But the question the obsessio cannot quiet is this: Am I a victim *alone*?

Turning to the arts, critic Waldo Frank identifies two basic traditions in literature. The first, characterized by visions of *possibility*, loosely includes our first four Worlds. The second tradition, which focuses upon the "common people," is the art of *probability*, giving us "not a vision, but persons." He is referring to our World Five: "They are frustrated, poor, often mad. They face grimly their resurgent hills, knowing the failure of their lives . . . yet . . . their dwelling . . . their acceptance . . . has given them even in defeat a fiber of strength, a smoldering spark of victory."[98]

Tennessee Williams' *Camino Real* is probably his most comprehensive effort to create a World. And it is World Five. In fact, his description of the playwright's task points toward what we mean by theological Worlds: "It is almost as if you were frantically constructing another world while the world that you live in dissolves beneath your feet, and that your survival depends on completing this construction at least one second before the old habitation collapses."[99] His dedication is from Dante's *Inferno*: "In the middle of the journey of our life I came to myself in a dark wood where the straight way was lost." That "dark wood" is modern society, caught solipsistically.

Kilroy, here meaning everyone, is stalked by Death's wheeled garbage can. He cries out that beyond the here and now, he "don't see nothing but nothing—and then more nothing." Gutman poses the obsessio: "Can this be all? Is there nothing more? Is this what the glittering wheels of the heavens turn for?" Without more, life is "the smell of an empty ice box."[100]

The gypsy asks, "Date of birth and place of that disaster?" "Your luck ran out the day you were born." In a World where "everything's for a while," where there are "no permanent guests," where "you got nothing to lose that won't be lost," the logic is that of "a funny paper read backwards!" "Lonely, lonely, lonely," comes the litany, with distrust emerging as the "only defense against betrayal." Then can one at least "leave with honor"? No, the "given" from which one cannot part is "the sort of desperation that comes after desperation has been worn out through long wear!"[101]

The transition toward epiphania seems signaled by the increasing reiteration of the word *pity*. "Pity the world and I pity the God who made it." From pity comes yearning: "Look down with a smile tonight on the last cavaliers . . . oh, sometime and somewhere, let there be something to mean the word *honor* again!" Such honor comes through the pity born of suffering: *to know and to endure the knowing*. "The wounds of the vanity, the many offenses our egos have to endure, being housed in bodies that age and hearts that grow tired, are better accepted with a tolerant smile."[102] It is this tenderness, says Quixote, that has "broken rocks!"

This parable of World Five becomes the legend of the foolish but tender Quixote who, with Kilroy, lives in the gentle dream of "nevertheless." This alone is able to set flowing the arid fountain in the town square. Since beyond the town walls is "terra incognito," all we can do is huddle together against the hearing of the piper's death tune. But in so doing, tender love is born among us who wait. It may not be much, but it is all we have. It is Archibald MacLeish who pushes the obsessio toward a finality, as if in conclusion. His quiet resignation is held in the irony of "Immortal Autumn":

> I praise the fall it is the human season now
> No more the foreign sun does meddle at our earth
> Enforce the green and thaw the frozen soil to birth
> No winter yet weigh all with silence the pine bough
> . . . we are alone . . . .[103]

If Frank is correct—that this World finds its connectedness not in vision but in the fiber of the strength of persons, the master painter of this World is Rembrandt. This is true not only of his profound self-portraits, but in the simplicity of *An Old Woman Cutting Her Nails*. Such life-drenched portraits emit a special mystery. Unlike the ebullient surface light that fascinates artists of World Three, or the symbolic transparency that points to a grounding mystery (World One), this is a light from within. This mystery so emanates from the subject that it illuminates the surrounding darkness. A light once reserved for saints and shrines becomes a gracious nimbus of endurance for the common folk and the commonplace. These portray a way of living that is in itself, of itself, for itself—self-authenticating. There is never the grandiose. Thus the common can take on a simple grandeur.

While Vermeer is often contrasted with Rembrandt, there is a continuity in these two painters of World Five. Rembrandt's inner glow, forged by suffering, is acted out in the sober mellowness of Vermeer's simple austerity. In paintings indicatively small, even the pouring of milk gives an enduring, eternal quality to the commonplace. It is as though the countless insignificant repetitions take on, through patient necessity, the marks of the quietly monumental.

In music, the obsessio of this World is distilled in Samuel Barber's *Adagio for Strings*. The music plods, as if each note ages as it is played. There is a slow ascendency, each mounting bringing a faltering pause, one step from each apparent topping. The apex is finally attained, tentatively, for a moment. Then the whole begins slowly to unwind, as the reversal comes dangerously close to ending where it began. Rather, it falters, almost stops, tries again, begins, stutters, wavers, and finally halts—unfinished, unresolved, worn through, exhausted. And yet, when apparently over, there persists in the listener that same relentlessness, working subtly what Ravel's *Bolero* achieves heavily. The strange closure is in the refusal to finish.

Words for this quiet resoluteness appear in Mendelssohn's chorale from *Elijah:* "He Who Shall Endure to the End Shall Be Saved." Samuel Becket's *Waiting for Godot* could provide the libretto for those who are held more closely to the obsessio: "The tears of the world are a constant quantity. For each one who begins to weep, somewhere else another stops. . . . Let us not then speak ill of our generation, it is not any unhappier than its predecessors."[104]

In finishing our exercises in obsessio for the five Worlds, it is important that the reader remember that far more is involved than the contrast in conceptual content. The powerful difference is grounded in contrasting modes of perception. We are talking about persons *living* in different Worlds. A strong case for the power of this lived reality appears in the reaction of a stellar resident of one World against an equally worthy resident of another. Ernest Becker is a resident of World Two. The damning critique of his brilliant work that follows makes sense only when we realize that the critic is functioning from a contrasting World, bringing the frustration of communication between Worlds to the point of hostility.

[Becker's] psychology and theology must be challenged. It is not just a matter of his giving us a one-sided picture which needs to be supplemented by views from other thinkers who have different perspectives. Becker is more seriously misleading. He often praises as virtues dispositions which are vices, and he proposes a piety which, though focused on what he calls "God," is merely a

strategy for self inflation. . . . The style of life and the religious
faith which he commends include evils which we ought to be
struggling against. And in this struggle we can draw on forces of
life and love whose existence Becker does not even acknowledge.[105]

This conflict is so intense that Becker's *Denial of Death* is
declared to be actually a "denial of life."

CHAPTER THREE

Anatomy of the Theological Answer— An Exercise in Epiphania

Our task now is to develop, in a more focused way, the epiphanias which, in dialogue with the obsessios, give dynamic to each theological World.

World One: Reunion as Homecoming—Neoliberalism

This World, as we saw, is characterized by a cosmos of infinite proportions, without seeming to have beginning or end. In fact, it seems to be without top, bottom, or sides. Life without parameters becomes tainted by a fourth dimension. Time places infinitesimally short boundaries on us within this Whole, giving to life the feel of arbitrariness. We are nameless, directionless, homeless, with *reality* simply the name for the incidental point where we happen to be.

Without a fulcrum for perspective, we seem caught within a vast movement that goes nowhere. Put more negatively, we *are* going somewhere—toward nothingness. To say even that much seems excessively certain. And yet this mood that suggests atheism keeps being pierced by special moments—the fragrance of thin remembrances, hints of new beauty. With these the enigma of obsessio sets in. Could these moments be rifts as in a curtain, stars in a firmament, which serve as holes into mystery? That would mean wagering that the meaning of this vast wholeness hinges on such moments as foretaste. Can the moment of a falling star be an intersection of time and eternity, bathing the infinitely meaningless with the unfathomably awe-full?

In such possibilities paradox is born. The cosmic abyss as tomb is a caldron of inexhaustible fecundity. It is as if the ache characterized as separation whispers that one's nature is, in fact, to belong—to the heart of being. Was this once upon a time, or now, or something yet to be? Time gets in the way of the answer; it separates things—into befores and afters, wheres and whens. It is the source of the feeling of abandonment.

Yet that feeling suggests a double negative. "Abandoned" implies "by someone." Absence implies presence somewhere. One essentially belongs, or why such homesickness? If so, then "the question is, itself, the answer. And we ourselves are both.'"[1] The strong metaphor that such moments proffer is that of prodigal offspring, but not of our choosing. We seem born to wander. As a result, at the heart of midnight musings, there emerges the distilled desire to undo, to return—from whence or from whom we came. Citizens of this World know what it would mean to go home, for the last time, to the harbor from which one set out on one's journey.

I remember, with fondness and pain, a colleague. Some nights, when I was too tired to care, I would walk from my office to the car. Sometimes he was there, sitting on a wall, looking at the stars. There was an invitation, then a question. "Do you think maybe?" One day I received a call. Evidently he decided that sitting on walls was not sufficient—or he couldn't wait.

Epiphania depends upon such moments; they point not in time, as toward resolution in some future, but must participate in a Now, an *eternal* now. In World One, such a moment is like a pinhole that serves as pupil for a shadow box. Such a reversed, shadowed image against the greased paper background is like a shadow of eternity. That is painful, for it discloses as well the gap between appearance and reality. Yet in recognizing this contrast, things can take on a transparency. After such a moment is experienced anywhere, anything can become a sacramental aperture. To recognize everything as appearance, of itself nothing, entails being grasped by the Ground in which all things participate in order to be. This infinitesimal moment is a homecoming, a transcendence of polarity, a foretaste of reunion, a touch of unity with the Eternal.

The Quaker Rufus Jones imaged World One by using the Platonic myth of an original unified self that had been cut in half at birth. Life is a search for one's other half. For Jones this longing for original wholeness is not sexual, but mystical. The alien soul, yearning for the Eternal, is opened to a mystic love birthed within the primordial division. What follows is the double-faced anatomy of life—our search for God within God's search for us, in an eternal rhythm.

Jones incorporates elements of World Three when he perceives evolution as the emergence of a new inward self. He evidences aspects of World Two when he holds to a vision of a Social Being in which Jesus Christ is the goal of the race. Yet World One remains foundational. Just as Christ's two natures are "intended for each other," so the human goal and the divine nature are one, a unity to which we must constantly return in prayer as "source and font." Love is the "longing to be united [with] the original whole. . . . The soul is alien here and its chief joy in the midst of the shows of sense is joy at the sight of something which reminds it of its old divine home."[2]

Contemporary Quaker Thomas Kelley gives similar witness: "For it is the Eternal who is the mother of our holy Now, nay, *is* our Now, and time is, as Plato said, merely its moving image." Therefore, for Kelley, the distinctive rhythm of separation and reunion follows: "The Life of God is breaking through into the world. Its execution is in peace and power and astounding faith and joy, for in unhurried serenity the Eternal is at work in the midst of time, triumphantly bringing all things up unto [God's self]."[3]

What we see in World One is that separation is the primal condition that births obsessio, longing is the impulse that points toward epiphania, and resolution coalesces around *revelation* as self-authenticating experience. Such illumination is the "still point of the turning wheel" (Eliot), serving as center of a new perspective. Through this new kind of seeing, things become new. Merton calls it spontaneous awe at the sacredness of life, of being. This eternal moment in time is the experiential fulcrum which discriminates the unreal and so intensifies the real that it becomes transparent to the inner unity of Being itself. The rhythm is that by losing all things finite, one is grasped ontically, so as to be found. Mystery becomes the epiphania when puzzlement becomes awe-drawn by the fact of life itself—any life, any thing. The mystery is not What but That.

Since one is not inclined to risk losing anything, death or any of its shadows is needed to haunt the self, forcing one to experience mystery in the sheer fact that one continues to exist. Why something rather than nothing? At the moment of death's threat, we are powerless to say No! Thus life is a gift over which we have no control—not only in this moment, but in every moment. *What* we do is ours to decide; but *that* we *are* is not in our power. This is the awareness that plunges us into a radically different dimension.

Schleiermacher calls this the feeling of "absolute dependence,"[4] and it is at the heart of epiphania for World One. For some it begins as the feeling of psychological fragility, until it is recognized as metaphysical fact—a dependency that grounds our existence in each fleeting and unconnected moment. Tillich calls this experience an ontic shock. Its positive correlate is a "vision of the new being," wherein the Unconditional (upon which all is dependent) radiates as sacramental presence through things. To perceive such transparency, one's idolatry must be punctured by the power of obsessio.

Such experience renders "transcendence" no longer as separation, but as Source. Resurrection is precisely such illumination, for to behold any moment as center point is to have the meaning of history revealed as no longer linear, but *kairotic*. The eternal Now is the readiness of each moment for transparency. Resolution means reunion, which entails a relinquishing of separation, a letting go, a willingness to be emptied. While we can now only experience foretaste, it as if we already participate in Being as All in all.

Words can only point to such moments—with feeble images like deathlessness, mystic oneness, unconditional belonging. But what once had no defining boundaries no longer needs them, for one is found standing in the center. Everything exists as circumference to this Center point, defined no longer by its edge but its common pivot. So seen, everything that is participates in the unbroken circle: union-separation-reunion.

The cosmos provides analogies. For some astrophysicists, the universe emerges from a center of infinite intensity, exploding in expansiveness. Then there will be a return into that dense beginning point. The self is a microcosm of such a rhythm. Both the journey outward and the journey inward are part of the myth of the eternal return.[5] This epiphania as reversal often results in a surprising toleration for ambiguity. How can it be otherwise, when moments that once haunted a person are rendered sacred as pointers to mystery. Odysseus speaks the paradox well: It entails staring "into the black eyes of the Abyss with gallantry and joy, as on one's native land."[6] Most mystics are embarrassed by the poverty of their descriptions.

Origen was one of the first Christian thinkers to develop an extended theology within World One. It is a World that continues as a recognizable strand throughout Christian history. Some versions have been Neo-Platonic, Gnostic, Augustinian, and/or mystic. Its mystic versions received classic expression from such persons as Jacob Boehme and Meister Eckhart. But it is with the brilliance of imagery in the writings of St. Teresa of Avila that one can feel this tradition afresh, culling from her works a richness of words that distill her epiphania: favors, graces, presence, recollection, union, taste, locution, rapture, ecstasy, vision, impulses, wounds, transverbations, pain, sickness, revelation, solitude, longing, illumination, consolation, torment, fire, possession, heavenly madness, sick with sickness, infused love, wisdom, flowering, foretastes, lavishness, promises, consummation, eternal, home.[7]

It is Thomas Merton who presently provides a theological entrée into World One for many. Dispersive as his writings are, there is a unifying rhythm which becomes visible when one perceives that "there is only one true flight from the world: it is not an escape from conflict, anguish and suffering, but the flight from disunity and separation." From the side of epiphania, one comes to recognize that this obsessio "is inspired by God in the depths of our nothingness." The epiphania occurs as "we pass through the center of our own souls and enter eternity."[8]

The faith that results brings "an obligation to preserve the stillness, the silence, the poverty, the virginal point of pure nothingness which is at the center of all other loves . . . at once the primordial paradise tree, the *axis mundi*, the cosmic axle, and the cross." What feeds one in this World is mystery, as "from moment to moment I remember with astonishment that I am at the same time empty and full, and satisfied because I am empty." Vision emerges in the "eternal now" as this "unspeakable secret: paradise is all around us and we do not understand." These are only foretastes, for at the deepest level is the yearning to "go home." Then we will participate in fullness, "the world and Time [as] the dance of the Lord in emptiness. [Here] the silence of the spheres is the music of a wedding feast."[9]

For Merton, to be born is to enter the world with a false self, emerging with a mask firmly in place, under the sign of contradiction.[10] For reunion from such separation, "We must withdraw ourselves . . . from exterior things, and pass through the center of our soul to find God."[11] Such a desire for solitude is in truth the hunger to disappear into God. In this life, however, the best that is possible is that "metaphysical consciousness" which is "beyond and prior to the subject-object division" as "a pure consciousness."[12] So grasped, one participates in the sweeping rhythm that unifies, "all of life as coming from God, sustained by God, and returning back to God."[13] A more succinct summary of World One is hard to find.

Tillich has developed the most extensive contemporary, systematic Christian expression of World One. Mary Daly, in *Beyond God the Father*, exhibits its feminist possibilities. Carol Christ identifies through certain modern feminist writers what she regards as the key female rhythm—an awareness of being grounded in what Doris Lessing calls "forces or currents of energy." These she interprets circularly, as "life, death, and regeneration; and being, non-being, and transformation."[14] In describing this defining rhythm, she quotes approvingly from Tillich. The central image is that of "grounding," from which emerges a new mysticism—opened, in this case, by the negative shock of the socializing process.

World One, from a feminist perspective, is sometimes interpreted in linkage with World Three. The rhythm begins with an experience of nothingness, emptiness, self-negation—as both outcast and alien. In the awakening there can occur a mystic identification in which the dualisms that infect common existence are overcome. This feminine perspective, however, is wary of images that suggest self-negation. The process must bring one *to* selfhood, not to sacrifice of it. As this happens, the earth becomes Sister, and one may be pulled toward World Three.

Nature, in contrast to history, plays the crucial role in World One. Nature is always enigmatic, sometimes fallen, yet ripe with epiphanias of presence through transparency. Annie Dillard is a powerful present-day sibyl of this convergence. As we have seen, it is precisely *because* the giant water bug "eats the world" that we are shaken into perceiving epiphania as red-winged blackbirds on frost-covered cedars. It takes only one such moment to send us on our way, as "my left foot says 'Glory,' and my right foot says, 'Amen' . . . in a daze, dancing, to the twin silver trumpets of praise."[15]

The arts provide multiple expressions of this World. The

reader familiar with European drama may recall August Strindberg's attempt to stage this World in *Ghost Sonata*. "The curse lies over the whole creation, over life itself." Consequently Jesus Christ's "descent into hell" was no more than his pilgrimage "to this madhouse, this prison, this charnel-house, this earth. . . . Savior of the world, save us!"[16]

And what, from such an obsessio, would it mean to be saved? It means the hope that

when you wake again . . . may you be greeted by a sun that does not burn, in a home without dust, by friends without stain, by a love without flaw. You wise and gentle Buddha, sitting there waiting for a Heaven to sprout from the earth, grant us patience in our ordeal and purity of will, so that this home may not be confounded.[17]

Such hope is anchored in an experience of that which is behind all appearances. "I beheld the Hidden," claims the hero near the end of the play. It is then that one dares face "this world of illusion . . . of endless change, disappointment, and pain. May the Lord of Heaven be merciful to you upon your journey."[18]

Such dramatic hints, surrounded by the weight of obsessio no less oppressive, become more sacramentally available in a masterpiece of the American stage—Eugene O'Neill's *Long Day's Journey into Night*. As his mother upstairs attempts to drink her homesickness into oblivion, Edmund shares for the first time his "sacred center." His obsessio is an awareness that he "will always be a stranger who never feels at home, who does not really want and is not really wanted, who can never belong, who must always be a little in love with death!" Yet there are the moments, when "the veil of things as they seem [is] drawn back by an unseen hand. For a second you see—and seeing the secret, *are* the secret. . . . Then the hand lets the veil fall and you are alone, lost in the fog again, and you stumble on toward nowhere, for no good reason!" This peace for which he searches is for "the end of the quest, the last harbor."[19] His foretastes occurred at sea:

I became drunk with the beauty and singing rhythm of it, and for a moment I lost myself—actually lost my life. I was set free! I dissolved in the sea, became white sails and flying spray, became beauty and rhythm, became moonlight and the ship and the high dim-starred sky! I belonged, without past or future, within peace and unity and a wild joy, within something greater than my own life . . . to Life itself! To God, if you want to put it that way.[20]

James Joyce's pilgrimage into World One takes place in novel form. His early fascination with World Two becomes increasingly impossible. "History," he concludes, "is a nightmare from which I am trying to awake." Likewise, his youthful fascination with the fulfilled self promised by World Three becomes parched. His experimentation with automatic writing is an effort to inveigle sufficient mystery from the unconscious to keep from suffocating. The resulting stream of consciousness is a desperate icono-clasm, intent on cleaving dry rock. Reminiscent of Plato, he picks the lock of what he calls "the prison gate of our soul," content if only for a moment he feels it quiver.

His famed *Ulysses* is a twenty-four-hour version of Homer's *Odyssey*. The hero wanders the streets of Dublin on his way home to wife and family. However, the epiphania occurs not in arriving, but through moments along the way. The power of those moments lies not in their content but in the transversion of words so as to give serendipitous hints of meaning. "Epiphanies," he calls them—extended moments in which present and future merge into an eternal now. Without these, he insists, we remain engulfed in the vulgarity of a nightmarish world, with only the "logic" of the dream-like but gratuitous qualities of free association. In the affirmation of one such moment the book stops: "Yes and his heart was going like mad and yes I said yes I will yes."[21]

In Hart Crane, lovers of poetry can recognize an interesting relationship between Worlds One and Two. While these Worlds tend to be at odds, there is an apparent fascination that seems to tug at the edges of both, drawing each to invert into the other. Crane senses that the chaos of modern culture rests in being bereft of landmarks of meaning. No mythology, or even a language, is capable of grasping an ideal order. The price is a forfeiture of vision. As a result, "realities plunge in silence be."[22] As critic Waldo Frank put it, Crane "began naked and brave, in a cultural chaos; and his attempt . . . to achieve poetic form was ever close to chaos. . . . Cities, machines, the warring hungers of lonely and herded [people], the passions released from defeated loyalties, were ever near to overwhelm the poet."[23] That is, Crane was bitten by the obsessio of World One.

A person of incredible and chaotic passion, he was never "ready for repentance," the fee required for entrance into World Four.[24] Instead, his passion drew him into fascination with machines—with energy, with the earthiness of powerful activity—he was a person of the city. But there he experienced the outer reef on which, for some, World Two flounders: the human carnage left in the wake of that which attracted them. Crane's responses, actually and symbolically, were sexual and alcoholic. The drive from within was to lose himself in a persistent alternation between ecstasy and dissipation. Caught in such tension, he was drawn by the poet's eye to discern an image capable of ordering that chaos into meaning. In the struggle, the dualism became severe.

The first organic image to emerge was the sea. Proposed in the closing of his "White Buildings" are strong hints of an epiphania that characterizes World One. We sense it as a mystic unity: "The great wink of eternity, of rainless floods, unfettered leewardings." The chaos of separation is promised a reunion, a coming home, as a primordial "return to a 'beginning' before the life of reason, and a unity won by the refusal of human consciousness." His metaphors invite immersion in the primal Mother, escaping from chaos in the restless unity of eternal repetition: "Sleep, death, desire, close round one instant in one floating flower." Only with such moments can one "draw in your head and sleep the long way home."[25]

But in his masterpiece, a contrasting image emerges—

"The Bridge." His poet's will for bringing order out of chaos was gripped by the engineering feat called the Brooklyn Bridge. Such achievement, symbolic of the march of history, is made microcosm for the poet's own pilgrimage. Here flirtation with World Two is strong. At the same time, it wars with a recognizable rhythm from World One. The poem is structured so that in the morning the crossing is from Brooklyn to Manhattan; the recrossing is at midnight—thus going forth and returning. The tension emerges when this circularity intersects with a vision of linearity. The bridge itself expresses continuity through human effort, a controlled order that connects past and future, spanning river and sea. What we have is a hint of circularity which, as a whole, has linear movement.

Such a vision is doomed to be unstable. At Crane's hand the "infinity" of such human creation keeps being drawn into a mystic wholeness. Thus the bridge is "launched in abysmal cupolas of space, toward endless terminals, Easters of speeding light . . . to course that span of consciousness thou'st named the open road."[26] But before the absorption is complete, we are launched into the image of Columbus moving toward Atlantis. Once again the paradox, if not the contradiction, is exposed. Atlantis functions both as the apex of striving and as a continent lost. While the journey begins by emerging from a darkened subway into the morning, it is to that same darkened underground that one returns at midnight.

Thus the powerful image of the bridge's linearity comes increasingly to capture a deep mystic yearning to bridge to another world: "So to thine Everpresence, beyond time . . . that bleeds infinity . . . one Song, one Bridge of Fire!"[27] In his subsequent poetry he returned with increased richness to the mystic images of the sea. At age thirty-two, he took off his coat, and at high noon, jumped from the bridge of a ship in linear voyage, into that primal unity for which he craved more than life.

For the reader weary of words, Mahler's Symphony No. 2 is sufficient. As one listens, it may or may not be useful to know what Mahler himself perceived: "My need to express myself musically—symphonically—begins at the point where the dark feelings hold sway, at the door which leads into the 'other world'—the world in which things are no longer separated by space and time." And of this symphony, he states that it moves into that other world where there is "no judgment; there are no sinners, no just. None is great, none small. There is no punishment and no reward. An overwhelming love illuminates our being. We know and *are*."[28] And so the contralto sings in the finale: "I am from God, and will return to God." And it ends: "I shall die, to live!"

Neoliberalism

To give conceptual concreteness, we have chosen for each World a representative modern Protestant theologian to illustrate how, even within one Christian tradition, the breadth of these five Worlds is present.

Tillich distills World One by drawing together both existentialist and ontological approaches to the theological task. Central for him is exploration of the logic of existing. This is known not through a process of logical consistency but by discerning, through living, that which brings fullness. The task is to become what I am ontologically. But such a task carries with it the paradox of coming to know God through the struggle to live without God.

Dostoevsky, too, explored the questions that result. First, Can we live *without* God? This entails tracing the deadly workings of idolatry. Both thinkers conclude that if there is no God, humans become lethal in assuming the role. This pushes us toward the second question: Can we live *with* God? Here one must face the issue of theodicy. If God's plan entails the suffering of innocent children, must we not hand back the ticket?

For Tillich, these dilemmas that form the obsessio are experienced as the separation of existence from essence.[29] If there is no God, we *are* existence, free to give ourselves any essence (i.e., to become God). So chose Sartre: "There is no

God; to be so is our task." If there is a God, we have an essence as an inescapable given—an essence one must become, or die of an existence warped and defrauded. So chose Augustine: "O Lord, Thou hast made us for thyself, and restless is our heart until it comes to rest in Thee."[30] How can one make such a choice? Precisely by living out that restlessness—struggling to live as if there is no God, thereby determining whether existence contains givens that cannot be avoided. If so, the question for World One becomes ontological.

Gathering these elements together, Tillich identifies the theological task as discovering a "courage to be" that enables authentic selfhood in the midst of alienation as separation. He begins by observing that to exist is to be anxious. But there is a fundamental distinction between pathological and ontological anxiety.[31] The first has its roots in my doing. Simple anxiety may have its cause in the fact that I have put off preparing tomorrow's lecture. If so, by identifying the source, anxiety becomes a problem to be solved: "Go prepare it now!" The same is true in pathological anxiety, where psychotherapy is needed to identify the cause within an unacknowledged past. When discovered, anxiety becomes a problem to be solved now.

But ontological anxiety is different. It resides not in my doing but in my being. It rests in the fear of being nothing. Since nothing is not something, it cannot become a problem to be solved. Something cannot undo nothing. Thus there is nothing to be done. Thus life is shadowed with anxiety, for we are ontologically powerless. By our natures, we are capable at any moment of experiencing this radical contingency as "ontic shock." While we know that people die, the best-kept secret is that *I* will die. Truly to know this is to encounter one's deadend as nightmare. It is here that the fabric of existing becomes clear. Standing before death, in any of its many forms, one cannot say No. Death is that over which I have no control.

Paradoxically, it is here that one can encounter epiphania. The reverse side of such shock is the encounter with mystery. The out-of-controlness true of the moment of death is the nature of every moment of life. *What* I do in each moment is mine to decide. But *that* I am is not within my power. Each moment of existence is sheer gift. To experience this mystery of "why something rather than nothing" graciously, to continue existing when there is no power in me to exist—this is to stand in the presence of a "whence."

Tillich conceptualizes one side of this experience as the Protestant Principle.[32] Here Luther's No against a finite institution that took on claims of being divine is universalized as protest against anything finite that claims the idolatory of being self-sustained. The positive side follows as the Sacramental Principle. Experienced personally, it is the "vision of the new being." Since everything is grounded in the power of Being, everything has potential for being perceived sacramentally—as transparent to that Power.

To illustrate, the shock to a person diagnosed as having terminal cancer is heavy. It is all over—so much so that the temptation is to capitulate. Yet that experience can become such an awakening that life lived in the face of death becomes new by refusing to take anything for granted. Each day, lived as perhaps one's last, becomes the miracle of gift. Each sunrise, each bird call, each moment becomes precious, as sacramental. Thus to be stripped to nothing is to be prepared to receive back everything; the Now is "graced."

Sin is the hemorrhaging of each Now—lost in routine, buried in tedious repetition, reduced to means for something else. Each pastoral call resembles the last one. Counseling sessions become weary replays of common themes. Faces blur into statistics. To be redeemed means to be awakened to what is immediately before one—intrinsically so: A pastoral cup of coffee is experienced eucharistically; a counseling session becomes a greeting of souls; meetings are latent communities calling to become manifest. Such freshness wars against the heaviness of modern culture in which so many have everything and have seen it all. Epiphania, on the other hand, evoked by obsessio, brings the amazement of seeing each of everything as if for the first time, with hands wide open.

One symbol for this ontic Ground is God. But Tillich purges this symbol of its traditional meaning.[33] God is not *a* being. God is Being Itself—the ecstatic heart of existence, the Eternal Now, the Principle(s) woven into the fabric of creation. Such a God does not will, or choose, or act, or reject, or disappear—or any other humanlike activity. To think otherwise would be to reduce God to an object, akin to rival objects. God must be the Ground of all these. Our yearning signals this, for that yearning cannot be stilled by anything finite, although the motive of our frantic activity is to do so. The depth of this craving marks our essence—to be united to that Ground from which our existence comes, from which we are estranged even in the act of existing, and to which we shall return. This eternal rhythm is "reunion of the separated."[34]

Authentic existence within finitude is "transparency." And to the degree that things are beheld as transparent (thus as sacramental), to that degree is the Kingdom here. Measuring any particular culture by this norm provides us with three categories. The ideal is *theonomy*, in which the expressions of a culture become fully sacramental to their ground. *Autonomy* is the opposite, characteristic of times of symbolic dissipation. In such situations, all that is left is the surface, as the game of self-sufficient finitude is being played. *Heteronomy* is an effort to impose meaning upon such a culture, an effort from the top down, attempting to avoid recognition of the meaninglessness bubbling from the bottom up. By this effort, a culture aims at avoiding the boundary situation toward which autonomy inevitably drifts.

As this dynamic functions within the individual, so in culture. To be driven into acknowledgment of the boundary situation that faces an autonomous culture is to undergo crucifixion. That encounter can effect resurrection for culture, in a manner paralleling the effects of ontic shock on the individual. What the vision of the new being is for an individual, theonomy is for a culture. The ideal is that everything becomes sacramental. Not only do bread and wine evoke the fundamental rhythm of separation and reunion, but also do such elements as wood, fire, or water. It should not be strange, then, that almost everything, at one time or another, has been a symbol for such ontic radiance.

Asked why he regarded the world as fallen, Tillich pointed to an altar and a desk—a Lord's Supper alongside a daily supper. Reunion as foretaste implies a daily shower as baptism, each eating as eucharistic, and every sleeping and arising as a death/resurrection.

Put biblically, faith rests in the promise that to gain life (self-sufficient finitude) is to lose it (idolatry), while to lose it (ontic shock) is to gain it (vision of the new being). For the Christian, "the New Testament portrait of Jesus as the Christ" is the most evocative symbol of this defining rhythm.[35] The moment of Jesus' self-loss in death is the moment of his greatest transparency. This event is the final norm, for as nonidolatrous symbol, it is the ideal against which every new kairos is judged and purified by being broken. This symbolic "nevertheless" is resurrection. It is kairos, a pregnant Now, freed of its historical confinements. Transparency is momentary loss into the whole, echoing as foretaste of the final completion in reunion. Consequently, the function of Scripture is not so much to declare historic fact as to provide a portrait that evokes other kairoi: "now" experiences of giftedness, known through finding by losing.

World Two: Vindication as Consummation— Liberation Theology

The *obsessio* that characterizes World Two stirs when the individual, in facing history, is shaken by the image of mindless repetition. History's plot is as constant as it is tragic. Only the players change. Power corrupts, ad nauseam. Furthermore, this historic struggle echoes the gamut of being. Life is based upon a hierarchy of death—weak vanquished by stronger, the lesser as food for the advanced. This arrangement appears everywhere as means/ends. Is anything alive that does not live as parasite off the life of others?

But such exterior death invades the interior as well. Microbes move throughout every system, challenging momentary weakness. Such conflict of being with nonbeing is so persistent that one ponders if it occurs as well in the Divine itself (e.g., Melville), perhaps as a "surd" in the Divine nature (e.g., Brightman), or as struggle in the Divine psyche (e.g., Kazantzakis). For Luther, mercy battles with justice within God, as the yearning to overwhelm with love wars with the anger to exterminate the world as fated nightmare.

For those less violent in temperament, life is like a closet of competing plaids. The conundrum marked obsessio, then, is conflict, within the fabric of everything. Yet there is one step more. Why do we, even when not in a survival mode, act in the same manner? Is it frenzy over the specter of Nothingness playing Pac-Man? In its face, we grip the sides of the black compartment and grimly play at all cost—until the quarters run out.

Are there any, then, who will not cheat when the odds are sufficient? Are there options beyond doublethink, betrayal, or the heaping up of absurd possessions against the door of our exit? This is not the willed arrogance of World Four. Rather, behind the idolatry of self and society, there is pretense, hidden by gaudy exteriors. Even at our worse, we can be discovered behind our masks and sets as the fragile workings of bravado. And for the less assertive actors in this World, the pretense is not pride but "hide"—the defensive posture of conforming into the mass of those already too frightened to death to acknowledge their situation.

Epiphania as vindication could result if a disclosure revealed that conflict is equitably distributed. Harsh though that might be, at least an eye for an eye is logical. But the contrary seems true. In fact, this destructive dynamic seems to express itself with particular fervor against those with integrity. The psalmist agonized, "These are the wicked; always at ease, they increase in riches. All in vain have I kept my heart clean" (73:12-13*a*). The poor, the aged, the orphaned, the widowed—innocent or otherwise—these are the losers heaped upon. The obnoxious ones never "go empty away." In a cartoon recently, Ziggy looks up with hands folded and quietly asks, "Have you noticed that the meek are still getting creamed?"

What is the import of this? Unlike World One, one is not drawn into some deep mystery behind it all. Nor, with World Four, is one plagued with guilty duplicity. Rather, one is distressed by the wrongness of the whole schema. It is as though a foe has contaminated the whole, much as excess salt ruins the soup beyond repair. What one feels is anger, as if tricked and used.

Even the atheist Ernst Bloch senses the yearning that seems inevitable: "Humanization of nature—that would mean the opening up of the cosmos, still closed to itself, to be our Home: the Home once expressed in the mystical fantasy of the new heaven and the new earth."[36] "Home," while characterizing the epiphania of World One, has the otherworldly weight of fantasy for World Two. In fact, it is a misdirected epiphania. The only home fit for vindicating this obsessio is on the plane of history. All that is unjust must be undone. As Berdyaev insists, such a home does not exist. "It must be created."[37] Thus, unlike World One, one does not search for an invisible design behind it all. The central issue is dealing with the design that is operative *now* within the empirical world, but doing so (for the Christian) without losing faith in the God who created it.

Among the unacceptable options for this World are Melville's malevolent God, Camus's agnosticism, Augustine's confession of ignorance, or Luther's insistence upon sin's blinding power. All these end by locating the dilemma in God *or* in us, much the way two friends destroy a relationship through counterblame. Rather, epiphania must provide a variation on the theme of a third party as interloper. For some, it may be the Nihil; for others, death; for the cosmos, entropy; or for the race, it could be Holocaust.

Whatever metaphor might emerge, the feel is deeply of the parasitic. There is an eating away at all that is, silent only when there is nothing left. We cannot escape it even on a daily basis, for whatever one touches is being relentlessly attacked by rust, rot, disintegration, decay, disease. Consequently, the struggle that is life begins to focus on the issue of choice. Shall one participate, acquiesce, or oppose this deadly dynamic?

Hegel finds that even logic partakes of this rhythm. For its realization, every thesis demands an antithesis as its contrary. Yet these lead to a synthesis greater than the sum of both parts, becoming in turn a thesis, birthing another antithesis—in a crisis of increasing fulfillment. On the other hand, there are those for whom this refrain, recognizable in biology, must, with the emergence of consciousness, be reversed: "Let us understand, once for all, that the ethical progress of society depends, not on imitating the cosmic process. Still less running away from it, but in combating it."[38]

Such expressions echo the biblical theme of transfiguration through reversal. Nothing will be vindicated unless the first shall be last, the fallen raised, the dead resurrected, the mighty pulled down, and the poor destined never again to go empty away. Marx identified such a hope as the logos immanent within history. Thus while the epiphania for World One is born in a timeless now, for World Two the epiphania is deeply temporal, emerging in a future tense. Vision focuses upon the transformation to be, vindicating what has been. Historian Herbert Butterfield belongs to this World, using such images as a weaver who redeems even the most questionable threads by incorporating them into the changing design of an ongoing fabric. Another image is a drama, in which whatever is said or done is made to function in subsequent acts as necessary to the whole. Or there is God, the Composer-Conductor, incorporating into the score the good and ill notes of each past moment, offering new harmonies. Faith is God's intent to orchestrate a whole, in which even the errors will appear as grace notes.[39]

Whatever analogies of vindication emerge, the role they broach for God is key. What matters is whether God is cause, watcher, or participant in this struggle. Epiphania must entail the disclosure that God is *participant* within history. If God is Designer or Spectator, the only response is one of rebellion, whether the action of "absurd hero" is the tragedy of Jesus as Prometheus, or the pathos of Camus's Sisyphus. But if God is Emmanuel, *God with us in the struggle*, we experience true epiphania. Christ becomes the pincer foray of the Promethean *God*, for it is the Deity who is heroine: "I have seen the affliction of my people . . . and have heard their cry . . . I know their sufferings, and I have come down to deliver them . . . to bring them up out of that land to . . . a land flowing with milk and honey" (Exod. 3:7-8). God's righteousness is righteous only if it is established in space and time, thereby vindicating creation.

While residents of World One are fascinated with the mystery that anything exists, in World Two the mystery is that anything continues to exist. Conflict renders fragility ominous. To exist means struggle, living each moment at the pulling edge of a tug-of-war. The thought of "just being" is inconceivable. In fact, it is treasonous, for it means capitulating. "Precisely," insists World One. "Surrender into the Whole." "Never," comes the response of World Two. The only Sabbath is the seventh day of history. But within the incompleteness of this sixth day, faith is in Promise. And to trust such promise is to hear the call to costly discipleship, based on the costliness of the Divine discipleship.

Epiphania entails a God declared innocent by the quality of involvement now within Creation. While it may be God's nature to be involved, World Two favors God's choice in the matter. For some, this entails God as triune. This is because the Creator so central in World One can appear to World Two as a demonic Designer. Likewise, the immanent Spirit characteristic of World Three can imply for World Two God's organic complicity in the world's condition. It is quite another matter, however, if God is triune, as ongoing Creator struggling as our companion in Incarnate Presence, on behalf of a world in which, as Spirit, God is wrenching a groaning creation into promised consummation.

Thus the christological center is often seen here as God's wedding to history, beyond the point of recall. Jesus Christ is the revelation in history, of history, for history. Consequently, as we see in Pannenberg and Moltmann, history as crucifixion, seen under Promise, is history moving toward resurrection. The one who came as promise must come again as vindication. Here is the God who comes back for the others. Thus the Christ Event, sometimes in contrast with World One, must be solidly historical. Austin Farrer, after completing his monumental philosophical case for the existence of God as creative Ground, insists:

As I wrote this, the German armies were occupying Paris, after a campaign prodigal of blood and human distress. Rational theology will not tell us whether this has or has not been an unqualified and irretrievable disaster. . . . It is another matter if we believe that God Incarnate also died, and rose from the dead.[40]

For World Two, without Jesus as the face of God, the specter of the Divine as foe is formidable.[41] Thus faith for some in this World is an either/or, a gamble heavy with doubt in the face of ongoing defeat. Thus concerning the resurrection, on which much can rest, one is inclined to want a second opinion—so much so that faith itself can appear as radical gift, for the kind of trust required needs to engulf the sweep of history.[42]

Such epiphania is a disclosure of narrative structure for the cosmos. The categories are act, not being; history, not nature; dynamism, not substance.[43] History must enfold nature as plot, establishing a forged meaning which vindicates because, as narrative, there is resolution. And the plot, which appears so often as tragedy, will be transmitted into comedy because it too is God's plot. Therefore crucifixion receives its narrative resolution in resurrection, its incarnation in ascension. Understandably, as in the book of Revelation, history is rendered into liturgical drama. This vision, charged by some as utopian, stresses not personal sin but the structures of evil. By changing structures, individuals are brought to their true humanity.

Strategies for such liberation vary. The more radical ecclesiology is to the sect type: "Salvation is the tough social formation of a colony, a holy nation, a people, a family, a congregation that is able to stand against the pretentiousness and illusions of the world."[44] Whether politically liberal or conservative, the call is to stand against, witness to, be leaven for, or even be subversive of existing society. Thus, liberation theologian Richard Shaull proposes the development within institutions of small groups "committed to constantly upsetting their stability . . . launching new experiments . . . and willing to pay the price of such subversive acts."[45]

Any charge of utopianism against the church as signal community could apply only to the future, for the present is a rehearsal of the End Time, a disciplined living "as if," rushing the future, as it were, by living it already. In contrast to World Three, the life-style of World Two is not one of self-realization but of self-sacrifice. The inclination is toward self-negation in behalf of a cause, either in witness or as protest. The hero(ine) is martyr, for reality now is a cross. Resurrection is future, now experienced as hope.

Consequently, such images as World Three's "development," "growth," and "wholeness" are viewed with suspicion. They hint of personal advantage. The saints are not fulfilled persons. They are "crazy" by most standards of their culture. Thus pastoral care might mean leading others not to enrichment but to a cross. It might entail wounding from behind, or pouring salt on open wounds. How else, since we must risk being losers, receiving marching instructions from another drummer? But most irritating, citizens of World Two are those whose tendency is to question every attainment as insufficient.

Understandably, then, the Gospel of Luke is a favorite for many in this World, the *Magnificat* functioning well as creed:

> God has shown strength with God's arm,
> God has scattered the proud
>   in the imagination of their hearts,

God has put down the mighty from their thrones
    and exalted those of low degree;
God has filled the hungry with good things,
and the rich God has sent empty away. *Luke 1:51-53, paraphrased*

Theologians who set up shop in World Two span Judaism, Roman Catholicism, and Protestantism. In Judaism, Arthur Cohen believes that "time is the medium, and history is the substance of divine actualization." In a manner following Berdyaev, "process within God is providence for [human-kind]."[46] Among Roman Catholics, Teilhard de Chardin's parable of humankind as crew is indicative. We sit with heads together, "telling time-honored tales." When startled by the lookout's cry, half of us leave, gazing with "fresh eyes" at the water against the hull and, with fresh lungs, feel the breeze. "And for these, all things, while remaining separately the same—the ripple of water, the scent of the air, the lights in the sky—become linked together and acquire a new sense: the fixed and random Universe is seen to move."[47] It moves as a whole, as if a ship set upon Polaris. Trusting the movement so that "I persevere courageously, I shall rejoin God across evil, deeper down than evil; I shall draw close to [God]: and at the moment the optimum of my 'communion in resignation' necessarily coincides . . . with the maximum of fidelity to the human task." Christianity bids us "plunge into Matter" in the call to create the future. There is a price, however, for this "entails deep inner turmoil," driving us distant from security and tranquility.[48]

In Protestantism, Bonhoeffer has one foot in World Two. He insists upon a consummation in which the concrete is preserved—not so much taken up into God as transfigured for the restoration of earth. Bonhoeffer's vision is that

nothing is lost, that everything is taken up in Christ, although it is transformed, made transparent, clear, and free from all selfish desire. Christ restores all this as God originally intended it to be, without the distortion resulting from our sins. The doctrine . . . of the restoration of all things . . . is a magnificent conception.[49]

World Two has powerful representatives in the liberation theology of Third World and ethnic thinkers. In this country, black theology is clear:

> In so far as [Christ] is the Conqueror of death and all the principalities and powers, he is the Black Messiah who was raised from the dead to liberate the oppressed by the power of the God who delivered Israel from the hand of pharaoh and revealed [God's self] as a strong Deliverer, and Liberator from every oppression of human existence.[50]

The Old Testament has been a particularly rich resource for this World. Yahweh is the Warrior God who "summons the earth" with a "devouring fire" that "executes judgment" (Pss. 50:1, 3; 75:7). This God will "trample under foot those who lust after tribute; scatter the peoples who delight in war" (Ps. 68:30*b*). This One will "gather [the] faithful ones" to God's own self with an epiphania of promise: to "defend the cause of the poor of the people, give deliverance to the needy, and crush the oppressor" (Pss. 50:5; 72:4). So grounded, the theology of black America, of Africa, and of Latin America must be recognized as "different expressions within the framework where they belong: the framework of the theology of liberation."[51]

This focus upon a liberated Commonwealth that is neither "other" nor "now" but "yet to be," can take richly varied forms—from revolutionary society to poetic eschatology, to literal apocalypticism. Inclusiveness can incorporate not only the living but "those asleep with Christ in God." And it need not be limited to history in a narrow sense, but may weave each moment of beauty into the enrichment of God, who, with and for us, shall be our All in all.

Certain feminist thinkers are uneasy about liberation as sometimes expressed in World Two. For Rosemary Ruether, an "Imperial Christ" can emerge oppressively from this World. For her, this tendency centers in the event of Nicea, where Hebraic messianism combined with Greek philosophy. There Zechariah's warrior-king combined with the Greek Logos to form the "great chain of being," condemning women, slaves, and barbarians to the bottom links. Yet her response discloses an intriguing alternative within World Two.

Needless to say, elements of this Christology might have been constructed in a different way. The victory of the Messiah as vindicator of the oppressed might have been seen as the radical leveling of all hierarchy and subjugation rather than installation of the New Israel as the center of a new empire.[52]

It is important to note the ambiguous role of White-headian process thought here. While it has possibilities that can be expressed within World Two, its impact is heaviest on World Three. In part, this is because Whitehead's under-standing stresses continuity more than discontinuity, affirms a rational design for creation, tempers dualism in a dipolar organic understanding of cosmos and God, empha-sizes a metaphysic of nature more than of history, and stresses immanence rather than incarnation. As incorporated by some within World Three, Whitehead's resolution of history is not upon the plane of history as a whole, but in more piecemeal fashion. Continuity is not within history, but through events taken into the Divine memory as enrichment. The focus is *process* rather than *telos*, with an unending future in which individuals as such will not participate. In addition, some residents of World Two claim that Whitehead does not take evil with sufficient seriousness. God appears impotent, restricted to luring the best from whatever is, refining the results by gathering the best into God's own self. Further, God's involvement is not by choice but by necessity. God cannot do otherwise.

Consequently, process thinking in World Two tends to become dialectic, the cosmic struggle often etched by harsh contours of pitched battle. The novelist Kazantzakis is illustrative. In *Saviors of God*, he articulates his theological conclusions, two in particular being indicative:

I believe in one God, defender of the borders . . . militant, suffering, of mighty but not of omnipotent powers, a warrior at the farthest frontiers, commander-in-chief of all the luminous powers, the visible and the invisible.

I believe in [the human] heart, that earthen threshing-floor where night and day, the defender of the borders fights with death.[53]

John Steinbeck is a self-conscious literary portrayer of World Two. His hope rises from anger: "In the souls of the people the grapes of wrath are filling and growing heavy, growing heavy for the vintage." Thus capitulation in the struggle "would never come as long as fear could turn to wrath." His emerging epiphania has nuances of other Worlds: "What made 'em bad was they needed stuff. . . . It's the need that makes all the trouble" (World 3); "We ain't gonna die. People is goin' on" (World 5). Yet the core remains within World Two: "You got to have patience . . . a different time's comin'." The hope is, "that ever' time they's a step forward, she may slip back a little, but she never slips clear back." Why? Because one had "foun' he didn't have no soul that was his'n. . . . He foun' he jus' got a little piece of a great big Soul."[54]

Such socialist tendencies are skillfully woven into a Christian fabric by the Italian novelist Ignazio Silone. His concern for "the kingdom of God on earth" brings him to the biblical idea of remnant as providing the continuity of history within history.[55] One character echoes the hope:

There'll always be someone that refuses to sell his soul for a handful of beans and a piece of cheese. . . . And at the end, when the worms think they've won, there'll come the angel. He'll take the trumpet from its hiding place and he'll sound full blast and he'll wake even the dead.[56]

Musically, the epiphania of World Two is distilled in Beethoven's sole opera, *Fidelio*. The story centers in Leonore, wife of the imprisoned Florestan, "that noble fighter for truth," who is being tortured in behalf of freedom. Disguised as Fidelio, Leonore liberates her husband, facing the possibility of death with "incredible courage." "I trust in God and justice," she sings. The prisoners respond from a common World: "We will with faith rely on God's help. Hope whispers softly to me: We shall be free." Leonore's vows move from a personal duty to a universal commitment: "Whoever you may be, I shall save you; by God! You shall not be victimized, I swear I will unfasten your chains, poor soul. I shall set you free!" It is in giving bread and wine to an otherwise dying prisoner that the heart of World Two is affirmed: "Providence watches over us all." And so we hear as Fidelio's climax:

> Blessed be this day! Blessed be this hour,
> Long yearned for, though beyond our hopes,
> Justice, side by side with mercy,
> Appears at the threshold of our grave.

The final movement of Beethoven's Third Symphony (*Eroica*) reaches a parallel crescendo of epic proportions. One experiences "such a monumental set of variations that it becomes a veritable musical arch of triumph through which the image of a liberated humanity joyfully passes in review."[57]

Handel's oratorios are especially expressive of the World we are describing. In *Israel in Egypt,* for example, Exodus 15 provides the coda for the double chorus: "Sing ye to the Lord, for [God] hath triumphed gloriously; the horse and his rider hath [God] thrown into the sea."

In Bach's music, however, World Two receives its finest expression. Indicatively, rhythms of triumph appear not only in his *Passions* and *Easter Oratorio,* but in his *Christmas Oratorio* as well. Here, written for the Feast of the Epiphany, appears the heart of epiphania for World Two.

> Lord, when our haughty foes assail us,
> Let not our faith and courage fail us,
> But with thy might and help be near,
> On thee we place our firm reliance.
> So to our foes we bid defiance
> And face them bold and free from fear.

The chorus responds:

> The triumph is completed!
> Our Savior, Christ the Lord
> Has vanquished and defeated
> The Fiend and all his horde,
> Sin, Death and Hell, and Satan.

Bach distills the whole: "Christ doth end in triumph the conflict he began."

Liberation Theology

Liberation theologians who belong to World Two claim diverse theological traditions. Yet it is intriguing that Protestant representatives as diverse as James Cone, Jose Miguez-Bonino, and Rubem Alves have their roots in the later theology of Karl Barth. The early Barth was central in restoring World Four as a widely viable contemporary option. There was a transition in this thinking, however, marked by his work on Anselm, in which a new theological climate was revived. While his earlier work centers on crucifixion, this later focus is upon the resurrection, functioning as the center point of the divine promise in and for history. Jesus Christ now becomes the triumphant Yes! spoken to all creation. Redemption, no longer narrowly individual, constitutes the restoration of all humanity to the status of heir. Thus regarded, we are invited to be co-creators with the Spirit in bringing history to completion.

Central to this transition in Barth's thinking is the awareness that if the Christ Event is the disclosure of "very God of very God," it follows that God has delivered God's very self into the flesh of space/time. This is an abandonment of Barth's previous World, in which God was remote and inaccessible, the "infinite qualitative other." God is now known precisely by where God chooses to stand. That choice is to be with the lowest class of the most despised—Jews. Thereby it is declared that in God's eyes, the world is reversed. To recognize that the rejected are those invited to the seats of honor is to see the whole cosmos anew. We see it under Divine promise.

The call that issues from Incarnation is an ongoing incarnation in solidarity with the dispossessed. Emphasis falls not exclusively on the Now, as if one's destiny rests on a "moment of decision." The tense turns radically futuristic. Earth yearns with us for adoption, so that God's transcendence is no longer spatial but temporal. God reaches for us not from above, but from in front, beckoning. Resurrection is no longer simply the confirmation of forgiveness. It is a proleptic event, the center point of history, as foretaste of what shall be, in and through history—not to us, but *with* us.

The vision becomes whole, for if resurrection entails God taking humanity into God's self, that essential motion identifies God's activities with the whole of creation. God's enrichment is through the glorification of Creation for its own sake. Time is the realm of increase, of becoming, so that Incarnation in history discloses history itself as a Divine-human incarnation. Consequently, Barth replaces the concept of eternity with the image of "God's time." God is in time, just as time is in God. Thus the Incarnation is God's ecstatic Yes! to the creation with which God has fallen in love, acting decisively in history, by taking sides for humankind against all foes.

Such a vision is no utopianism, for it never can be known or realized through the world's own immanent possibilities. As Alves puts it, "We are impotent. To hope for liberation in capacity is to hope for the impossible: the unexpected. In the idiom of religion, it is to have trust in a God who summons things that do not exist into existence and makes the barren fruitful."[58]

Life is lived under promise, the promise of what God will do with us as covenant partners. God risks all—in order for the cosmos to be completed by God for us, and by us for God, together. This changes the syntax of faith. What we hear is no longer "thou must" but "thou may." Demand becomes invitation. The imperative becomes indicative.

Consequently, every human enterprise—culture, philosophy, economics, art, politics—may contribute in this World as the theater of Divine/human glory. These are creative gifts, recognizable as exchanges in the cosmic love affair, anticipating the wedding night of the Lamb and the cosmic Bride.

Christians of World Two, like their God, tend to become intoxicated with living. The earth is less instrumentality and more sabbatical theater for its own sake. Marianne Micks calls such "useless" joy the "future present." The church is where such living occurs—the community wrapped in the joy that what is true for it now in foretaste, is true for the entire cosmos by promise. The task is so to struggle that the good news is seen as good.

Barth's morning ritual gives clues to this World. He had a Bible at one hand, a newspaper at the other—with Mozart on the stereo, and coffee and pipe waiting on the table. When too old to attend church, he listened to the radio every Sunday and heard the Promise declared twice—once Protestant, once Roman Catholic. The Word continued to remind him where we must stand in order to see, for that is where God has chosen to stand. For World Two, this often means setting up shop beside the empty tomb, outside the walls.

World Three: Fulfillment as Enriched Belonging— Process Theology

Central to World Three is a concern for the self. Its *obsessio* is experienced as an aching void, marking a self alienated primarily from itself. One's negative energies often focus in a frantic effort at facade. Yet even if outer acceptance is achieved, it cannot quiet this emptiness. One's insides continue to be chewed by nothing—and by everything—"To be or not to be." But to be is not the simple task of willing it. One is socialized early into roles, expectations, postures—assigned, conditioned, educated, compensated, fitted, picked—until one feels trapped, with one's needs as conditioned as one's responses. Destined to take on the boredom of infinite repetition, one watches from behind a "me" that "I" regret knowing.

At the height of her Hollywood success, surrounded by lines of admirers, Marilyn Monroe quietly cried, "I feel so neglected." In the quiet hours, one cannot hide, caught between two tugs. Inside there is the deadness of repressed feelings that won't stay dead; outside there is the lure of seductive comfort through invisibility. Augustine quaintly named it sloth. And society's task is that of Dostoevsky's "Grand Inquisitor," rewarding with security the forfeiture of freedom through conformity.

Eliot captures this obsessio in the figure of Prufrock. His is a distillation of vacuity, boredom, and impotence, resisting with tedious habit the "overwhelming question." It is a life of indecisions over revisions, while at the edge stalks the question, "Do I dare?" Emptiness trivializes even the question, "Do I dare to eat a peach?" And so I continue as always: "I have measured out my life with coffee spoons"—until "we drown."[59]

The sin of pride in this World actually becomes another form of sloth. Pride is the frenzied action of trying to escape the hard question, a posture of bravado that superficializes the game, a loss of selfhood through vicariousness, with belonging the reward for serving well.

Epiphania in World Three begins with arrest, with encounter, with awakening—often at the painful intersection of unbearable emptiness and unimagined possibilities. For others, it is more negative, as when a life transition or the aging process becomes an unexpected mirror for a face only strangely mine. It may entail adding up one's string of zeros, until the sum of the total equals each of its parts. Yet painful as experiencing bottom lines may be, sometimes the most devastating mirroring eyes are those of kindly invitation.

The opposite of love is not hate, but indifference. It is out of indifference that one must be shocked. The death of Christ is not the work of powers and principalities or of the arrogance of the vicious. Crucifixion takes place through the apathy of the frightened many.)Thus awakening brings not the feel of guilt (World Four) as much as a profound sadness. The focus is not on what I have done as much as what I have not done. The grief is for omission, not commission. The title of Frost's "The Road Not Taken" captures the epiphania, while the obsessio lies in taking the well-traveled route.

While an awakening often undermines one's carefully constructed props of self-justification, this is generally not a World where epiphania entails harsh condemnation. In fact, here guilt does not function well as an emetic. It is counterproductive; it hardens self-alienation by reinforcing an already shabby self-image. "Why try? I'd only fail again!" Guilt is like stuffing one's mouth with ashes in an attempt to silence the dry heaves.

Consequently, orthodox Christology is often difficult for this World. Against Lenten grimness, the Christ portrait needs to be more welcoming. And the one who welcomes must be the One who mirrors us to ourselves, having gone before, looking back and beckoning. The path is firm. The river is manageable. Most important, then, is Jesus' humanity rather than his divinity. Jesus is "best friend," One with whom I dare imagine. Presence means the secure space in which to dream enough to believe in myself, because he cares enough to believe in me. Blockage to fulfillment is in not daring to feel again. Paralysis through fear of failing is not likely to be overcome without companion support. Thus others can become Christ to me, in believing, long before I believe, that "I can do it." So understood, Christ is the invitation to be, to risk, to live. In this, Jesus is *teacher*, for the word means "one who nourishes."

Jesus can be twin representative—of me to God, and of God to me. Because God sees me as he sees Jesus, I am able to see myself as the one believed in by God. And as believed in by God, I become lover, as was Jesus. That means I see myself loved by God not so much because *of* Jesus, but *as* Jesus was loved. By seeing in this person a divine humanity birthed by love, I can understand what God is about in the process called creation; I can begin to trust myself as part of it. The christological mirror, then, becomes increasingly convex, displaying our selfhood as no longer vacuous, repetitive, restrictive. Selfhood is an ongoing birthing, an event in progress, a process of being led out—never finished, never totally determined—a project always in the making. What was once a life of distraction and dissipation in past and future, now converges in the present as potential. But the portent of such moments appears not as transparency but as intensity, and thus expansiveness.

However one is awakened, there tends to be agreement with Harnack that the essence of Christianity is anchored in the "sanctity of the self."[60] It follows, with Ritschl, that Christian beliefs are value-formed. Thus, for example, to speak of the divinity of Jesus means that for me, Jesus has the value of God in effecting the process of self-maturation. Consequently, this World finds very unacceptable the atonement of "imputed righteousness" (World Four), in which God sees us as if we were what we are not. To be seen as one is not?—that is not a distillation of epiphania, but obsessio. Thus some residents of World Three regard as unfortunate Luther's insistence on grace as forgiveness of sin, rather than as empowerment of self. As over against his insistence that the self never changes qualitatively, here one must be enabled to believe in oneself. The epiphania unconditionally affirms one as self. The change must be in *me*. Unless I am enabled to love myself, it makes no sense to love my neighbor as myself.

Socrates was early mentor for this World. Freedom is the wholeness belonging to self-discovery, self-growth, self-risk. What is to be unloosed is already within, lured from imprisonment through an atmosphere of acceptance of each self as unique and sacred. Carl Rogers' form of counseling is based on this process.[61] Epiphania occurs in the context of "unconditional positive regard," within which "mirroring back" can resolve self-estrangement through decision. Significant change requires such an affirmation of one's potential that growth becomes not so much a choice as an inevitability. Even the grim determination to be other than one is needs to melt into a "flowering forth."

In the end, two things are clear. One can only be loved into love. And one cannot love others if one does not love oneself.

More than a century ago, Horace Bushnell gave strong voice to World Three by challenging the theology of World Four characterizing New England.[62] There is no need for a traumatic crisis as a means of conversion if a person has been surrounded from birth with nurturing love. Salvation means that the self is so affirmed in love that fear no longer creates the paralysis of death during life, which requires the threat of life through death. What is more, if radical conversion is needed, this is a confession of church and society's failure to nurture.

Since such failure is characteristic of the individualistic, competitive, hierarchical nature of present society, World Three can make common cause with the process of "conscientization" used by certain Third World theologians—a participatory method by which role expectations and oppressive institutions are desacralized through perceiving their contradictions. Such disclosure of hypocrisy is necessary for selfhood, for it creates distance from those institutions to which one conforms without question. Social control requires veneration sufficient for deference, at the expense of the self. For freedom, then, such veneration must be tempered, if not undermined.

Literary critic Robert Graves expresses this attraction of World Three for the feminist sensibility. This is Graves' own World, captured for him in the rhythm of classic Goddess worship. Epitomized in terms of the poet's love of the muse, the rhythm is: birth/initiation/consummation/repose/death. We must regain the priority of nature over history, he insists. For this, one must become disengaged from the historical Jesus, the one who declared war against the Goddess, thereby establishing the parameters of World Two. In contrast, one must lay claim to the "mythical Christ" who "loved the filial Queen of heaven rather than, like Jesus, the Incomprehensive Father."[63]

This stress on organic and natural rhythms makes connection with certain current transitions in feminist thinking. While some women see childbirth as confining, often socialized into a demeaning restriction upon women's wholeness, others are beginning to see in it not only a uniqueness but a paragdigm of Divine meaning. Birthing is the Divine sacrament, its liturgy enacted as the defining cosmic rhythm—the womb wherein emptiness becomes fulfillment.

The rhythm of World Three is that of reaching out and enfolding, bringing fullness through embrace. Life is development, a pilgrimage of unfolding. Sam Keen recognizes this commingling of birth and death and birth as a lifelong process, calling *life* the serendipity of "beginnings without end."[64]

Understandably, for many in this World the Gospel of John has special appeal. Here the eschatology is not future but present. *Now* is the acceptable day of the Lord, for this is the One "who is *coming* into the world" (11:27, italics added). This is the One who can give the "living bread" now, for the "void" which is judgment has already occurred. Open before us is a lyric sacramentalism which marks our daily passing "from death to life." And so the key question: "What do you seek?" (1:38). To "have life, and have it abundantly" (10:10). And the epiphania? It is an invitation: "Come and see."

Such a biblical understanding for World Three is masterfully exegeted by Rudolf Bultmann. The inauthentic self is one smothered in the "has been," paralyzed by the "can be," hiding from authenticity through mass anonymity and/or material accumulation.[65] The locus of epiphania is in the Now, where in each moment, crucifixion becomes the imperative to let go of the past. Resurrection is the corollary of responding with the courage to pick up one's bed and walk. Consequently, faith is a resolution made and remade, moment after moment, for it is resolve that provides life's continuity. The life-style that results is one of owning as if not owning, of loving with open hands.

Such existentialist understandings can belong to World

Three, but sometimes a grim edge of determined "never-theless" can move the Bultmannian toward World Five. Either way, however, it is a perspective that tends to be conative, while it is the affective mood that most often characterizes World Three. This World recognizes the surge of libido, life's lyric love of life.

While the epiphania of World Two tends to be teleological, that of World Three tends to be cumulative. Put another way, the eschatological question is not so much Where do events lead? but Will they be lost? The concern is not so much to reach Canaan as to rerememer freshly the moment when Yahweh and the maiden Israel first made love in the desert—"Still Crazy After All Those Years." It is not so much building one's consummate dream house as recapturing as recurrent present the strange joy of one's first cold-water flat. Here World Three comes within hailing distance of the sacramentalism of World One. But there is a difference. The latter depends upon a transparency that points beyond itself, while the lyricism of World Three resides in an immanent pregnancy. The former involves emptying; the latter, a rich filling.

Because value is understood intrinsically more than instrumentally, no future can compensate for present loss. Thus a key question: "Will each pregnant moment, experienced in itself, be forgotten?" There is a fascination with the idea of enriched belonging. While such an image can exhibit multiple interpretations, process thinking is helpful. For Daniel Day Williams, the obsessio of emptiness centers upon the theme of loneliness, experienced as the yearning to belong.[66] Correlatively, the epiphania has two focuses. On the human side, the church is inclusive community, incorporating persons into an organic whole. On the Divine side, in God's "consequent nature" nothing of value is ever lost but is taken up, as enriched belonging, into the refining fire of God's memory. The Kingdom is the ongoing enrichment of God as growing experience and deepening consciousness. History will have no telos, but in each event we can experience, as possibility, the rich

convergence of memory and imagination in God, and thus
for us.

Such a process orientation has further appeal for members
of World Three because the personal venturing called for in
this World necessitates trust. A process metaphysic can
provide this through the analogy of the World as organism,
resulting in two affirmations. First, the World is ordered, and
thus predictable, dependable, intelligible, and trustworthy.
Second, since organism requires novelty for growth, growth
is an ordered process. The result is change, intent upon the
maximization of ever new possibilities, in whole and in part.
Since these dimensions belong to the nature of life itself, the
feel of the cosmos is that of home, a domicile amenable to
enriched humanness.

While for some, World Three has a mark of modernity, it
actually has a long tradition. The ethos of the Middle Ages,
for example, focused on the dilemma of self-impotence.
Thus the elaborate sacramental system which developed
can be understood as response to such an obsessio. It was
grace as infused, enabling power that provided epiphania.
The Eucharist, especially, provided the nourishment
necessary for faith, hope, and love—the characteristics of
the fulfilled self. Even viaticum was provided—the final
food for the dying, nurture for the journey into eternity.
This is why excommunication is so cataclysmic. Without
such empowerment, one cannot become who one truly is
created to be.

Earlier, Irenaeus insisted that "the glory of God is the
living human, and the life of the human is the vision of
God." God became human in order that the human might
become divine. The task followed—"to be fully alive." St.
Francis elaborated this World, living out this fulfillment in
resonance with Renaissance awakenings. Within half a
century, Meister Eckhardt focused on what Matthew Fox
calls creation spirituality, in contrast to the penitential
emphasis of World Four. So understood, World Three's
invitation lay in the lure of upward ascendency in the
Gothic cathedral, only to be threatened by the Reformation
preference for the confines of the confessional booth.

In literature, a provocative exploration appears in the seven novels that compose Marcel Proust's *Remembrance of Things Past*. The characters are deliberate composites of Proust's own experiences, in the attempt to fulfill the ideal character toward which each person tends in actual life. Through the creative intersecting of memory and imagination, Proust believed that a symphonic, structural whole could emerge as an epiphania for life itself.

Proust's effort at a fulfillment which life itself resists emerged not only because everything that exists is less than ideal; even more, everything that exists is tyrannized by time. He encountered this fact with what he called "fascinated terror." Thus his novel begins with a description of restless nights spent in an effort to capture memory losses. His hope was that, in establishing lively associations within memory, even such trivia as the taste of cake can become part of an organic whole. This is an aesthetic expression of what Hegel called a concrete universal. Each thing is what it is because of its relation to everything else.

Yet such associational connections are fleeting. Thus for fulfillment to be real, we must somehow escape the relentless erosion of time, for which the finite memory is endemic. This ongoing hemorrhaging of lyric moments calls for atonement, for even the past must be recovered and saved. Proust had no formal religious position with which to undergird such hope. Therefore his hope came to rest in the power of imagination, in a manner that anticipated Whitehead's resolution. Imagination alone has the power to bridge past with present as future, gifting time with a oneness that stops linear destructiveness.

Chronology provides no meaning. Nor is memory sufficient; at best it only collects. What is needed, and what Proust gained through the aesthetic process, is a sui generis experience that is both sacramental and mystic. What his novels provide as hints and guesses suggest a theology characteristic of World Three. He flirted with a static eternity characteristic of World One, but in the end he rebels against the loss of each fresh detail in symbolism.

What fascinates him is *this* earth, experienced in its full sensuality. Thus his obsessio is not only emptiness yearning for fullness, but emptiness *after* fullness—the hemorrhaging of time. His is the yearning for an ordered and eternal peace within the lyricism of an experienced wholeness.

Process Theology

Contemporary process thought illustrates well the parameters of World Three. Its base image for reality is not the Greek changelessness bequeathed to orthodox Christian theology. That God is One for whom yesterday, today, tomorrow, are always the same. Such an image encourages a conservative stance toward reality—one of maintenance, restoration, or preoccupation with another realm. But, Whitehead insisted, since change is the primary dynamic of the world we know, conservatives are pitting themselves against the very impulse of the universe.

Charles Hartshorne suggests analogies from human behavior to criticize such orthodox views of God. An unchanging parent is pigheaded, arrogant, inflexible, unhearing, indifferent—in a word, unloving: "You do as I say!"; "I've said it once, and I won't hear another word about it!" Thus if love is at the heart of the Divine, God cannot be Aristotle's Unmoved Mover. God is the most moved of Movers (Hosea)—that is, totally responsive. By contrast, Greek philosophy, being antifleshly and antihistorical in its otherworldliness, so influenced Christian theology that it has undercut the world affirmation of Hebraic thought and, with it, the Christian gospel.

The Christian can appropriate the process perspective in at least two ways. Daniel Day Williams and Marjorie Suchocki adopt the approach of "faith seeking understanding," using process analogies for interpreting Christianity.[67] The resulting portrait of the human condition is liberal and positive. Sin is "misdirected love," hate is "frustrated love," despair is "self-betrayal." Emphasis falls upon the humanity of Jesus, the continuity between God and the world, and redemption as being lured and completed through nurturing community. The crucial categories are love, belonging, potential, realization. Divine activity, as evident within these human processes, is "love in process." The power of God is the "worship God inspires," "evoking human response." God's ideal for us is "communion" as the "mutual sharing of community." All of this is done so that God's "willing" is consistent with human freedom: "Self-giving without self-affirmation is meaningless." ✳

On the other hand, the Christian may use the process perspective also as "understanding seeking faith." Thus John Cobb finds in process metaphysics an understanding of the world with which Christian faith can have a point of contact.[68] Its metaphysic insists upon a universe in which the principles of existence and logic apply both to God and to humans (uni-verse). Our minds are drawn to explain three basic phenomena—order, novelty, and preservation. These became understandable if God is dipolar. As "primordial," God is pure potential, the envisaging of all that is possible ("eternal ideas"). As "consequent," God is becoming, experiencing the world in its temporal flow, preserving positive occasions by memory. Since humans are dipolar too, we are affected by God's "eternal ideas" as they converge with past consequences to form new possibilities. This gives novelty to each moment, luring us toward maximization of beauty through fresh "initial aims" for our choosing.

To use an organic analogy, God is to the world as mind is to body. Thus, for Hartshorne, God has no need of *this world, but God does have need of a* world. Without a physical world, God is empty possibility. Thus events are ingredients for the fulfillment of God, actualized by the Divine memory through suffering, as a refining fire. God "resurrects" into God's self that which is redeemable, rendering it eternal as part of God's fulfillment.[69]

For others, the analogy of mind is more suggestive. It is *in* God that we live and move and have our being (panentheism). Thus all that is is energy, spirit, mind (panpsychism). Either way, we are part of a whole in which mind/body, self/world, divine/human are misleading polarizations. Not only are we not foreigners to the cosmos, but we are not separated from one another. Jesus was metaphysically right: "As you did it to one of the least of these, you did it to me." To deprive anyone of fulfillment is to deprive myself. To enrich others is to enrich God as well. This means experiencing the world as home and one's self as participant, in a cosmos of enriched belonging.

The best analogies for understanding this process as epiphania may be aesthetic. Michelangelo, for example, was able to envisage in a marble block the figure yearning to be unlocked. Dostoevsky, as novelist, discovered meaning in the process of giving independent life to his characters. Correlatively, the life-style that tends to represent World Three is not one characterized by obedience, morality, or will. It is more of a divine-human exchange, a midwifing of beauty in mutual discovery. At its best, each moment is exciting—lively of beauty and staggering in novelty, a world to be prehended into fullness. Epiphania, in the end, occurs by realizing that there is nothing whose outer edge is not touched by the lure into freedom.

Yet there may be a sadness to this World. Choice entails nonchoices, and each realization entails possibilities forever lost. It is this hemorrhaging that invites belief in the eternity of God's memory. But, for Whitehead, such eternity is for God, not for us.[70] We contribute and will be forever remembered, but as past. We will not be there. This can result in a heroic spirituality, contributing selflessly to the fullness of a God in which one will not participate. The parable is Moses, standing on Pisgah, to which his life has brought him—looking over at a Promised Land he will never enter.

It is sad, but enough. God is not to blame, for God has not created things this way. God does not create ex nihilo. Rather, God orders what is, much as an artist strives to make the best of what is available. Thus we cannot rail against God, for God is doing all that God can do—luring forth the maximization of beauty in each new situation. There are other process theologians, such as Marjorie

Suchocki, who insist, from Christian convictions, upon personal resurrection. And there are still others in World Three for whom death is part of life's organic rhythm. There is room for each in this World.

God can do one more thing. God is companion sufferer with us. Whitehead calls this the experiencing of God's superjective nature. One can grasp, through his appreciation for the Romantic poets, the difference this might make. Their works have a self-justifying melancholy. By the capturing, through a ruined castle, of the ephemeral quality of all that is finite, we are grasped by a rare quality of fragile beauty. Sharing such experience, if only fleetingly, has a feel of the eternal. There is no supernatural realm behind a veil that can be drawn back. Yet we are not alone, and in sharing such loss there is beauty. It is no surprise that "Abide with Me" was Whitehead's favorite hymn.

It may help to anticipate the contrasting Christologies that characterize these Worlds whose epiphanias we have explored this far. In World One, "Jesus as the Christ" can be the normative symbol that evokes awareness of the transparency of all things. In World Two, Jesus can be seen as the proleptic event, giving promise of God's vindication of creation in and through history. For World Three, Jesus is not God's final word about us, but "our final word about God."[71] Jesus' humanness is the model for our fullness, through our relation both to God and to the cosmos.

Likewise, the role of Scripture in each of these Worlds is different. For World One, Scripture does not describe reality as much as it evokes moments of unifying experience. In World Two, Scripture intoxicates with vision. And for World Three, Scripture distills the authentic posture of humanness, finding in Jesus, as human representative, the lens for illuminating both human and divine.

World Four: Forgiveness as Reprieve/Adoption—Neoorthodoxy

The impact of World Four on Western civilization is recognizable in the primacy of guilt within its obsessio. The condemnation from which it issues focuses not so much on infractions, or even their temptations. The obsessio festers underneath as a nameless fear of being known. *Sin* is what the state is called, of which "sins" are symptoms. This condition precedes every action, and in fact would be present even if one never did anything. It is inescapable—marking the forehead and serving as logo over the terrain.

The words *diseased* or *tainted* are often used to focus the obsessio. The condition isn't something that happens to us. It is the way we are born. One feels one's life needing justification just for being—even before it starts. While the key epiphania, justification by faith, may sound archaic, it is in fact the key for understanding what is happening all around us.

Living is the dynamic of seeking justification through works. In legal parlance, *to justify* means to have satisfactory reasons for something that has been done. Yet even if one could provide good reasons for everything one does, that is still insufficient. The justification whose absence eats at us is the absence of a satisfactory reason for existing. How do I justify the fact that I am? Is there any way, other than to work with such drivenness that in the end I can say my life was worthwhile? It is this compulsion to make one's life "warranted" that reduces living to a fearful and self-defeating chore to be done. This drive makes us irreparable perfectionists. Dare we try to label the nameless fear directly under the surface? A leading contender is *failure*.

Birth entails awakening to a checking account already overdrawn. For some it feels like a sixty-five-year mortgage, found at retirement to have been a second loan. For my friend who battled cancer for three years and lost two days ago, it meant living as a body constantly in danger of being repossessed. Foreclosure is never a question; only the date. To live is a matter of deficit spending, on borrowed time. There is no such thing as a free lunch—someone must pay the bill, even if the lunch has already been eaten. The central nightmare is to run out of time. Those of us with fragile talents realize that, at any moment, "from [one] who has not, even what [one] has will be taken away" (Matt. 13:12). Someone always has veto power.

This obsessio is experienced as the frenetic hyphening of life and work. Genesis knows this well—an awakening to guilt brings with it the laboriousness of living: "In the sweat of your face . . . cursed is the ground . . . in toil shall you eat" (Gen. 3:19, 17*b*). No wonder the cry for epiphania here sounds so total—it requires rebirth. Scraping bare the cellar floor of the obsessio, *the* question appears: "Can [one] enter a second time into [one's] mother's womb and be born?" (John 3:4). The feel is a need to refinance one's life, start it all over again. Common-day language is seasoned with such sentiments: Get up on the right side of the bed; Wait till next year; Start with a clean slate. For those who need to interview a citizen of this World in order to understand, the firstborn of an alcoholic family (the "hero") will be more than sufficient.

Things will be different once one's list is completed or one's job is changed. But sooner or later, one is driven to a conclusion—resolution is beyond us. If recompense is needed for acts done, perhaps it is possible—one's work can always be more frantic. But if the obsessio precedes even the first act, then one is always a step behind. Even a life perfectly lived would end where it started—not yet at zero. One never quite measures up, is never quite good enough. This is not a matter of being too hard on one's self. "Poor self-image" is simply a euphemism for honest self-knowledge.

There is reason to believe the dilemma lies still deeper. In justifying my life, it is the *me* who wants to do the act. Therefore its anatomy edges upon idolatry. To be self-justified is a stance that rivals God—as "pure act," being self-constituted, needing nothing outside one's self. Thus the guilt into which I was born, the guilt that spawns frantic activity, turns out at its heart to be intertwined with the drive to be "as God." This presumptuous and self-defeating urge does not come upon me. When first detected, it is already within my will as desire.

World Three makes much of new beginnings in the potential of each moment. World Four finds the dilemma otherwise. To be awakened to the need for decision is to be awakened to how much one's acts are predetermined. In a way, they seem not to be willed at all. They follow inevitably, even spontaneously, from our fundamental orientation. Yet even though we seem "factory set," there is no escape from guilt. When the will *does* attain the capacity to reflect upon itself, it would not have chosen otherwise! But even that is to put things too passively. Part of the lure for doing what I do is precisely that it is forbidden: "You shall not eat . . . . It was a delight!" (Gen. 3:3, 6). Reverse psychology for the child is humorous. Its operation in adults is deadly.

Yet is there not something heroic in such rebelliousness? Perhaps, but World Four rarely experiences it that way. Instead, the typical words for acting out the obsessio are "Who, me?" If accused, one tends to blubber, weakly unwilling to acknowledge not only what one has done, but who one truly is. And when found guilty, clean confessions are an endangered species. Instead, the phenomenon is one of self-deception—postures of indignant selflessness, in defense of blatant but unacknowledged egotism. Here reason, the so-called mark of our dignity, becomes the second-rate rationalization of a third-rate mortician of the soul. Tragedy keeps unraveling into pathos.

Christopher Marlowe's *Doctor Faustus* captures this drama. It begins with the temptation to greatness: "A sound magician is a mighty god: Here, Faustus, try through brains to gain a deity!" The increasing disclosure of motives for divinization is damning. They begin with the arrogance that none shall "live but by my leave," ending as a disclosure of his real condition: "The God thou servest is thine own appetite." Then the base level—self-deception. When evil appears in its true form, Faustus cannot face it: "I charge thee to return and change thy shape; thou art too ugly to attend on me."[72] The ending gives no chance for the heroic; potential tragedy becomes pathos, as pride reduces the self to sick pomposity.

The beginning of epiphania is *condemnation*. Christians who have walked the dark streets of World Four acknowledge a Christ while still unknown, haunts us down the corridors of our lonely nights. This haunting persists as an ache that sinks every excuse, exposes each motive, and pricks with deadly precision the seduced conscience. To be good news, Jesus must first be bad news. The wages of sin are death (Rom. 6:23), whether understood as penalty or as some variation of self-destruction in the downward spiral of the sinning process. This is so true that a Luther can see death as welcomed contrast: "For this our life is so full of perils—sin, like a serpent besetting us on every side—and it is impossible for us to live without sinning: but fairest death delivers us from these perils and cuts our sin clear away from us."[73]

We call the Friday of crucifixion Good; yet it is, for it is our undoing. "Thou wouldst not be seeking me," Pascal heard God saying ironically, "hadst thou not already found me." Francis Thompson describes such seeking as the work of One who hounds us as we flee the relentless pursuing. The haunting continues "adown Titanic glooms of chasmed fears," until in the dead-ends of days "crackled and gone up like smoke," may it be known that "all things betray thee, who betray Me."[74]

This is where World Four can make contact with other Worlds: Simone Weil speaks of "Christ's terrible love"; Merton, of Christ of the "burnt [ones]"; Eliot, of "Christ the tiger." But the only sacrifice that will suffice on the edge of this epiphania is a "broken and contrite spirit." The will cannot will to break itself. Thus we stand before the primal paradox in a World characterized by paradox.[75] Self-crucifixion is a self-contradiction, so that even to want to seek it is a miracle of the Spirit's workings. It is for this reason that World Four is drawn toward the language of election. Since life is so deeply interspersed with sin, every effort to right the situation is inevitably motivated in sin. Whatever way we turn, the posture is arrogant, intent not on *serving* God but on *emulating* the Divine.

Since resolution has no basis on our side, it must be gift, in no way our own doing. This is election. God has every right to show no mercy. In fact, it is God's moral duty to condemn. Thus each part of the redeeming process—motive, access, empowerment—is gift. To think of such impossible acceptance as anything other than a "nevertheless" is to debase the unconditional act.

Yet the human condition is such that accepting a gift is difficult. Instead, we want rewards. Gifts place us in someone's debt, exacerbating the obsessio. Even Christmas, the season of gifts modeling the Divine gift, we undermine by obsessio. "Have you been good?" A gift, to be a gift, cannot be deserved, claimed, or earned. Thus even the capacity to accept a gift as gift must be a gift. Here we find ourselves at the edge of epiphania. Restoration of childlikeness depends on the primal awareness that one deserves only coal.

Who killed the Christ, the One "guilty" of love? It was those of us who prefer to destroy the judge rather than hear the judgment. But such attempted escape never has the last word. The Christ crucified is the Christ raised, intent upon haunting those who prefer death to life. He is the scapegoat who infuriatingly refuses to stay out of sight in the desert. It is he who discloses the universality and interrelatedness of condemnation. No white has hope without the judgment posed by blackness. No male can know epiphania without the knowing gaze of the female. No "American" can experience resurrection without the pleading eyes of a Nicaraguan child.

Nathan tells King David the story of a person who owns a solitary lamb, so deeply loved that "it was like a daughter" (II Sam. 12:3). As the story leads to its deliberate slaughter by a man who owned many, David shouts, "The man who has done this deserves to die" (12:5). Precisely. This is the timeless moment where epiphania is birthed through obsessio—"Thou art the one!" The Christ story is clear. From God we hear, "He was like a Son to me."

Such analogies point to the reason this World tends to

insist that God needs to be a "Person." The obsessio is rooted in broken relationships. World One can speak of God as the Ground of personality, and World Three sometimes focuses upon Spirit as Energy, impulsing growth in all things. But World Four is emphatic. God is not Being Itself, but *a* Being, capable of a relationship that is more than the arrangement of whole to parts. God is even more than personal. God is Person—One who wills, intends, acts, loves, suffers. God even repents. It cannot be otherwise, for value, by its very nature, is relational. The relation of God and humans is a matter of "value forness."[76]

Joachim Jeremias sees the uniqueness of Jesus' ministry precisely here. "There is *no analogy at all* in the whole of Jewish literature or practice" for Jesus' use of Abba in addressing God. For Jesus, the Sovereign Creator of the Universe is "daddy." In teaching the Lord's Prayer to his disciples, Jesus invited them into that familial relationship with God which encapsuled Jesus' own uniqueness.[77] Thus for this World, the clue both to Christology and to epiphania resides in the nature of this relationship.

Such intimacy does not suggest easy sentimentality. Sin is so serious precisely because it is rooted in relationship. Peter is paradigm. He who shared bread at my table, walked and talked with me on the road, laughed with me over a shared cup—it is *he* who said, "I do not know him." Not once, but three times in one night. Taken by week-fulls, we pass seventy times seven exponentially. No wonder Luther considered confession a third sacrament—on a par with baptism as washing, and eucharist as the Word of forgiveness.

In World One, sin means taking one's relation for granted. In World Two the relation has been externally disrupted. In World Three the relation has not yet been ventured. In World Four it has been desecrated. Betrayal is at its heart. I lie, deceive, dishonor the confidence give as sacred trust. What's more, I do it easily, with self-adjusting, self-justifying self-righteousness. The feel of this obsessio is that of having broken a priceless vase, the only one of its kind. If only I could take back that moment, alter the

"instant playback." But it is done—irremediably, irreplace-
ably, irrevocably—beyond all hope for Elmer's Glue. And
what is worse, I am brought bolt upright to the awareness
that my purpose in life is to take care of that vase. And at
this moment, the owner/friend is at the front door, excited
at the prospect of greeting me after all these years.

What began as a birth into deficit spending soon loses the
feel of a fallenness that *precedes* me. I myself am part of the
web. As one person put it during confession, "I keep
wanting to trade food stamps for a porn video."

Because relationships can be richly varied, epiphania in
World Four has many images. Yet each stresses the
necessity of atonement, beginning with the costliness of
sin. It is unfair to caricature World Four, as some do, with
analogies of God as sadistic disciplinarian to a well-meaning
child. In fact, punishment language often misses the point,
trivializing the predicament. Thus we must be careful with
analogies such as paying the debt or balancing the account
or appeasing the banker. Such metaphors are helpful in
emphasizing the cost, but they can convey a crude feeling of
a demanding God, alien to Christianity. They make it
difficult to avoid seeing the dynamic as other than an eye for
an eye—in this case, a perfect life for a diseased world.
Therefore to understand World Four, we need to go behind
such analogies.

A beginning point is to be aware that condemnation
hurts, not only to receive but to give. Correlatively,
forgiveness costs, both to give and to receive. Suffering is to
the resolution as guilt is to the dilemma. On our side, to
miss the costliness is to trivialize forgiveness. On God's
side, to miss the costliness is to lose God as the Incarnate
One who works on our behalf.

Hosea captures this costliness. A betrayed relation
wrings from the victim a spectrum of feelings. You "shall be
utterly cut off," screams God (10:15). "Yet it was I," groans
God, who "took them up in my arms" (11:3). Still the
remembrance of deceit arises again to sear into God with
anger: "The sword shall rage . . . and devour them" (11:6).
God vomits it out, until weary with wrung passion. Then

God falters, as the world might well wait in terrified silence. God gasps, "How shall I give you up?" (11:8). God's agony is that of a lover spurned, a daughter violated, a friend betrayed, a painter's final work slashed, a dream turned nightmare. On and on the analogies tumble forth, until nothing short of images of bloody carnage can give full vent to the cost. "O sacred Head, now wounded . . . / What thou, my Lord, hast suffered / Was all for sinners' gain."

Yet there is difficulty. When such imagery is held together, it is rich. But when the parts are separated to provide conceptual logic, images are led into conflict with one another. What is lost is the meaning of the whole cloth from which they were torn. Held together, the question is clear: "Who is this suffering figure?" Some say, "He is as we." Others say, "He is as God." Says Chalcedon, "He is both." Precisely so, says World Four.

Consequently, in the images of epiphania that result, it is imperative that these two dimensions be somehow held together. This is part of what makes World Four incurably paradoxical. Luther's posture illustrates it well:

[One] is under law, and yet not under law but grace; [one] is sinner, and yet righteous; [one] believes, as a doubter; [one] has assurance of salvation, yet walks along the knife-edge of insecurity. In Christ all things have become new, and yet everything remains as it was from the beginning. God has revealed [God's self] in Christ, but hidden it in [this] revelation; the believer knows the One in whom [one] has believed, yet walks by faith, not sight.[78]

This paradoxical nature of the Christ Event as epiphania finds analogy in the strobe lighting of drama. Each event-figure, for a split second deprived of organic continuity, is an image in its own right. We receive such moments seriatim: the crucifixion as God betrayed/as humanity pitied/as Divine condemnation/as human dereliction/as Divine humiliation/as forgiveness claimed. There are both Divine and human elements, separate but commingled, movement without logic, gift but received—

yet there is an arrival together. But to arrive is most paradoxical of all. Only in being forgiven does one truly know oneself as sinner. Only in being loved do we know the meaning of condemnation.

The epiphania of World Four loses its power when it strays far from such relational imagery. The fact that "forensic" is often used to identify the atonement theory of World Four indicates how often legalistic translations have been seen wrongly as normative. Kept imagistically open, the crucifixion is far richer than payment. It condemns, resolves, offers, and consummates. Likewise, resurrection provides a contextual temper for the whole, rather than separate content—that is, what happens must be within the flavor of incredible impossibility. Forgiveness is the miracle of God's willingness to restore. Thus the resurrection confirms the miracle of the cross as the center point of history, the distilled plot of the Divine relationship with humanity. This Divine-human relation in Jesus Christ relates to epiphania much as the saga of Adam and Eve relates to obsessio. The plot of salvation history is the Divine and human in a cruciformed relation, seen first from the human side, then transformed by being disclosed through the eyes of God.

Just as this restored relation through epiphania is better grasped analogically than conceptually, so is faith. This is why such a great split within World Four is possible at this point. "Justification by faith" was explicated by Calvin in trinitarian fashion: The Spirit now bears witness to what the Creator did for our salvation in the cross of Christ. Such a Spirit experience witnesses to God's decision to bequeath the benefits of this act individually. Such a dynamic is best stated as justification *by grace*, through the gift of trust. *Grace* is not substantive, not something that one either has or does not have, that one can possess. Grace is adjectival—"graciousness" as a quality of God. Thus grace signals a *new relation* based on God's graciousness. Such an epiphania is purely God's doing, with faith the gift of trusting that graciousness. But the untrusting self cannot begin to trust by willing it. Therefore God not only forgives, states Barth, but by that forgiveness creates in us the capacity to accept that acceptance.[79]

Barth's Nein! to any point of contact in us willing to accept God's gift seems consistent with the obsessio of World Four. A mistake has not been found, warranting a new trial. The reprieve sets all trials aside. It is in spite of all evidence, without qualification—it is gift. One is staggered. Could it make any sense to imagine a criminal on Death Row, overwhelmed by the announcement of reprieve, saying, "I want some time to think this over"? If a recipient needs to decide, it is not reprieve but calculation. In fact, the worst sin of all would be our desire to have the final say about it. That way, epiphania would finally depend not on God but on *me*. As a result, the obsessio, not the epiphania, would have the last word.

At the foot of the cross our condition is exposed. It resides in our unwillingness even to receive. "Shall we never permit our hands to be empty, that we may grasp," paradoxically, what only empty hands can grasp? This is why epiphania in World Four is often stated as a double negation: Christ "is the negation of the negation. . . . He is the death of our death, and the non-existence of our non-existence." Such a confession can be blantant: "The individual is not more than the stage upon which election and rejection take place in the freedom of . . . the individual who rests in God and is moved by [God]." If we refuse, faith "is completely abreast of the situation. It grips reason by the throat and strangles the beast."[80]

This is strong, overstated language—but how else can residents of World Four preserve epiphania as resting in grace as sheer gift? It is neither earned, deserved, nor worked for. "The [one] who boasts that [one] possesses something which justifies [one] before God and [human-kind], even if that something be [one's] own insecurity and brokenness, still retains confidence in human self-justifica-tion." We cannot lay claim even to experience. "Our [real] experience is that which we have not experienced."[81] Again the theme is echoed: Epiphania is gift and gift alone. And the test is whether one's will is relinquished in childlikeness. What one feels is the joy of knowing that one's destiny is in the hands of the God who is foolish Lover.

Thus the person of faith, says Calvin, is not only "saved from," but "saved for." This entails living a life of glorifying God and enjoying God forever. Even Calvin hoped for universalism. Although redemption is God's doing, it is our prayer, he stated, that none shall be excluded. How better can one express the triumph of grace?

There are others in World Four, however, who understand justification by faith by defining it more as "belief." Emphasis falls more heavily on choice than on gift. Salvation is primarily a salvation "from," with personal decision marking the fragile difference. These interpreters are uneasy about election, for it seems to deprecate human responsibility, cheapening the costliness of grace from the human side. They are sometimes criticized, however, for making salvation depend upon us. Paul does well in holding both these postures in paradoxical tension, providing the contours for World Four at its best: "Work out your own salvation with fear and trembling; for God is at work in you, both to will and to work for [God's] good pleasure" (Phil. 2:12).

This paradox is fundamental to any deep relationship. To fall in love is to experience a miracle, for in no way does one deserve to be loved this way. One is puzzled to the point of amazement: "What can she/he possibly see in me?" Yet in the next strobe, responsibility is reversed. Such a relationship cannot be a 50-50 arrangement. It is all or nothing. I give my whole self, as if making it work depends totally on me. Expressed theologically, before the metanoia, responsibility is totally mine. Afterward, I know that the whole is gift, for which I cannot do enough in gratitude. The Heidelburg Catechism captures this dynamic of World Four. All we need to know, it insists, are three things: The first, how great my sins and miseries are; the second, how I may be delivered from all my sins and miseries; and third, how I shall express my gratitude to God for such deliverance.[82]

The need for change in World Four is clear. Less agreed upon is the degree to which epiphania can transform the grimness of obsessio. For Luther, we are forgiven, but sinners we remain; the epiphania is the ongoing forgiveness for our ongoing sinning. For others, epiphania bequeaths no such "alien righteousness," but a genuine conversion, signaled as "new birth." For Wesley, such sanctification as "growth in grace" through perfection into glorification becomes so central for each self that he straddles the boundary, moving into World Three.

Reprieve is the best image for capturing the impact of epiphania for the first of these options. The image of *adoption* is best for capturing the second, for it involves both offer and acceptance. Justification is accompanied by a gift of Spirit, so that "through God you are no longer a slave but [a child], and if [a child] then an heir" (Gal. 4:7). Forgiveness is the negative part. What follows is positive—the forgiven are showered with "unsearchable riches" (Eph. 3:8). True, the prodigal child bespeaks a family relationship squandered, reduced to swill, with nothing left but to connive to become a slave. But the reception at home will permit neither confessions nor apologies. There is a fatted calf, a robe, a ring, and a banquet—with merriment (Luke 15:22-23).

An analogy from Death Row also can capture the result of epiphania, possibly for either case. One needs to picture the final day. There are absurd questions: Any last requests? Last words? What do you want for your last meal? One chokes down the roast beef, medium rare—for the last time. It stays down better with a sip of coffee, the last ever. Then comes the walk, completed with the last step—never again. One feels the last coldness at one's temples. One sees the last person. One looks into the last set of eyes. One breathes one's last breath—five, four, three, two—the phone rings!

It's the Governor: *Reprieve!* Free—a new life, a new person! "Never again" has become "again and again." One races up the steps, waving. There is even a hug for the executioner. Then one bounds through the heavy doors. Skipping through grass, a dandelion behind each ear, one giggles at a sky that has never been so blue. Even curious glances from each stranger are special—one of a kind. And then comes the climax. The biggest orange juice McDonald's can pour surpasses any vintage wine. To experience each thing, every moment, each person, as if for the first time, is the gift opened for one who, in experiencing the last "condemnation" is enabled to live *again* as if reborn.

Bernanos' country priest uses an analogy for life lived in epiphania—the childlikeness sensed on a motorcycle:

> "Like to have a ride, Father?" . . . Beside this machine of blazing light, my cassock was like a sad black shadow. By what miracle can I have felt so young at that moment? . . . My youth had passed me by. . . . I was never young because I never dared be young . . . had drugged myself with work. . . . I was never young because no one wanted to be young with me. . . . Joy! A kind of pride, a gaiety, an absurd hope, entirely carnal; the carnal form of hope, I think, is what they call joy.[83]

Reprieve promised as adoption can cancel the drivenness to earn the parental love one never had. It means letting go and being fed by *the* Parent, as one is given permission to become the child one never was. Such rebirth can betake a simple craziness—collecting stones, smelling flowers, watching snails. Anything will do, as long as done in wonder. Naive? Certainly. "Second naiveté," says Ricoeur. Such rebirth can crack the encrustations of world-weariness built as wall against the futility of self-justification.

However the consequences are spelled out, it is the "conversion moment" that residents of World Four understand best. Powerful testimonies appear in Dostoevsky's *Brothers Karamazov,* where the evidence of epiphania is traced over three generations. The first step is the condemnation, which brings awareness of guilt. Second, through the suffering born of guilt, a freedom is opened as decision. Dostoevsky's favorite text is from John: "Unless a grain of wheat falls into the earth and dies, it remains alone; but if it dies, it bears much fruit" (12:24). And what is the fruit of the epiphania? It comes first to Father Zossima, who on his deathbed declares that one is tormented by conscience until one is willing to confess and suffer punishment. Only thereby can one be brought to assume responsibility for all sins.[84] At such a moment, he insists, one is swept with the Love which organically unites all with All, bringing one to

> kiss the earth and love it with an unceasing, consuming love. Love all [people], love everything. Seek that rapture and ecstasy. Water the earth with tears of your joy and love those tears. Don't be ashamed of that ecstasy, prize it, for it is a gift of God and a great one; it is not given to many . . . but only to the elect.[85]

Through Zossima's death, Alyosha's epiphania is enabled. He is much younger and thus not yet so tormented. But even so, epiphania can never be without confession and suffering. After that, he throws himself on the earth: "He kisses it weeping, sobbing and watering it with his tears, and vowed passionately to love it, to love it for ever and ever."[86]

Through Alyosha, in turn, comes the epiphania for one still younger, as the rhythm of condemnation and forgiveness is played out again and again. Through the atoning death of another youth comes the confession: "'Let us never forget him. May his memory live forever in our hearts from this time forth! . . . We love you, we love you!' They all caught it up. 'Forever. . . . Certainly we shall all rise again, certainly we shall see each other and shall tell each other with joy and gladness all that has happened!'"[87]

Such events usually occur once in a lifetime, and to live at such a miraculous crescendo is uncommon for World Four. Perhaps that is why this World is characterized by storytelling. On the one hand, the need is to tell the story as anamnesis, remembering again and again, so as never to forget. Whether in preaching or in testimony, in church or in A.A. meeting, the word is a variation on one theme: "Once I was blind; now I see." In the words of Katherine Hankey, "I love to tell the story, / It did so much for me; / And that is just the reason / I tell it now to thee."

The obsessio for World Four, in summary, centers in our condition of unworthiness. On the one hand, this births an enslaving temptation to cloak our finitude by arrogance. On the other hand, one is driven into works-righteousness. Hobbled by impotence, claimed by guilt, angered at self, fearful of punishment, we flounder in self-hatred and self-flagellation. One image is that of the fugitive leper, running from the specter of one's own self. The epiphania is miraculous, not only in the fact that God forgives me, but that God would even want to do so. There is nothing grudging about such forgiveness. It entails God leaving the ninety and nine, risking the darkness, in order to treat me as the pearl of great price. To love the unlovable, God embraces as "only child" the slobbering village idiot. I am that one.

Neoorthodoxy

Twentieth-century Protestant thought began with the reemergence of World Four as a lively option. This occurred through the publication of Barth's second edition of *Epistle to the Romans* (1921). The central themes are these:

1. The utter transcendence (freedom) of God in regard to the world.
2. The idolatry of all human effort. Given World War I as context, the arrogance of nations, threatening to destroy Western "civilization" in their self-righteousness, disclosed *God* as a name for their idolatries.
3. The presupposition for one's thought and being must be either God or one's self—not both. Only such an either/or hears the radical No of God's judgment. There is no point of contact by which the self can reach God, for all efforts from our side are variations on the themes of rationalization, projection, self-justification, control, self-aggrandizement.
4. The hope that we might hear, in the darkness of our pretentiousness, God's No, experienced as the tumbling of nations and the swallowing of the individual in the threat of death. Even such purgation is God's doing.
5. This breakthrough by God centers in the absurd act of

Jesus Christ, so irrational that to believe it is itself a gift. From our side, it resembles a meteor plunging to earth, leaving only an empty crater. Psychologically considered, faith is a leap into the void in an abandonment of reason. Thus God acts objectively in Jesus Christ, as the atonement of sin; and subjectively in one's heart, as the Holy Spirit bringing us to faith.

6. Christian life has the strangeness of paradox. One believes, but without reasons. One sins, but is forgiven. One's death has taken place, but not yet. One knows, but only that one is known. One sees, but through a glass darkly. The No is a Yes in being the negation of my negation. Faith is never a possession, but a gift resting in God's graciousness.

7. Jesus Christ is the paradigm for all things. As human, he is "without form or comeliness that we should look at him." Being meek, weak, limited, unimpressive—in a word, a failure—he is hardly the model for human emulation. Therefore faith rests in the declaration that this is God. This is not a human paradigm of successful religiosity. It is *God*, who has chosen the despised and lowly as the recipients of Love and Forgiveness.

8. Likewise, the church is paradoxical. Inept, hypocritical, and often self-contradictory, God has nonetheless chosen it as Divine vehicle for declaring the good news.

9. Scripture, too, is paradoxical. Some of it is poorly written, contradictory, tedious, error-filled. Yet although Scripture is not revelation, God has chosen it to bear witness to *the* revelation—Jesus Christ. Why should it be otherwise? *The* paradox is that the Christian—sinful, arrogant, like other humankind—is chosen as recipient of God's undeserved forgiveness.

10. One's life is in but not of the world, for eschatology is not temporal. There will be no historical consummation. The end is personal, in anticipation of the life to come with Christ in God. Wesley's "Watch Night Service" captures the resulting life-style:

I am no longer my own, but thine. Put me to what thou wilt, rank me with whom thou wilt; put me to doing, put me to suffering; let me be employed for thee or laid aside for thee, exalted for thee or brought low for thee; let me be full, let me be empty; let me have all things, let me have nothing; I freely and heartily yield all things to thy pleasure and disposal.[88]

Being emptied of self to be used by God—this is the central theme. As a result, the Christian may not be outwardly different from others, for faith is never a possession. The difference is an inward life grounded in remembrance, nurtured by gratitude to the One who has ransomed me, branded me, renamed me as God's own. It is enough to wait without idols, letting God be God.

World Five: Endurance as Survival—Existentialism

To be is to be overwhelmed. In World Five one often feels so threatened that survival requires feigning either indifference or a cynical fatigue. The *obsessio*, experienced as undeserved suffering, cannot be made into a problem to be solved. In World One, ontic anxiety can open one to mystery and to the sacramental. But here such an epiphany is regarded as fantasy, a luxury for the leisured. Breathlessness in this World can mean only near-suffocation, a hyperextension of directionlessness. The "given" over which one stumbles is not cosmos, history, or self—either as potential or as guilt-ridden. The given is one day at a time, to be lived *very* carefully. Each day is much like every other day, with little to be changed. Yet, coping as simply getting by won't do either.

Ironically, the craved *epiphania* doesn't change anything. Rather, in facing the whole, it gives a quality of *perseverance*. The fiber of its hope is *endurance*. Faulkner pushed this quality even further in his Nobel Prize speech: "I believe that man will not merely endure: he will prevail . . . because he has a soul, a spirit capable of compassion and sacrifice and endurance."[89] Yet prevailing is not to be understood here as it is in World Two. There is no *telos* whose resolution can flow back over the whole as transforming shroud. Any vindication comes not from the result, but through *the quality of life effected in facing the inevitable*.

One is reminded of Schopenhauer, sad apostle of determinism. He insisted that in knowing that one is bound, one transcends that fact. Will, as a practical response to life, precedes reason. It is the fundamental craving to exist, often bequeathing suicide and endless murder to history. It is this will to be other than we are that renders the drive for self-preservatio into an obsessio. Thus the only resolution to a drive so blind, irrational, and immoral is to stop the will. This eliminates hope and dispels fear, so that we can become timeless and will-less. What results through such epiphania is that one wills nothing more than emptiness. And it is here, ironically, that morality emerges. In having nothing, doing nothing, being nothing, wanting nothing, one comes to sense the universality of all in a common poverty. To truly experience this commonness is to render violence insane and compassion spontaneous. The result is a gracious living, sharing the little that one has with all—an "all" made up of all other little ones. An endurance that prevails, then, is the miracle of the shared loaves and fishes.

Pascal insists that Jesus will be in agony until the end. His greatness and ours is in *knowing* our misery. This is the dignity of being human. Relatedly, Bonhoeffer insists that "we must learn to regard people less in the light of what they do or omit to do, and more in the light of what they suffer."[90]

A musician friend and I enjoy listening to new jazz musicians. Sometime during a set, I expect him to lean over and ask, "Does she know?" Yes, if she's good, she knows. Knows what? As a resident of World Five, his question translates roughly this way: "Does this musician know that there is no knowing, that the nightmare comes after the dreaming is over, that the end is no resolution, but a stopping?" But in music birthed in such knowing, one can hear an indefinable transcendence. A jazz pianist himself, my friend plays "Help Me Make It Through the Night" so that the song is the help. He knows.

One senses this irony in the self-contradiction of Samuel Beckett's plays. Why would someone bother to portray the absurdity of life? It is because "keeping on," in the full face of knowing the way things are, is an act of nobility. There is a quality in such living that is tried, tempered, annealed, and thereby honest. "Outside of here is death," warns Hamm, as in *Endgame*, Clov threatens to leave the dingy life-room of a center-stage crippled tyrant and the badgered slave. Why doesn't he leave? One critic suggests that beneath the turbulent sound and fury, there is echo of a relationship which goes beyond that of master/servant, husband/wife, father/son, playwright/actor, actor and addressed.[91]

This hunch relates to director Jack Garfein's observation that Beckett's plays work only with humor.[92] Strange though it be, epiphania is contained in the laughter evoked as Hamm's withered parents keep popping out unexpectedly from their ashcan retirements. The backdrop is painted with pathos in huge strokes, touching the etymology of the word. What relates us is the dilemma of common "suffering." For such suffering, nothing is to be done, except . . . except, perhaps, to experience the meaning of being able to laugh at it all.

We are not permitted the luxury of the heroic in this World, or even the important. Settling over all is dust as vestment of the commonplace. Even Aida has bad breath. We are in the world of opera, with the music turned off.

What is it, then, that can atone? It is the aura of a toothless grin and a furtive glance. Epiphania entails snickering at the death rattle of our sameness. It is to *refuse* not to "know." It is the courage to render endless repetitions comic. It has the flavor of children making believe, in the very act knowing better. Above all, it involves refusal to "check out" at any point, but to live death out to its very turnstile, armed only with a rope too short for suicide.[93] Images flood this

World—the laughing skull, the weary clown—anything that proposes a serious refusal to take seriously that which is undeserving of even quiet respect. It is no wonder that Rouault's sorrow-cured clowns merge indistinguishably with his Christs.

I experienced hints of such epiphania in the raspy laughter of uplifted steins after each shift at Rosie's Grill, outside Gate 11 of Bethlehem Steel. A picture of the Virgin Mary hung over the bar, as if an honorary barmaid. Perhaps we knew beyond knowing what John Phillips discovered through research: that Mary is no solution for Eve's sinful obedience; she is the model of endurance.[94] Fowler calls such knowing the "sacrament of defeat."[95] Camus's Sysyphus acted it out. Condemned to roll a stone up a mountain, only to have it roll back down, his epiphania was that as he walked down the hill to begin again, he knew that "the struggle itself toward the heights is enough to fill a [person's] heart. One must imagine Sisyphus happy."[96] Defiant. Determined. Courageous. *Enduring*.

Genesis paints the backdrop for life in this World: "In toil you shall eat of . . . thorns and thistles," for "in the sweat of your face you shall eat bread till you return to the ground; . . . you are dust, and to dust you shall return" (3:17c, 19). Life is not right. It is an existence cursed. So it is, and so it shall be. And while other Worlds tend to be concerned with *why*, this World is concerned with *how*—how to live life, deeply, to its core.

Eucharistically, the wine of sweat commingles with the bread coaxed from the dust. Even cigarette ads and beer commercials hint at this epiphania. The end of a hard day's work, done together, is worth drinking to. Homo faber points to an integrity of living, whether it be the fish well caught, a house well built, the bottle well drunk. The circumstances are indifferent; what matters is *how* it is done. Such work is measured not by goal or compensation or instrumentality; it is done for its own sake, with the quality of an alien grace. Rembrandt's self-portraits testify to such qualities of endurance. When the soundings of this World are taken, Oscar Wilde reveals its deepest level: "Where there is sorrow, there is sacred ground."

While World Four sees suffering as the result of guilt, bringing confession, this World sees suffering as the undeserved refining fire through which integrity is forged. Paul experienced his pilgrimage that way. On the one hand, his thorn in the flesh was the reminder that God's "power is made perfect in weakness" (II Cor. 12:9). On the other hand, suffering was a clue to Christology: "For the sake of Christ, then, I am content with weaknesses, insults, hardships, persecutions, and calamities; for when I am weak, then I am strong" (12:10). Or again, "I know how to be abased, and I know how to abound; in any and all circumstances I have learned the secret of facing plenty and hunger, abundance and want. I can do all things in [the One] who strengthens me" (Phil. 4:12-13). This strength can be found in following the footsteps of one who has done it before. Nothing changes except the fiber of strength within. This change is sui generis. It is *how* one lives out the No that determines whether it is a Yes.

Christology is often central, for the citizens of World Five are ambiguous about nature as a resource for meaning. Naturalist Joseph Wood Krutch puts the issue bluntly: "The God who planned the well-working machines which function as atom and solar system seems to have had no part in arranging the curiously inefficient society of plants and animals in which everything works against everything else."[97] Since "there is no coherence in nature, there can be no coherence of nature with the Christian concept of God."[98] The world, as a "quirky mass of imperfections," can find resolution only within the human—in a caring that has the quality of epiphania. "Remember those who are in prison," we are reminded, "as though in prison with them; and those who are ill-treated, since you also are in the body" (Heb. 13:3). Thus Christology is more a *how* than a *what*.

I propose a weak analogy: When I was a graduate student at Yale, there was an annual massacre, inappropriately called the Yale-Army football game. Each year the bleakness grew, with scores increasingly outrageous and injuries more alarming. But one year this indignity, rather than bringing the usual resignation, evoked determination. The end itself, of course, was never in doubt, but the way the game was played merited headlines even in the *New York Times:* "Yale Wins Moral Victory." The epiphania in World Five is a moral victory over life—so played as to protest the game.

Biblical hints of such self-transcendence appear with the proposal that in contending with "the principalities, against the powers," one must be "strong" by putting on "the whole armor," for what counts is that "you may be able to stand" (Eph. 6:10, 12). One is reminded of Tolkien's *Return of the King.* Pippin and Beregond await the climaxing battle, pitting good against evil. "If we fall, who shall stand? . . . Do you see any hope that we shall stand?" Pippin does not answer. As he looks at the walls, the sky, the gathering gloom, the "winged terror of the foe," he shudders. Hope withers as he hears a cry, "faint but heart quelling, cruel and cold. . . . 'It is the sign of our fall. . . . The very warmth of my blood seems stolen away.' " They sit with bowed heads. But when Pippin looks up, he sees the sun still shining, the banners still in the breeze. "It is passed," he says. "No, my heart will not yet despair. . . . We may stand, if only on one leg, or at least be left still upon our knees."[99] That is to endure.

Yet there may be more. The response may have about it the mark of heroic faithfulness. But to what? Certainly not to life, nor to the way things are. Rather, it seems to reside in the tension of "unresolved betweenness" itself. In a real sense, crucifixion is resurrection, lived as the tension called Holy Saturday. The "too late" and the "not yet" somehow belong together. Put another way, there are hints that the essence of endurance is *shared* suffering. The redemptive quality in endurance is compassion, born from being in it together. Here can arise a powerful analogy for the Divine-human relationship. Royce arrived at this point philosophically, concluding that the heart of Christianity is a loyalty to Loyalty.[100] Here it is compassion with the Compassionate.

Contrasting the spirituality of Worlds One and Five can be helpful here, using the images of mountain and desert. Mountain spirituality exists for the sake of experiences that make life meaningful. The spirituality of World Five, however, is the way of the desert, the via negativa. It rests on "irrevocable commitment" alone; there is a turning point from which "one knows, deep in the heart, one is no longer free to turn back . . . with fidelity." These two spiritualities contrast, in that one is emotional; the other, volitional. The latter, says David Knight, is "indifferent to consolations, satisfactions, or reward." His summary is a capsule of World Five: "The desert is a place in which to endure. Just to endure in the desert is to survive, to triumph."[101] Such commitment to see it through, no matter what, expresses what the Scripture means by a covenant God and a covenant people. It begins when God says, Go—and Abraham and Sarah discover that the "why" is in the going.

Faulkner's novels provide profound interactions of Worlds Four and Five. The obsessio, as we have seen, rests in the former, the epiphania in the latter. This is possible because Faulkner's World is a composite of white and black. The white inhabitants are held within World Four, overwhelmed by the unrelenting obsessio of guilt. Yet it is this white obsessio that forges an epiphania for the exploited. We explored the rotting center of *Sound and Fury* in the guilt-ridden white clan. Yet the beginning and the end belong to Dilsey, the black servant. Hers is the novel's epiphania—one that begins on Maundy Thursday and ends on Easter Sunday. Suffering is the crucible that forges endurance. Such a backdrop of epiphania remains steadfast, while stage front, white families in crumbling houses live out the tragedy of guilt unconfessed and unforgiven. The blacks and native Americans watch, as if a Greek chorus. It is through these people that the epiphania is declared: "They endured."[102]

Faulkner's quest is for the marks and character of endurance. In story after story, only the annealing process of suffering emerges as redemptive. Classic is the description of Dilsey in church. As the black minister preaches, he becomes the cruciformed epiphania: "His monkey face lifted and his whole attitude [was] that of a serene crucifix that transcended its shabbiness and insignificance and made of it no moment." The whole event is transfiguration: "Dilsey sat bolt upright . . . crying rigidly and quietly in the annealment and the blood of the remembered lamb."[103] The only white present is the idiot, crying beside Dilsey in quiet and blubbering unknowing.

However, the epiphania is not restricted to such uncommon moments, although they are its sacraments. Epiphania is a quality of living. This emerges in Faulkner's portrait of Quentin. His family, symbolized by the tradition of land, has sold part of the heritage for a golf course, the profit from which is to send Quentin to Harvard, guaranteeing continuity of the family honor.

He is traveling north, intent upon enduring Harvard for one year so as "not to squander that inheritance," thereby becoming free to end the family guilt in suicide. As the train slows to a stop at a crossroads, he sees a black man on a mule. It is "as if they had been built there, there with the fence and the road, or with the hill, carved out of the hill itself, like a sign put there saying you are home again. . . . 'Hey Uncle,' I said, 'Is this the way?' " And as if in answer, Quentin is grasped by "that quality about them of shabby and timeless patience, of static serenity." It was then that he knew: "A nigger is not a person so much as a form of behavior, a sort of obverse reflection of the white people he lives among."[104] The oppressors cause the suffering that bequeaths to the victims the power of endurance by which to outlast them. *Agnus Dei.*

Bernanos inhabits World Four. Yet the brilliance of his writing is such that a major sub-theme provides an important ingredient in completing the epiphania of World Five. Bernanos develops, as analogy, the contrast between the suffering of the rich and that of the poor. The epiphania centers in a poverty born of knowing "the emptiness in your hearts and your hands," from which childlikeness is born. For the arrogant, however, admission of such metaphysical emptiness has the likelihood of belonging to camels and needles. Thus they must be broken, brought to a point where they can perceive nothing except "in the form of agony." Epiphany for these residents of World Four can be found only when they stand face to face with their "inexplicable incompetence, superhuman clumsiness."[105]

But what of those already broken by life, those living in World Five? It is very easy to surrender to God's will, Bernanos insists, when it is proved to you day after day that you can do no good. We sense the significance of this sacrament of suffering in the deep unspoken communication between the dying atheistic doctor and the dying priest. Resignation before anything immovable can bring the posture ripe for epiphania. Bernanos calls it joyous resignation, the grace of true poverty, true simplicity, childlikeness.[106] Bonhoeffer knew such epiphania through the experience of imprisonment: "In the prison yard there is a thrush which sings beautifully in the morning, and now in the evening too. One is grateful for little things, and that is surely a gain."[107]

It is not by chance that Bernanos' doubting priest is drawn out of his parish into the ghetto. His conversation there with a poor woman provides a classic portrait of World Five. Characteristically, obsessio and epiphania have become so intertwined as to become one. She becomes a symbol of

the ageless voice, the voice both brave and resigned, which soothes drunkards, scolds naughty brats, lulls naked babes, argues with relentless tradesmen, beseeches bailiffs, comforts the dying, the voice of the working woman who goes on through time probably never changing, the voice which holds out against all the miseries of the world.[108]

In the face of such suffering, the priest is forced to query why she does not despair, or rebel. With her answer, we perceive epiphania:

I don't understand no more. [That's when] I think of all the people that I don't know of like me—an' there's plenty of 'em, a wide world it is—beggars ploddin' through the rain, kiddies with no home, all the ailin' and the mad folk in the asylums cryin' to the moon, an' plenty, plenty more! I slip into the crowd of 'em, makin' meself small, and it's not only the livin' but the dead as well who was sufferin' once, and those that are comin', an'll be sufferin' too, with 'em. I can hear it like a great murmurin', sendin' me to sleep. I wouldn't be changin' places then with a millionaire, it's so happy I'm feelin'.[109]

Suffering forges a near-cosmic ingrafting, whereby endurance becomes not an idea or even a hope. Endurance is experienced as essence. Thus to speak of God for such a World is to sense a God who is long-suffering.

Bonhoeffer's prison experience suggests a christological link. We must abandon an omnipotent God, he insists, for "only the suffering God can help." In fact, it is precisely in experiencing "the hands of a godless world" that we are claimed into this epiphania.[110] In knowing such forsaken-ness, we discover that we "must . . . manage our lives without [God]." It is at this point, strangely, that we come to know God. This God is the One who, like us, is knowable only as "weakness and suffering." Bonhoeffer's musings have about them the makings of a Christology fit for World Five:

It is only by living completely in this world that one learns to have faith. One must completely abandon any attempt to make something of oneself. . . . In so doing we throw ourselves completely into the arms of God, taking seriously, not our own sufferings, but those of God in the world—watching with Christ in Gethsemane.[111]

The corollary follows. In the cross God throws God's self utterly into our arms. God's screams are shared agony *with us,* over the way things are for God too. Jesus becomes one of us—as the feeling incarnation of God. Nothing can separate us from such a God, who participates in it all. Such Divine-human intimacy grounds community as well, as a universality with all those who have nothing. With God, so with us: to die well is key for living well. Yet such faith is rooted in irony, for it means that since God is experienced as the void, God's absence must be wagered upon as presence. God is most present in God's own experience of absence. Faith, then, becomes an intense wager in the face of all evidence to the contrary. It is based on so little, yet means so much.

Integrity is the defining quality of life so lived. It emerges as the inconceivability of quitting, annealed through facing our misery without deception. While faith begins in resignation, it is a refusal to submit. What matters is the quality of living, not its quantity. What matters is the depth of experience, not its height. And this depth is attained by living, stripped of motivation for reward. When one accepts that there is to be no more than there is now, everything depends upon how one receives the now.

A neighbor had a fire. He was underinsured, and the agent encouraged him to lie when turning in his claim, but he refused: "No. I don't have much, but I got my integrity. If a person's word ain't worth anything, it don't matter what he owns."

A musical elaboration of World Five appears in Leonard Bernstein's *Mass*.[112] It begins with the quadraphonic confusion of the *Kyrie Eleison*, echoing from the theater-world's four corners. At "a point of maximum confusion," a young man enters as celebrant. Simply dressed, he "wipes out the sound" with a sung praise: "God loves all simple things, for God is the simplest of all." The Latin of the Mass proceeds, translated periodically and prophetically by blues and rock singers or by street chorus and band, in each case providing variations on the recurrent themes of the *Confiteor*:

> What I say I don't feel
> What I feel I don't show
> What I show isn't real
> What is real, Lord—I don't know,
> No, no, no—I don't know.

And the "gospel"? "We wait in silent treason until reason is restored and we wait for the season of the Word of the Lord." And so we wait, rehearsing the commonplace, desperate for a litany of endurance by which we might chant, "And it was good, and it was good." But each effort at *Credo* ends in scepticism: "Possibly yes, probably no." And so it follows: "Dark are the cities, dead is the ocean."

A hint of epiphania leaks out as a question: "I believe in God, but does God believe in me? . . . From the depths I cried to you." There are suggested dimensions of forgiveness, characterizing World Four. But these hopes too are short-lived, as fetishes of the golden calf lurk in the shadows, threatening to engulf the attempts of Moses-Jesus-Celebrant to mount Sinai-Golgotha. The doubt that results is battered into a preface for a World Five credo:

> If tomorrow tumbles and
> everything I love is gone
> I will face regret
> All my days and yet
> I will still go on . . . on . . . .

Attempting to still go on, the celebrant makes one final struggle to ascend. Chalice-Commandments in hand, he arrives, only to see the whole world-stage in "disarray and turmoil."

> You worked six days and
> rested on Sunday.
> We can tear the whole mess
> down in one day.

"Paa . . . cem" screams the celebrant, in desperation throwing the chalice-Commandments to the ground. He flings the altar cloth as if for a banquet without guests. He tears off the vestments, as relevant here as a wedding bouquet at a divorce court. There is to be no burning bush in Bethlehem after all.

> Take a look, there is nothing
> But me under this.

Then comes the moment of irony. Intended as a negative conclusion, the words become prophetic: "Any one of you can be any one of me!" But he feels only its underbelly as despair. "It's so easy if you don't care," he sobs, descending into the final grave-pit.

"A prolonged silence . . . " is the stage direction. Then, as if from the dead, rises a flute solo. A boy soprano sings, just as in the beginning: "Laude, laude." But now the simple song is identified as the "secret song." The former celebrant, now dressed simply, takes his place "unobstrusively." The "peace" is passed through the church-audience by the Joshua-Christ-choir, now visible as the enduring ones. What has happened is happening, and will happen. It will be on and on.

This Mass is humankind, in its ascent and its descent— daily, lifelong, eternally. This is the way things are and always will be. The quiet, even melancholy "Amen" is meant as credo for those of us who know the song of World Five: "So be it." It is chanted best to notes that are gentle, persistent, enduring, as if themselves annealed in the suffering.

In a real sense, World Five is a World in which life is lived not as symbol but as liturgy. The Liturgy of St. Mark (ca. A.D. 451) provides the eucharistic prayer for World Five:

Have mercy on all those who are held in prison, or in the mines, (under accusation or condemnation), in exile, or bitter slavery (or tribute), and free them all. For you are (our God) who loosens the bonds, who restores the broken, the hope of the hopeless, the help of the helpless, (raising up of the fallen), the harbour of the storm tossed, (the avenger of the afflicted). To every afflicted and hard pressed (Christian) soul give mercy, give relief, give refreshment.[113]

Existentialism

To choose a contemporary Protestant expression of World Five, one is drawn toward some form of existentialism. Kierkegaard holds that those who best understand faith are not the wise, but the most ordinary. This is because it is through struggling with "life's circumstances" that faith is forged and maintained. On the other hand, one must strive "with more and more effort in proportion as [one's] culture increases." He himself knew such lonely suffering in a special way—disabled, deformed, ridiculed by children and cartoonists alike. One cannot become a Christian, he insisted, without the intensification of pathos.[114]

This irony of finding the "knight of faith" to be a sufferer thrusts one into awareness of the Christian as "belonging entirely to finiteness." It is by immersion in that finiteness that the "stages along life's way" are traversed.[115] The pilgrimage for authentic existence is marked by the dynamic of frustrated effort, aborted at each step, until one leaps as if for one's life. The pilgrimage begins with the Aesthetic Stage, populated by such persons as the sensualist, the dabbler, the vagabond.[116] While this stage is exciting at first, one becomes drawn into a whirlpool of decreasing intensity. More and more is experienced as less and less. And so one is driven by boredom to the edge, until one leaps—not *to*, but *from*.

Here the Moral Stage begins, as one wills to be a committed person.[117] The vagabond takes a job. The seducer gets married. The professor makes up her mind. Yet this answer too is doomed. The harder one strives to do one's duty the more one is driven into impotence: "The good that I would do, I do not." Thus a second time the leap—now into the Stage of Religion, Type A.[118] This leap is to a Creator God. But again the dead end. It is one thing not to be able to do what *I* will to do; *it is quite another to be impotent before God as Lawgiver*. The name of this edge is *guilt*.

The inevitable pilgrimage into darkness is from irony to boredom, to impotence through guilt, and into despair. They have a unifying thread—"the distinguishing mark of religious action is suffering."[119] This is what brings one to the final stage. It is sin-consciousness that brings a breach with the immanence of Religion, Type A, forcing one to confess the sickness of despair, which is "the greatest misfortune one can endure." Only then can one begin to hear the witness of the gospel. We can begin to identify with the Christ—"the man who of all [people], absolutely all, suffered the most; never was there born, never shall there or can there be a [person] who shall suffer as He did." Yet he is the one who has put himself in my place, making an eternal pledge by suffering and death, so that against everything that may come, I may stand behind him. This does not mean that anything external happens. The circumstances remain quite the same. "It does not mean to become a new [person] under happier circumstance, but to become a new [person]" within the old, in "consoling assurance."[120]

Faith is more living than believing, attempting to become who God wishes us to be. For this, what matters is that God has existed in human form, in this precise form of suffering, in that concrete situation which demands the endurance that is now mine. No, one thing more: God did this, and then died. We must not forget that. Authentic living is staking one's life on that death, and thus on one's own dying. One's living depends on this infinite risk, making of life an ongoing test. "To believe, to wish to believe, is to change one's life into a trial; daily test is the trial of faith."[121]

The foe is "false spirit," the parching of the passion to persevere. The focus is not on the *what* of living but the *how*. The how that matters is that of passionate existence, made possible by those whose circumstances make it impossible to forget their "objective uncertainty"—knowing what it means to be "out upon the deep, over seventy thousand fathoms of water."[122] Genuine living is to recognize oneself as a living paradox, for that by which one is being encountered remains the Unknown—so much so that while we may use the word *God*, that word "is nothing more than a name we assign to it."[123]

Yet this Infinitely Exalted One "is quite close to thee, closer than [those] who are about thee daily, closer than thy most trusted friend before whom thou dost feel free to show thyself for what thou art." What follows is "so simple"— one loves God because one needs God.[124] And both need and answer rest in the fact that suffering/endurance is the Divine rhythm itself. God let God's self be born in lowly station, and thereafter live in poverty, despised and humiliated. Indeed, no [one] ever lived in such humiliation as He. Even the poorest [person], on comparing [one's] life with His, must come to the conclusion that, humanly speaking, [one's] own life was preferable in comparison with the condition of His life.[125]

Here is the final dimension—inwardness. The changes are not external but inward, grounded in the awareness of God as suffering *with* us. "Christ never desired to conquer in this world; He came to the world to suffer—that is what He called conquering."[126] Outlasting. Enduring.

To endure with God entails faith as living deeply—an inward taking delight in everything that goes on, from children's play to the new omnibuses. The Christian is an earthly creature, tending to the work at hand so that "one might suppose that he was a clerk who had lost his soul in the intricate system of book-keeping." The difference is inwardness, for one "buys up the acceptable time at the dearest price, for [one] does not do the least except by virtue of the absurd."[127] One so suffers the absurdities of existence that in the intensity which results, the common is transformed.

With infinite resignation [one] has drained the cup of life's profound sadness . . . knows the bliss of the infinite . . . senses the pain of renouncing everything, the dearest things [one] possesses in the world, and yet finiteness tastes to [that one] just as good as to one who never knew anything higher.[128]

The blocking of one's outer circumstances thus becomes of no consequence, for the essential is in willing the internal, the subjective, as primary. Privation can give one a taste for enduring.

Yet if one is left with only the subjective, one is bankrupt. We must make the supreme leap "into God." But that is as much beyond our capacity as it is necessary. The more intensely we experience the need, the more we are repelled. Since the finite cannot reach the Infinite, the key affirmation on which all else hangs is that the Infinite once became finite. But I cannot possibly believe that, for it is like believing in square circles. Reason cannot conclude any such thing without abandoning itself—which is not in reason's ability to do. It is clear, then, that the belief needed to be a Christian is a gift. The leap into the void of such unreason can be only from God's side.

This is the importance of Christianity—that its heart is so absurd that it cannot be acquired by human decision. It rests on paradox—drawing meaning from Otherness as sheer gift only after "fear and trembling" discloses one's irremediable "sickness unto death." Then one knows from within, through the suffering of soul and body, that "God" is the name echoing from the cry at life's center. Only in unbearableness is there born a serenity invisible to others. It marks absurd living in the face of the absurd, moved by a voice that is "nevertheless," insofar as no one speaks. Even more astonishing, one finds oneself obeying, while perennially on the edge of embarrassment—because to be seen so acting is to evoke ridicule.

Meaning in World Five, then, has its birth in the fact that through the power to say No to life *as* suffering, there comes a life of Yes *in* suffering. Endurance lives as Promise. Faith is risking, its intensity paralleled by a suffering that is life-wide. It becomes "soul size" only by staking one's life on something that endures, known to be such when one "lives entirely full of the idea, risking [one's] life for it; and [one's] life is the proof."[129] In a strange sense, one opens into the Divine embrace, and dies into belief.

CHAPTER FOUR

Anatomy of the Theological Dialectic—Atonement as Christology

We have faceted the obsessio and epiphania which function in each of the five theological Worlds. Our task now is to develop more in depth how these two interact as the dynamic through which resolution is accomplished. The term *Christ* ("to anoint") is not a proper name. It is a title that acknowledges the One who functions as epiphania for one's obsessio. Thus each person, consciously or not, functions with someone or some thing as messiah, the anointed. Such a "messiah" renders it better for that person to live than to die. These five Worlds are not uniquely Christian. Each is Christian only when one confesses a particular World to be one's own because of Jesus of Nazareth as the Christ. Within each of these Worlds, then, Jesus functions as the Christ if that event provides epiphania—a Yes that renders the obsessio pregnant with promise. The name for this dynamic is *atonement*. Christology is an explication of the nature of that One who has effected such a dynamic. Thus atonement and Christology are inextricably linked, as *how* is to *who*.

Christian theology agrees on two issues: (1) The human situation is discordant, requiring that something be done. (2) The human being, in itself, cannot effect this reconciliation. Atonement occurs when an epiphania is of such a magnitude that the obsessio, while not removed, is transformed by being taken up into that epiphania. On the other hand, atonement has not occurred if the potential

185

epiphania continues to be swallowed by the obsessio, functioning only as respite for a craving still insatiable. The term for the effective intersection of obsessio and epiphania is *conversion*. The Who for this conversion is explored as Christology.

The church has never agreed on atonement theory because it could not discover a common obsessio. Our attempt will be to focus on the obsessio that characterizes each World, thus recognizing the options for atonement and Christology available within these alternative contexts.

Scripture is a central vehicle for the Christian in this process. Its power lies in evoking a pluralism of atonement expressions which interact with a richness of alternative christological imagery, because Scripture itself is a composite witness of writer-editors who operated from contrasting obsessios and epiphanias, and therefore inhabited different theological Worlds. Such pluralism is not to be lamented, but celebrated—for the same is true of the readers. To help draw these connections, we can enumerate resources for tasting each World, in the language most familiar to Scripture:

World One—From Alienation to Citizenship (e.g., Luke 15; Eph. 2:12-13; Heb. 11:10; Rev. 21)

World Two—From Hostile Powers to Freedom (e.g., Mark 10:45; Luke 10:17-20; II Tim. 1:7; I John 4:18; I Peter 1:18-19)

World Three—From Darkness to Light (e.g., Gal. 4:26f; Col. 1:17; I Peter 2:9)

World Four—From Guilt to Pardon (e.g., II Cor. 5:14-15; Gal. 3:13; I Peter 2:24; I John 4:10)

World Five—From Suffering to Healing (e.g., John 15:18-19; Rom. 5:3-5; II Cor. 4:7-12; Col. 1:24-5; Phil. 2:1-11)

World One: The Experiential as Revealer—
Love as Tearing the Veil

In World One, the focusing issue is the cosmos, for the inhabitant experiences the human condition as an isolation resulting from a sensed abandonment. One is conscious of obtuseness, opaqueness, thrownness, mystery, distilled by absence into a sense of longing. One's state of being is as an alien. The epiphania capable of drawing the inhabitant from such an obsessio is the vision of a transcendent final harmony, grasped now as foretaste. The viable options are variations on the theme of coming home. What should be explored, then, is how this particular set of obsessio and epiphania interrelates as atonement. Having done so, we are able to describe as Christology the nature of the event necessary to effect such an engagement.

Atonement in World One is fundamentally *experiential*. A "tearing of the veil" is needed, whereby a different dimension of reality is opened. It is through such experience that we gain an aperture for a contrasting perspective regarding the Whole. Such experience is mediated through One who functions as *Revealer*. Enablement occurs most often through a process of evocation, as when the event of Jesus as the Christ is seen as grounded in, and thus is transparent to, such Otherness. Such an experience, centrally evoked for the Christian by the Christ Event, can be experienced through any object or event, for all things that exist have God as their grounding. Such experiential moments, which transcend the subject/object dualism characteristic of our finitude, are foretastes of a promised and final overcoming of separation in the fullness of reunion. The key, then, is mediation through a unique Now experience which illuminates the unifying nature of All in all.

The veil that shrouds our existence needs to be lifted; therefore *reconciliation* is *a new way of seeing*. The relation of human to Divine does not essentially change. One is facing an ontic given, so one's perspective, in contrast to one's previous way of seeing, must change. Previously we have been shrouded by the ignorance and blindness that result from separation. Plato called such an epiphania noetic. O'Neill identified it as eternal moments. Eliot used the image of the rose garden, giving ecstatic "hints followed by guesses."

All such moments point us toward *the* lens for such moments or, perhaps better, the lens of lenses. Such a "final norm" for Tillich is a christological transparency that serves as standard for all transparencies. In such symbolic interchange, through which two disparate spheres are rendered intervisible, any lack of transparency is idolatry. In contrast is Jesus, who, in crucifixion, underwent that emptiness which is resurrection—total openness to the Spirit in which we all are grounded.

Such an experience of the eternal now as crucifixion/resurrection provides that comparison of before and after which Plato likens to the shadows on a cave wall, as contrasted with real objects in morning sunlight. This is the contrast between experiencing alienation as subject/object dualism and the mystic immediacy that transcends all distinctions of separation. While ordinary life entails seeing through a glass darkly, epiphania is birthed by moments of such intensity that one is claimed with the promise of a permanent seeing, face-to-face.

Although Abelard's understanding of atonement is usually is identified as moral, not ontic, there is one important point of contact. Jesus makes it possible, Abelard insists, for us to see God in a new way. It is helpful to apply this insight to Job's resolution. The Divine address to Job is an epiphania because it reveals the true nature of the human situation: "I have uttered what I did not understand." Being ignorant and blind, it is we who populate a cosmos that is screened—opaque, concealed, mantled.

Eliot's hints of incarnation tend to be gentle—wild thyme unseen, winter lightning, music in which we lose ourselves. Job, by contrast, needs to be plundered by the cosmic sweep. His awakening comes from the ontic "foundations of the earth"—from the doors of the sea to the cords that bind Orion (38:4-11)—because the human condition, to mix metaphors, is suffocating from myopia of the spirit. Only when cataracts fall from one's eyes can one say, "Now my eyes see thee." The result is a new way of seeing—akin to the freshness that belonged to the "morning stars" when they first "sang together." It is the kind of seeing with which God beheld the first dawn coming forth and declared it to be good.

The center of atonement is clear: It entails experiencing in a new way. Schleiermacher interprets such atonement as a deepening of "God-consciousness," in that a growing harmony with the universe is effected. This is evoked by the orienting perspective of Jesus; we are enabled to see as he saw.

This understanding of atonement is misleadingly called subjective, humanistic, or psychological, because the locus of change is in the self. Yet this is true of each World. The theologizing process should be from function (atonement) to theory (Christology), and not the reverse (as is so often the case). Otherwise, denizens of these contrasting Worlds would have pushed upon them christological options which may fail functionally within their particular World. For example, if one begins with Christology, one is limited by logic to the understanding of Jesus as human, or as divine, or as a tenuous balance of both. With these as the only options, atonement theory in World One is forced toward the human. But that is simplistic.

No change can be monolateral, for by nature, all knowing is relational. Thus the transaction required here is reciprocal, in the sense of being mediational. Etymology is helpful. *Mediatus* means "in the middle," much as a pinhole functions in a shadow box. By beginning with atonement, it becomes clear that not a figure, but an *event*, is central for the process of reconciliation in World One—so much so that Tillich, pressed by the above logical options, insists that the historicity of Jesus is a nonissue. Using an aesthetic analogy, epiphania is illumination through an event whose verification is its possibility of being lived now. An aesthetic experience is sui generis, for independent of the aesthetic transaction, a work of art has no existence as art. Likewise, Jesus is the Christ in being so recognized. The value of life evoked anew through this event is independent of some so-called objective estimate of who Jesus "really" was.

Thus, if my life is transformed by experiencing the drama of Hamlet, am I undone if I discover that Hamlet never lived? No, for what I now know through that play is true, independently of that drama or the historicity of its ingredients. Therefore Tillich's Christology is formed around the image of the New Testament *portrait* of Jesus as the Christ. Since it is the portrait that effects the transaction, its truth rests not on its historicity but on its experiential functioning—"*Now* I see."

So understood, the best term for the reconciling dynamic we are describing is *experiential atonement*—that is, atonement in World One is mediation which functions symbolically as illumination. It is revelational by being focused in an experience worth hoping upon, unifying the present with a primal wholeness known as one's promised home.

World Two: The Constitutive as Messiah— Love as Taking Our Part

The defining issue for World Two is history as the stage on which our purpose is defined. Yet this linear process is infected by the meaningless repetition of evil, the directionless rise and fall of things—as if everything is out of control. The human condition is characterized by the normlessness resulting from such chaos. Entropy, wrenchedness, the sense of being invaded—these intersect emotionally in evoking the response of anger. To live out such a competitive ethos means being pressed into some variation on the role of warrior. Thus any epiphania capable of laying claim in this World focuses in a dream of consummation, promised as "a new heaven and a new earth." In Shakespeare's words, all's well that ends well. It is this end which flows back to become more than the sum of the parts and, in doing so, renders each part more than the defeats or gains of the individual.

In this section we will explore atonement as the manner in which this obsessio interrelates with this epiphania, describing as Christology the nature of the event necessary to effect such an interrelation.

Atonement here, unlike that in World One, is not primarily

experiential. To escape the charge of sound and fury that signifies nothing, one's role upon life's stage must be *constitutive* of the meaning of the whole. In the epiphania, something must happen—not a change in perspective, but in fact. And that fact, which changes the present, must have its verification in the future tense. *Love, to be love, must take sides.* To be involved in the combat, it is necessary to express the seriousness of Love—to disrupt the forces of evil with commitment.

Christologically, this requires a messiah understood as Liberator. The resulting vindication must be *in* history, creating a vision capable of sustaining Divine/human co-creativity in the struggle for creation's completion. A pledge is needed, ratified by costly action, that God has taken sides within history, committed beyond the point of recall to history's vindication.

In World Two, everything changes, so that nothing can be seen as completed. Thereby the question regarding everything is, "What is it for?" Thus the answer regarding the essence of things as vindicated is promissorial. Hope resides in the one thing that does not change—God's faithfulness to promise. The heart of this promise, declared as Messiah, is God's commitment to the struggle of Being against nonbeing. The result of this combat is open-ended—so much so that Barth, in his later writings, insists that success is not in our hands. Ours is the call to be faithful—to God's faithfulness.

Regardless, residents of World Two are clear that faithfulness to the promised vision requires human struggle. Human creativity must contribute to history in the long run. The foe to be combated may be imaged in many ways—as the demonic, death, systems, cultures, the satanic, law, sin, entropy, or as nothingness. Whatever the image, this power functions as invader, trespasser, encroacher, oppressor—tempting humanity to subvert God's struggle for history's completion. Thus the epiphania which can change us brings trust in God's capacity to do what God has promised. Epiphania is acknowledged when the response is a call to action.

As we observed, theologians of World Two draw heavily upon the Old Testament, salvation often having as its core meaning, "to have victory in battle" (I Sam. 14:45). This follows from the nature of the obsessio. The one "who needs salvation is the one who has been threatened or oppressed, and [whose] salvation consists in deliverance from danger and tyranny or rescue from immanent peril. . . . To save another is to communicate to [that other] one's own prevailing strength."[1]

Thus understood, salvation entails deliverance from danger, peril, and tyranny, so as to gain victory, security, and freedom (I Sam. 4:3, 7:8, 9:16; Ps. 98:1; Job 40:14). It is significant that thirty of the one hundred fifty references to salvation in the New Testament refer to a historical completion. Such oppressions as captivity, disease, devil possession, and death are identified as eschatological demons to be vanquished in the end.[2]

African liberation theology draws from this base: "To be saved [means] that one's enemies have been conquered, and the savior is [the one] who has the power to gain victory."[3] Central American liberationist Ernesto Cardenal goes even further. He sees such victory as the birthing of God:

> And Yahweh said:
> I am one who is not.
> I am one who will be. . . .
> We will know God when there are no
> more Acahualincas. [a Managua slum]
> —*Epistle to Jose Coronel Ertecho*[4]

The need for liberation is so deep, then, that it is mutual—for human and for Divine. This makes life a matter of living in hope as radical futurity.

Irenaeus was one of the first clear advocates of a view of atonement characteristic of World Two, in a way that can overlap certain dimensions of World Three. In the Incarnation, God filled the vacuum within creation to its envisaged fullness, breaking the limits of a diseased creation caused by human sin. This act in Christ was a *recapitulatio,* a recreating from within, so that the finite can take on a completeness previously known only to God. While World Four follows Anselm in centering Jesus' action in the cross, effecting forgiveness, Irenaeus' stress is on creation and incarnation.

As a result, two focuses have developed, in contrasting directions. For World Two, the stress is upon incarnation as *struggle* unto death with the demonic, reclaiming enemy territory. For World Three, the stress centers upon incarnation as enriched fufillment of the voided self. God became as we, in order that we may become as God.

The first interpretation was predominant in early Christianity, for perhaps a thousand years. It has been called the dramatic view of atonement. This is appropriate, for World Two not only has a Divine-human-demonic drama as its defining rhythm, but analogically, the Playwright makes a personal appearance upon the stage.[5]

It also has been called dualistic, for it insists upon a third party to account for the dilemma of history. Relatedly, the title "mythological" has been given, for the means by which vindication occurs has encouraged poetic descriptions more profound than their analytic translations. When the early rich imagery began to be formed into a conceptual schema, the result became increasingly legal. A major theme for such coalescing was "ransom." As an image, it is a faithful reflection of the etymology of redemption (*redemere*, "to buy back"). It is unfortunate that more literal minds have permitted the poetic license of early World Two thinkers to be destroyed by forcing them from metaphor into a logical schema.

The point at stake is the costly struggle required for liberation. We sense the initial meaning through the Mercedarian Sisters, organized in A.D.1218 during the time of brutal Turkish kidnappings for forced labor. Even today these sisters take a fourth vow: to give their lives as ransom for those they are called to serve. This vow was made in the clear knowledge that to gain freedom for those to whom they ministered, they might need to place themselves into slavery as ransom for the release of others. Such an exchange required a dear price—rape, torture, martyrdom.

It is the power for atonement of such an image that makes solid connection with the sociopolitical dimensions that are reemerging as World Two in current liberation theology: "He who has called things into being is with the oppressed, and . . . will guarantee that [our] liberation will become a reality of the land—and 'all flesh shall see it together.' "[6] The current image of such costliness for some in this World is revolution.

This image of atonement helps to recapture as well the heart of prayer for World Two—it is intercessory. This World is uneasy about cheap prayer—a reminder to God as an excuse for our own passivity. For World Two, intercessory prayer is costly. Julian Hartt sensed this in suggesting that intercession is one's willingness to take the place of a particular person in need. This, truly, is the request to be ransomed, and several weeks ago, I experienced this powerfully. My prayer was for a friend struggling the last days of a battle with cancer. I prayed *for* him—but no matter how I tried, I could not bring myself to ask that I might take his place. Such an exchange would have meant liberation for him.

He died yesterday. The faith that characterizes World Two says that God has made the exchange, taking on God's own self the battle with such powers. The costliness comes in knowing that God is doing what I could not bring myself even to entertain.

Other rich imagery is available, if the poetic stance is maintained. There is value even in the crude imagery of God baiting a hook with Jesus in order to catch Satan. Such imagery witnesses to the life-death struggle that characterizes World Two. Its power is still to be found moving beneath the surface of such contemporary expressions as Hemingway's *Old Man and the Sea,* although it can move as well toward World Five.

This leads to the central feature of atonement in World Two—the objective. *The Christ Event must be constitutive of the vindication itself.* Since it is the situation that needs to be changed, Incarnation-Crucifixion as central christological event must be rooted in history. Gone must be the Divine Watcher. What must be revealed is a God who chooses to look out upon creation *from within.*

Even this disclosure is no vindication, if it happened only once. But if, in the fleshly Christ Event, we have "very God of very God," one can see revealed therein that God is radically involved in history from beginning to end. This approach to atonement insists upon God as Actor at every point: "[Christ] partook of the same nature, that through death he might destroy . . . the devil, and deliver all those who through fear of death were subject to lifelong bondage" (Heb. 2:14).

This ongoing incarnation of Divine-human activity constitutes a New Creation. In Barth's words, "He who from eternity willed to become [human] for our good, will be and remain [human] in eternity for our good—that is, Jesus Christ."[7] Jesus Christ, then, as God's self, not only brings God into human history, but brings the human into the Divine—as constitutive of the Kingdom. Bathed in such promise, all of creation is atoned in joy, for present life is taken up into God. In Cardenal's words, in God "are concentrated the beauty of all women and the flavor of all fruit and the drunkenness of all wines and the sweetness and bitterness of all the loves on earth, and to taste a drop of God [as proleptic] is to become crazy forever."[8] Atonement so understood means that letters written from a Birmingham jail, and a dream proclaimed from the steps of the Lincoln Memorial are hyphened by God, as obsessio is to epiphania. The present never again can be seen as final. The future edge of every moment throbs for a "more."

The atonement theory which characterizes World Two has been so central to Christian history that Aulen calls it the classical view. So it was for such Greek Fathers as Origen, Athanasius, Basil the Great, Gregory of Nyssa, Cyril of Alexandria, and Chrysostom. In the West, key representatives were Ambrose, Augustine, and Leo the Great.

World Two's atonement must be *constitutive.* Thereby the Christ Event within history constitutes resolution. Its import, unlike that in World One, is not in manifesting what already is so. Its import is in *making* it so, even if this is promissory. The Christ Event upon which one wagers is that, from advent to ascension, we behold God's involvement in history as macrocosm. So seen, we are gifted by a vision of the end so transforming in promise that history is made worthy of the conflict.

A powerful literary expression of atonement imagery characteristic of World Two appears in the tenth-century Anglo-Saxon poem, *The Dream of the Rood*. Early Christian history avoided depicting the suffering of Christ realistically, and in time this led to the unfortunate separation of the work of Christ from his person. In this poem, they are permitted to merge again. The crucified One not only is fully human, but stands for the whole of creation. He suffers on the archetypal world-tree, his appendages stretching to the four corners. The cry is from creation itself, as onto the cross leaps the heroic Warrior Christ:

He is a young and confident champion striding from afar. . . . Vigorous and single-minded, he strips himself for battle and a kingly victory. The action is entirely his, an eager sacrifice; there is no question at this point of his being nailed to the cross. Instead he climbs to embrace it.[9]

The author needs only mention the harrowing of hell, for no longer is it something additional to be done. All that is living or dead or yet to be is part of the vindication embattled on the cross. The sovereign Christ will return, as the poem ends, to consummate in finality the vindication already won for the Divine-human struggle that is history.

Aulen draws the implications of this atonement understanding, identifying the obsessio and epiphania of World Two as his own: "I am persuaded that no form of Christian teaching has any future before it, except such as can keep steadily in view the reality of the evil in the world, and to meet the evil with a battle-song of triumph."[10]

World Three: The Enabler as Model—
  Love as Filling to Overflowing

The contours of World Three center on the self, for here the human condition is experienced as self-estrangement. Key are self-images of insignificance and impotence, experienced in relation to others as emptiness, invisibility, loneliness, rejection. Such a state becomes distilled into an (ache) and a (void.) One is identified as outcast. Epiphania begins as a dream of personal whole-ness, invited as possibility through being grasped in some form of enriched belonging. In this section we will explore atonement as the manner in which this particular obsessio interrelates with this concrete epiphania, describing as Christology the nature of the event necessary to effect such an interrelation.

Atonement in World Three has the weight of *enablement*. For this, love functions to fill one to overflowing. For the Christian, this occurs through the ministrations of One who models such fullness, both as example and as representa-tive—evoking the power by which to fulfill one's human-ness. The image of God as our intended nature is so disclosed in that one human life that we are discovered and empowered. Such overcoming of emptiness not only occurs through this luring forth by One who models us to ourselves; but it is done in such a way that we may receive it not in frustration but as affirmation. At the root of obsessio, the need is to be loved with such sufficiency that we dare to risk loving, becoming who we truly are.

This approach to atonement claims Abelard as a mentor. His imagery is drawn not from the medieval legal/penal system, as in World Four, but from an alternative image operative in medieval piety—the imitation of Christ. As perfect exemplar, drawing us to our ideal selves, Jesus is the head of the race. While this approach has often been called subjective, such a term robs World Three of the rich atonement possibilities inherent within it.

to imitate Christ is to

Here the Old Testament root meanings for the term *salvation* are promising. The first definition, as we have seen, is most at home within World Two—"to have victory, to do battle." The second moves us into World Three—"to be wide, to establish spaciousness," resulting in "development without hindrance." Here one can make rich contact with the image of blood, which, in the physiology of the time, was synonymous with life. Atonement, then, is the spacious release of life for the empowerment of living. Such a perspective is more characteristic of the Synoptic Gospels than of the Pauline epistles. The problem for the Synoptics focuses more on present sins (missing the mark) than on Sin (as in Paul, an originating condition beyond our remedy). Therefore Jesus is the teacher-model *par excellence*. Both titles—teacher and model—must be held together, for either alone is misleading. Together, they function much like the contemporary image of player-coach, uniting telling and doing. In this way, self-consciousness, self-awareness, self-affirmation, and thus action, are brought about.

The Jesus Event in World Three focuses on the human. Jesus is "very man," truly human, representative humanity, the fulfilled self. This is axiomatic, but in a reflexive way. Jesus, in the very act of being fully human, as model exemplar, can be perceived conversely as a decisive disclosure of God's love for humankind. Discovering in Jesus the true nature of the humanity God has created, one is overwhelmed by the love of a God who invites us to be but a little lower than the angels. Epiphania occurs when, on the one hand, I perceive through Jesus the God who loves me by creating me to become who God envisaged me to be. On the other hand, in knowing myself through Jesus as the one so loved, I am enabled to follow as example the One already loved by God into uniqueness—just as I am loved.

In this sense Jesus is mediator, the one who "stands in the middle." One looks both ways in seeing the biblical picture, and thus in looking at all life—for "the Christian indeed cannot look into [humanity] without seeing Jesus and cannot look into Jesus without seeing God."[11]

Such an approach is best titled *enablement atonement*. The New Testament proclamation of Jesus as the Christ enables the process of emptiness to fulfillment. One question that follows concerns the issue of Jesus' uniqueness. Bultmann insists that one may know about such authentic existence through nonscriptural sources (e.g., the philosophy of Heidegger), but the *attainment* of such authenticity is possible only through the proclamation of Jesus as the event which lays claim. Such encounter comes as an imperative indicative. While Schubert Ogden and Fritz Buri agree that such authenticity can be known through multiple sources, they disagree with Bultmann's insistence that only the proclamation of Jesus as the Christ Event has enabling capacity.[12] However this quarrel be settled, it is intramural within World Three. There is agreement that, *for the Christian*, authentic existence has its enablement in Jesus proclaimed as the Christ, so named for precisely that reason—Jesus is the Christ *because* he enables fulfillment.

While for World One the historicity of this event can appear less than necessary, one dimension of atonement for some in World Three requires a stress upon the historicity of Jesus. By living life to its fullness, Jesus not only identifies but proves that the *imago dei* within each of us is lively and possible. In this, he is a precursor of a new threshold in humanness. Others, however, stress the imaginative, poetic, evocative power of the Jesus narrative as told, so that past facticity is less important than existential functioning. For these, historic reconstruction is not important, the value of Scripture being in the fact that it is written from the experience of those who witness to their own fulfillment through Jesus.

The Renaissance fascination with the human Jesus unearthed an interesting, but often unrecognized, christological perspective, anticipated in imitation by St. Francis and his followers. The more free-spirited members of World Three can be lured by the power of fantasy into becoming, for others, Robin Hoods of the spirit. These are the lyric, childlike, animal-loving earth mystics who turn maturity on end.[13] Other expressions of this creation-centered tradition extend far back into Christian tradition. In developing World Two, we indicated that in Irenaeus there appears a strong affirmation of the ongoing goodness of creation. The work of Jesus as the Christ was such a living of humanness from within that humanity is restored and elevated beyond even that authenticity aborted by sin. Jesus made this possible by ascending the stages of humanness into the fulfillment of our created Divine likeness. It is in this sense, for Irenaeus, that Jesus is the teacher/participant, who "through his transcendent love become[s] what we are, that he might bring us to be what he is himself."[14] "We could not otherwise attain to incorruption and immortality except we had been united with incorruption and immortality."[15]

Ritschl has been one of the most influential modern representatives of atonement understandings within World Three. He understands the atonement/Christology dynamic in terms not of metaphysics but of axiology. Jesus is the Christ because, in modeling fulfilled integrity, he possesses the *value* of God for the self. Relatedly, the image of Jesus' faithfulness in the face of emptiness reorients our outlook of mistrust. Even if we cannot see as clearly as he, by trusting him, we can trust as he did. However this be imaged, we are pointing through Jesus to a new relation with God that enables self-realization.

Interesting variations within this approach to atonement/Christology are not hard to find. "Representative Christology" holds that God, by seeing us through Jesus, takes a more hopeful view of humankind. In Protestant Pietism, we find a movement away from new birth as made possible through justification (World Four), toward new birth as the Spirit's internal process of growth.

Prominent in World Three understandings is the insistence that God's attitude toward us always has been one of love—seeking the misplaced coin, the lost sheep, the insignificant and worthless. Thus the change needed is not in God or in the structures that define life. The change needs to be in the self. From within, I must be brought to know what is already so, independent of my knowing. The focus is the subjective, but the reality to be appropriated is not. Thus what happens through one's relation with Jesus is a personal experience that is life-changing. Van Buren calls it Jesus' contagious freedom. Jesus is one of us who has done it—and so can I. However that may be explained, I know myself as loved by the God who leaves the ninety and nine *for me*. Then a strange thing can happen. With such an epiphania, the emptiness inside, which once was suffocating, can take on a peacefulness, like the rests in good music.

Contemporary theologians whose atonement views illustrate World Three include Daniel Day Williams, J.A.T. Robinson, Marjorie Suchocki, and John Cobb. For Williams, Jesus reveals love as the image of God, thereby becoming the human exemplar of the Spirit that is God. The power of God, then, lies in drawing us to ourselves through "the worship God inspires."[16] For Robinson, "Jesus is the prototype of the new humanity." Our fall occurs when "the possibilities of the human scene are measured by something less than 'the full stature of Christ.' " Therefore "the humanity of God" is the "glory" of humankind, and therein the Christian is "distinguished by the divinity [one] sees" in the human being.[17]

For Marjorie Suchocki, God is the source of possibilities available to us through love that evokes love. Jesus makes this possible in two ways. On the one hand, he manifests the love to which he also calls us; on the other, he reveals God by loving the way God loves.[18] Cobb basically agrees with these understandings, seeing therein a breakthrough on the plane of human evolution, for in Jesus we pass over a new threshold of human consciousness. However the dynamic may be described, the result is a life of self-affirmation in communion with others.

We can summarize now these strands that appear necessary for atonement in World Three. Jesus functions as the Christ by being the One who:

—*focuses* the unconditional love of God for the self by revealing this in, to, and through his human Godlikeness;

—*fulfills* humanity in modeling the lyric joy that lures us

from emptiness into the process of authentic selfhood;
—*combines* these two functions, distilling in himself the
Divine-human meaning of nature's process, as enrichment and home to our becoming. Therein is established
an intelligibility worth living for.

Jesus realizes in principle every divine possibility that
defines humanness (imago dei). As the One who awakens,
models, and contexts us in this process, he is also the One
who believes in us.

World Four: The Compensator as Savior— Love as Forgiving the Unworthy

The anatomy of World Four is focused by a sense of the
demonic, with which we struggle as temptation and sin.
Consequently, the human condition is characterized by a
state of powerlessness, resulting from, and in, idolatry.
Diseased, fallen short, and condemned, we experience guilt
in our deepest parts, exacerbated by a powerless fear that
renders us fugitives. The epiphania for which one yearns is
reprieve, which entails newness in the undeserved relation
of adoption. In this section, we will explore atonement as
the way this particular obsessio interrelates with this
concrete epiphania, describing as Christology the nature of
the event necessary to effect such a transfiguring relation.

In World Four, atonement must be *compensatory,* because
Love, in forgiving the unworthy, must replace what must
be removed and make up for what has been ruined. This is
not a matter of taking sides, as in World Two, but of taking
the place of. Christologically speaking, what is needed is a
Savior—One who can take away that which poisons and
blocks a restored relationship with God.

The diseased life shaped by the obsessio of this World has
about it an almost substantive heaviness, a not-rightness,
which causes a creeping paralysis. Consequently, atonement theories in World Four are transactional, centered on
the theme of propitiation. The profound sense of guilt

present is an ingredient over which we can do nothing. All efforts, in the end, are reducible to cul-de-sacs of self-deception or self-justification. Reason, reduced to rationalization, loses its capacity for freeing. Instead, it controls consciousness with a defensive cloak to hide our true motivations.

Therefore, one of the deepest issues in atonement is condemnation. The hardest moment in existence is the moment of public confession—clear, unambiguous, total: "I am the one!" Almost without exception, confession is never pure. Almost never is it born of genuine sorrow. On the contrary, it issues from either being discovered or fear of being discovered. And even as one is confessing, the unspoken self-chastisement is for "being so careless." The deadly game is always one of plea-bargaining for a lesser charge.

The way beyond these games of self-deception is through them. Morning comes only after the darkest hours. One's hope is in the feeling of dereliction, when all distractions are asleep and the gnawing won't be reasoned away. This unshakable persistence is able to turn self-deception into guilt, exacerbating one's frantic efforts at self-justification, moving one toward confusion.

Liza, in Dostoevsky's *Brothers Karamazov*, is an intriguing figure—weak, self-pitying, defensive, spiteful, unloved and unloving. Yet she is being surrounded and redefined by a new context—Alyosha's unconditional love. The startling newness is in being accepted, no matter what. Yet instead of accepting the gift, her response is violent, as if she is being attacked. To respond positively would entail the acceptance of a centering outside herself. When, in exhausted dead end, she discovers that she cannot hurt him sufficiently to either contaminate or destroy his love, she waits until he leaves. Then in her bitterness, she deliberately crushes her finger in the crack of the door. In bearing the pain, she will justify herself. By paying the cost, she will warrant continuation in the grim confines of self-centeredness. And there she sits—alone.

Resolution entails an event of suffering that is outside the self, condemning one not for any particular act or for any portion of one's life, but for the whole of one's being. Resolution needs to be accomplished without corridor or closet, or any other hiding spot of escape. Thus such judgment must be done by one so innocent that there is no question that the suffering is absurdly undeserved. And as undeserved, it is freely chosen. With such motive, true love is disclosed. In the words of the old hymn, "What wonderous love is this / That caused the Lord of bliss / To bear the dreadful curse for my soul?"

Psalm 38 structures this twin dynamic: (1) "Thy hand has come down on me. . . . My iniquities . . . weigh like a burden too heavy for me" (vss. 2, 4); (2) "For thee, O Lord, do I wait; it is thou, O Lord my God, who wilt answer" (vs. 15). There is no necessary connection between the two—none at all. Confession is not a work that necessitates or earns forgiveness. Waiting is all that can be done, for waiting is the desert that connects the seemingly unconnectable poles of obsessio and epiphania.

This so-called forensic, objective, or substitutionary view of atonement, which we are calling compensatory, centers in crucifixion. The perfect One undergoes undeserved sacrifice. The focus is upon expiation sufficient for acquittal: "Without the shedding of blood there is no forgiveness of sins" (Heb. 9:22). Christ becomes "the Lamb who was slain," through which we, the enemy, are "reconciled to God by the death of his Son" (Rev. 5:12; Rom. 5:10). It is he who is "wounded for our transgressions," and God "made him to be sin who knew no sin," suffering both the consequences and the penalty of sin (Isa. 53:5; II Cor. 5:21).

Despite tensions in the way these atonement declarations are translated within World Four, we can detect common features. It is important to develop these in some detail, for while the atonement/Christology dynamic of this World has tended to dominate Protestant Christianity, it has not always had the application of imagination needed to make it a living option.

Creation as Positive Condemnation

In Genesis, we have the story of a restructured creation in response to sin. As a result, creation is sown with suffering. While this can be understood as Divine punishment, there is portrayed a God who provides fur garments to replace our harsh fig-leaf improvisation. Some find in that act a suggestion of God's positive motive for the austere recontouring of life. Among the themes that have resulted from this exploration are trial, testing, chastisement, annealment, correction, discipline, teaching, and corrective suffering. In each case, they are explored as Divine instruments for reconciliation. Even frustration and despair have been seen as evidence of the Divine pursuit.

It is through these eyes that the crucifixion, as the epitomy of exile, can be understood as being, on the personal level, the redemptive paradigm for which the Babylonian captivity served on the communal level. Recent studies of the function of wilderness and desert in Scripture show them to be designed by God as preparation—for Israel, for Jesus, for us. From the perspective of epiphania, suffering as condemnation can be beheld as positive.

But the cross is not only preparation; it is also consequence. Jesus is, and becomes for us, the *imitatio Christi*: "Take up your cross and follow me" portrays faith as a call to lifelong crucifixion. If the cross is the center of history, it is likewise the center of one's pilgrimage. The only thing that matters is how one dies one's death. If this is understood as a work, life is grim. But crucifixion becomes epiphania if self-sacrifice is rooted not in the motive to receive, but as response to having been forgiven. It is a matter of loving as one already has been loved. So seen, it is clear that the Divine motive for condemnation *is* forgiveness. *It is God as the imitatio Christi who discloses the motive behind all of creation, even in its harshest contours.* Luther is so clear about this that he insists that anyone who is unwilling to suffer as much as possible deprives Christ of his proper titles—Savior and "the crucified One."

Thus while creation is "restructured" as condemnation,

crucifixion discloses the Divine motive as profoundly positive. Punishment for its own sake, or as an end rather than as a means, is no longer a possible understanding of God. Whatever images are used, if God bears punishment for us, then God has nothing to do with punishment that is not a Divine gift. The rugged contours of life are calls to repentance, as perpetual recalls to life rooted in forgiveness. Therefore the circle of atonement defines not only the pattern of life as a whole, but each moment as well.

Consequently, belief in "the crucified One" begins a process which subsequently loses any clear "before" and "after." Repentence is as much a response to forgiveness as its precondition; and forgiveness is as much the precondition for repentence as its consequence. Thus, as Luther insisted, forgiveness is not once-and-for-all, but ongoing. It changes not our condition, but our relation, so that while justification is abiding, the dynamic of condemnation-forgiveness is the defining flux of daily existence. Understandably, World Four insists that worship without confession is not Christian. It is in being condemned that one knows again that one is forgiven, and it is in forgiveness that one is open to humility, enabled to hear condemnation as positive. This is why we dare to call Friday good.

Legal Analogies

World Four has tended to draw heavily upon juridical imagery for insight, with the focus falling upon guilt and punishment as the dynamic for restoring relationship. In part, this reflects the historical periods in which such understanding developed, as well as the kind of training received by key theologians (e.g., Calvin was trained as a lawyer). While today we tend to draw legal illustrations for atonement from personal offenses, one of the most penetrating images used in the past involves the public crime of treason. That is our situation: We have been unfaithful to the One who left the castle totally in our charge; this One returns, to find not only that we have dropped the drawbridge but that we are making love with the enemy, in our friend's own bed. The dilemma so posed suggests that three requirements need resolution:

—*disclosure*, of such a nature that we will never forget.
—*punishment*, so paid that there is preserved the moral structure of the world, for morality without enforced sanctions is anarchy.
—*catharsis*, which effects restoration of the full relationship.

If one shifts the analogy of broken relationship to that of a king or queen who discovers a cavorting spouse, one senses that the needed catharsis involves more than the relation itself. It is internal, for the condition is operative even if one never had been discovered. In fact, the dilemma would be present even had the act never been done: "One who looks . . . lustfully has already committed adultery." *Betrayal can be reloved away only by the one betrayed, in an agony defying description.* One who has never experienced it personally can never know. Thus the hymn "There Is a Fountain Filled with Blood" insists not only on loss of "guilty stains" but on a catharsis by which "to sin no more."

Understanding the fuller possibilities of such legal analogies, then, requires the distinction between retribution and rehabilitation—a distinction very lively in contemporary penology. It is crucial to insist that in understanding Devine punishment, the only motive faithful to the heart of World Four is rehabilitation (to redeem)—not retribution (to avenge).

The history of World Four's wrestlings with legal analogies shows significant variation. In Anselm, for example, as in Cyprian and Tertullian, Christ's death is seen as satisfaction for God's injured honor. For most Protestant Reformers, the focus was upon penalty for sin. For Grotius, Jesus as the Christ shows that God does not hold God's own law in contempt. The christological emphasis that emerges is determined largely by which dimension receives emphasis. These are some of the possibilities:

1. A representative Christology emerges when satisfaction is seen as entailing not only depth, as in the crucifixion, but breadth, as a fulfillment of the law throughout Jesus' life. In seeing us through Jesus' accomplishments, God accepts us—weak but well-intended.

Relatedly, lawyers are called advocates because they defend others by risking their own honor and reputation on behalf of the clients, standing between conflicting parties. So is the case with Jesus. His perfect life, as law-abiding both in letter and in spirit, is risked by taking on our case.

A further analogy appears in Roman law. The head of the household was responsible for maintaining order. Therefore the head was personally punished for the public misconduct of any members of that household. In Jesus Christ, God assumed such responsibility. Again, while some lawyers will take on any case for a fee, the analogy is powerful as it pertains to those special lawyers for whom the cause of the client is indistinguishable from their own. It is in this sense that we stand represented in the cause of Jesus.

A last analogy occurred several years ago in North Carolina, when a husband went before a judge to ask that he be sent to jail in place of his convicted wife, who was pregnant. Such surrogate punishment was granted. The pathos of this story, which makes it even more poignant as image for the Divine act in Jesus Christ, is that the woman, after bearing the child, filed for divorce. The husband was required to remain in jail, paying the price for one who had abandoned him.

2. There is a problem in conceiving how the price paid by one person, no matter how perfect, can give *full* legal satisfaction for the guilt of all people in history. This is because the problem goes even deeper. If the payment that changes the relationship comes from Jesus as human, how is forgiveness to be seen as a Divine gift, rather than as a human achievement? Aulen's critique of this atonement theory seems right—at the crucial point of sacrifice, the

reconciling act as payment is the work of Jesus as *human*. Consequently, to be faithful to World Four, it is important to stress the Trinitarian connection of "Father" and "Son." In that way, the distinction between condemnation and forgiveness refers not to the distinction between Divine and human, but between Divine functions. To preserve this connection, the weight of human analogy falls heavily upon the full emotional meaning of "only begotten Son." God gave out of his own agony and heart-breaking grief, for the tragedy was of his own "flesh." Without this close tie, the image fails as epiphania—one cannot shake the feeling that any crucifixion in which God simply watches and is pleased discloses the sadistic perversions of a Divine voyeurist.

3. Some thinkers within World Four have dealt with this issue further by acknowledging that any price paid by Jesus, no matter how perfect, carries only the weight that belongs to one finite life. Consequently, the satisfaction given by Jesus draws on the metaphor of token payment. This provides a creative tension sufficient to support the element of grace. Since Jesus' suffering can be only token, God is in no way obligated to accept it. The fact that God does accept it discloses that the final, determining act is the work of Divine graciousness. This does not discount the importance of what Jesus has accomplished. But rather than a heroic act, it is accepted by God much as the poor widow's mite was heralded by Jesus as "more than all." Thus the atoning act creates a tension between Divine and human, but in such a way that the initiative of grace is maintained throughout. The gift of a dandelion by a child to it's mother hints of such sacred exchange.

Sacrifice

Many atonement views not of World Four hesitate to hold that atonement *changes* God. This uneasiness about seeing a movement in God from wrath to love often rests in the refusal to entertain the possibility that the God revealed in Jesus Christ is willing even to consider eternal damnation.

Yet Paul is clear: "Since, therefore, we are now justified by his blood, much more shall we be saved by him from the wrath of God" (Rom. 5:9).

Some in World Four are willing to risk such difficulties. For Protestants, deathbed repentances have had a special importance, as for our Puritan ancestors. In the traditional Roman Catholic Requiem Mass there is a crucial section titled *Dies Irae,* the Day of Wrath. The sounds of that section in Verdi's *Requiem* make the meaning more than clear. A scattering of words is sufficient: trembling/throne/judge/ hidden becomes clear/remember kind Jesus/do not forsake/ groan like a sinner/burn in everlasting fire/separate from the goats/blessed contrition.

It is understandable, then, why World Four evidences a tendency toward intermediation: "Remember me kind Jesus to the Father"; "Holy Mary, ever virgin, speak to thy Son who will not turn away from Thee." There are more than seven hundred fifty official saints, each evoked for one reason: "May their prayers rise to Thee."

However one interprets this tendency, its evidence is inevitable in World Four—the issue of moral inaccessibility. Applied to God, moral is to immoral as infinite is to finite. Analogies from daily life are legion: Put in a good word for me; Do you have any friends who . . . ?; Who do you know at . . . ?; You have friends in high places; Doesn't she work for your dad?; Who does he listen to?

By analogy, it is Jesus who has paid the price for access. It is Jesus who has the ear of the One who matters. The saints have secondary entrée, with Jesus the cornerstone of all hagiology. They all have known Jesus well. Even in deeply secular circles, there is still a deep respect for those who have paid their dues.

Yet serious attempts to understand how God's anger is inverted into good favor have always moved deeper than interdiction—toward the theme of sacrifice. Sometimes this is expressed in crude terms that barely escape cannibalistic urges hardly worthy even of sinners. Nevertheless, a promising possibility occurs in the Gospel of John, where there is a shift from moral to aesthetic categories. It is the lamb without blemish that is genuinely *pleasing* to God, for the act of being perfect resides for Jesus in the intent to be pleasing to the One by whom one is sent. Throughout the detailed instructions for sacrifice in the Old Testament, this same theme is echoed: "The priest shall burn it upon the altar for a pleasing odor to the Lord" (Lev. 4:31). The Johannine Christ perpetuates this sacramental tradition. He is the One who takes in the vinegar of condemnation, and from his side flows water and blood commingled—the purifying water of baptism and the joy of the eucharistic wine. "It is finished," he declares. And genuflecting his head, as it were, offers the elements of his body and blood to God as sacrament, as a pleasing gift to the God whom we know is "well pleased."

Seen from the outside, from the perspective of the Potter's Field in Matthew's despairing portrait, this is a grim sacrifice. But when seen from within the Johannine World, it takes on the lyric interchange of lovers. Perhaps this is why Mary Magdalene had such a sensitivity toward the resurrection (John 20:1-18). We grasp the fragrance of such exchange in Luke's description of Jesus' relation with "a woman of the city." Clearly pleased, Jesus celebrates her: "She has wet my feet with her tears and wiped them with her hair. You gave me no kiss, but from the time I came in she has not ceased to kiss my feet" (7:44-45). Again the water of cleansing and the joyful fragrance of ointment commingle. *Therefore*, "her sins, which are many, are forgiven, for she loved much" (vs. 47). The astonished response comes as question: "Who is this, who even forgives sins?" (vs. 49). And the unspoken answer? Lovers! Surely no debt has been paid, but something beautiful has been done—and it is enough.

One can develop this theme into sacramental reciprocity as *mutual* sacrifice. At the same time, it ascends and descends, for it is as Divine as it is human. This event which atones serves as offering and as Offered, as guest and as Host, as invited and as Invitee, as lover and as Loved. And is God changed by the event? "Truly, I say to you, wherever this gospel is preached in the whole world, what she has done will be told in memory of her" (Matt. 26:13). "Do this in memory of me."

Louis Evely captures poetically this eucharistic flavor of atonement as it can be explored within World Four:

The Eucharist itself is so powerful that it is capable of making the whole world participate in the death and resurrection of Christ, of making everyone in the world pass from death to life in one definitive Easter. To celebrate the Mass is, so to speak, to hasten the end of the world.[19]

In fact, the end of the world is consummated in Eucharist. So understood, one can see a dual functioning in the liturgical furniture of the upper room, holding in tension both pre- and post-Vatican II emphases. Altar and table need to be one, functioning as both sacrifice and communion, offering and reception, pain and ecstasy, carnal and spiritual, carnage and feast, Divine and human. How better than in one simple act of Eucharist to grasp the complexity of atonement? In so doing, the logical contradictions of orthodox Christology are functionally resolved. "Fully God and fully human" are experienced creatively as inseparable.

Eucharist without the carnage of the crucifix is sentimentality; without a table, there is no joy. Therefore residents of World Four need this dimension of pleasing God. Without it, sacrifice partakes of the grim accounting of a Divine miser, or the silly caricature of a melodrama in which the rent must be paid. Clearly the God of Scripture savors the offering. And on the reverse side, the insignificant gift so given becomes, beyond all our doing, a gift returned a hundredfold. It is pleasing to us, just as it is pleasing to God—just as God created it to be.

If atonement patterned upon Eucharist is transsignification, then all of life is sacramental. Beginning in the Christ Event, the eucharistic rhythm expands to define the world itself. The New Testament understands this sacrificial rhythm to be true of the Christian's own relationship with God. The atoning act named *the Christ* is model for the life of the Christian. "I am now ready to be offered. . . . I have fought a good fight, I have finished my course. I have kept the faith" (II Tim. 4:6-7 KJV). This ongoing Divine-human exchange is the dynamic known best by lovers. May my life be lived as a gift pleasing to God, for it is rooted in God's gift to me, which has been so pleasing.

Therefore, while Protestant understandings of atonement in World Four tend to draw upon analogies from jurisprudence, Roman Catholic explorations tend to be fed by the image of sacrifice as sacrament. For the one, the Lamb is scapegoat. For the other, it is the Lamb of Passover. The one takes away; the other marks one for life. The one focuses upon sin; the other struggles with death. There is good reason to believe that the heart of World Four is best reached by holding these two understandings creatively together.

Obliteration

This option for atonement brings us close to the boundary between World Four and World Five. Crucifixion is the only perfect gesture a human can make toward the Divine. Death, said Luther, is the only way to settle accounts with God. A saint, said Tillich, is one who is utterly self-sacrificing, so that in transparency, one points totally to the Ground that is not oneself. Acting out such postures within World Four begins to make sense only if it emerges from a desperate knowledge that there is nothing of recompense that one can possibly proffer to God. At the heart of World Four is the bottom line to every account: overdrawn. All that is left to offer are the empty hands of a derelict spirit. That is precisely what Jesus did—not as hero, but as a broken reed, a dampened wick. In so doing, it was a perfect sacrifice, not as "full and sufficient," but as broken and empty—and thus enough.

Here the emphasis no longer falls on the "what" of sacrifice, but on the "that." Sacrifice becomes the posture of faith itself. The blood metaphor is appropriate, for one's life is to be offered as total renunciation of self. For Wesley, it was the supreme promise of faith as imitation of Christ: "I am no longer mine but yours."[20] This is kenosis as atonement, as Christology, and thus as life-style. In a Roman Catholic prayer, the tone is similar: "Take all my freedom, my memory, my understanding, and my will. . . . Your grace and your love are wealth enough for me."[21] The one who loses one's life for His sake shall find it, we are told.

This self-negation is rendered as atonement by the clear awareness that there is no guarantee of receiving it back at all. There is no means-end connection. Barth's early writings insisted upon this abandonment of self, but later became uneasy lest it be misunderstood as laying claim upon God for forgiveness. Thus the key is that one offers it all up, knowing that the only value lies in awareness of the futility of offering up even one's futility. The connection between crucifixion and resurrection is *ex nihilo*—that is, there is *no* connection. Therefore the total sacrifice of Jesus is at the center of the cruciformed nature of life; whatever else may occur, it is God's totally free act. Therefore the *imitatio Christi* is the perfect act—crucifixion. And God's perfect act is resurrection. Viewed from our side, they have no connection; viewed from God's side, they are one.

These atonement ruminations we are discerning as native to World Four can be summarized in the Hebrew word *kaphar*, which carries two meanings: atoning directed toward God (propitiation); and atoning directed toward the offense (expiation). Both meanings are developed biblically, and both appear in World Four. In the first, propitiation, the wrath of God is turned. In the priestly tradition, as we have seen, this occurs through what is received as "sweet savour" (Gen. 8:21). The morality intrinsic to relationship insists that restoration cannot be bought, thus the reciprocity of propitiation is recognized. Here the suffering servant *"makes himself"* an offering for sin," as the "chastisement that made us whole"; "it was *the will of the Lord* to bruise him" (Isa. 53:10, 5, 10, italics added). The heart of atonement is touched best when these two dimensions are held in tension. In *kaphar*, Jesus, as human event, nevertheless originates in the will of God.

In the second meaning, *expiation*, atonement directed

toward the offense focuses upon *kaphar* as blotting out sin, rendering it harmless, nonexistent, inoperative, annulled, purged—in a word, expiated. In a Christian context, this requires a creative tension between the imperative to "take up your cross" and the indicative, that in the cross of Christ it has been done. Jesus is the propitiation for our sins (I John 4:10), but only because the sending of the Son is not a matter of our loving God, but of God loving us. Nothing short of an epiphania held by this tension can do justice to the heart of atonement: "For our sake [God] *made* him to be sin who knew no sin, so that in *him* we might become the righteousness of God" (II Cor. 5:21, italics added).

God, him, we—these are the referents whose functional need for organic relation require the paradoxes that connect "God" and "him" in a transactional unity. At Nicea, this was confirmed as Trinity. "Him" and "we" were affirmed at Chalcedon, as the incarnate exchange of Divine and human. In providing such channel markers, World Four declares that the mercy seat of God, once veiled in inaccessibility, has become, through the cross, history's crossroad (Rom. 3:25).

World Five: The Assumptive as Suffering Companion— Love as Outlasting with Long-suffering

The issue in World Five is life itself. One is overwhelmed by the apparent meaninglessness of the way things are. The feel is that of being engulfed, controlled, wronged, so that one takes on the state of refugee or victim. The epiphania capable of claiming the inhabitants of this World effects the quality of integrity, forged in survival as endurance. In this section we will explore atonement as the way this particular obsessio interrelates with this concrete epiphania, describing as Christology the nature of the event necessary to effect such an interrelation.

Atonement in World Five is *assumptive*. Here, what needs to happen is not, as in World Four, a "taking away *for* others," but a "taking on *with* others." The only love that matters is that which remains for the long run. Outlasting with long-suffering, God writes off human foibles as inconsequential *when experienced from within*. Thus Christ is companion, disclosing God as suffering servant. In its *obsessio*, this World knows the weight of Pirandello's play *Six Characters in Search of an Author*, the hope that in the dynamic of endurance, there is to be found a hint of plot. Yet a more persistent question is not so much whether life has an author, or even perhaps whether there is a plot—but is the author one of the actors? Here one comes, for a moment, within hailing distance of World Two. Yet it is not vindication promised in a *telos* of resurrection that is sought. Rather, epiphania emerges at the point where suffering, Divine and human, intersect as a cross. Yet this is not in order that something should be done, as in World Four, but that we and God are in it together.

Atonement ruminations in World Five may seem strange when viewed from more traditional understandings. While the resulting theory is subjective (for it is a changed perspective that is needed), the cause is objective (e.g., a radical act of Divine incarnation-crucifixion). This epiphania remains opaque and, perhaps as a result, often has remained undeveloped. Nevertheless, the heart of atonement for many World Five inhabitants resides in the Divine assumption of the human plight with such intensity that suffering becomes a sacrament of presence. Expressed as hope, life is a companionship of endurance.

From such a basis in atonement, Christology varies. It may be grounded, for instance, in God's resolve to be incarnate in the plight of the discarded—traveling into the far country of our estrangement. Or it may draw insight from Luther's insistence upon God's own inner struggle, resolvable only through a change in God's perspective. This is effected when God comes into our experience, enduring our dilemma from within.

For other inhabitants of World Five, Jesus discloses a God who is no longer either omnipotent or omniscient. Claiming this from within World One, Tillich concludes that "substitutionary suffering . . . is a rather unfortunate term and should not be used in theology. God participates in the suffering of existential estrangement, but [God's] suffering is not a substitute for the suffering of the creature."[22] Likewise Whitehead, within World Three, affirms a God subject to the same conditions as humanity. This is a *univ*erse, he insists, so it is a given for God as well. Thus God is the sympathetic companion who anguishes with us in a communion of suffering. And for Brightman, evil issues from a surd—not only in nature but in God. Thus existence is a profoundly personal Divine-human sharing of dilemma.

Such thoughts are permitted to converge powerfully in World Five. We see the condition of life quite differently if God experiences creation as we do, from within. Atonement occurs when the human plight becomes known as God's own inner history. It is the cross that marks the disclosure of this Divine-human point of identity. Indicative may be the contrast between black theology and that which characterizes many poor white and blue-collar believers. For the former, Christ is the liberator who shapes World Two, disclosing God as the One-for-us. For the latter, Jesus becomes One-*of*-us. In the first, God identifies with our situation in order to change it. In the second, God identifies *with* us in order to *endure* it—indeed, to outlast it.

A Christology for World Five is further suggested in the contrast between Japanese Christianity and that of the American/European church. Describing the work of Roman Catholic lay theologian Shusaku Erdo, Roy Sano exhibits a God in clear contrast to the God of World Two, the One who acts. Instead of speaking and doing, the God of Japanese Christians is silent. Expressed christologically, the best image is a *fumie*, a plaque of Jesus on which Christians at one time were forced to trample as a renunciation of faith. This is no Jesus embellished with halo. Here Jesus is bordered in black. In contrast with the fulfilled Jesus of World Three, we see a Jesus of hollow cheeks. "Fullness is associated with the divine in Europe and the U. S., [but in

Japan] holiness is associated with the hollow," as convex is inversely related to concave.[23]

The God of traditional completeness, then, stands in heady contrast with the empty and void Oriental Divine. Even the bells of the two Worlds are different. The Japanese *bong* is "out of the void," while the Western *clang* issues "out of fullness." Thus the Jesus who distills the uniqueness of World Five is a Japanese Jesus—ugly, unfinished, trampled on. Relatedly, as C. S. Song indicates, "In Chinese one is required to say the two words love and pain almost in the same breath." The word is *thun-ai*.[24]

The epiphania of such Divine identification with human living can be lived in a manner that resembles Bonhoeffer's secular spirituality, or the "worldly transcendence" of Kierkegaard's knight of faith. From the outside, Christians are no different from others. From the inside, however, they are utterly different. They exist knowingly in a depth of seventy-thousand fathoms—the insanity of living the insane and still trusting the impossible. There is a dim recognition that on a clear night the wilderness *is* the Promised Land, and the Eucharist, at its best, is a brown-bag lunch shared with a stranger on the road. More than any other World, life in World Five is a life of "as if," waged in the face of all evidence to the contrary.

This image of basing so much on so little finds analogy in the paintings of Morandi. His whole life was spent capturing bottles on canvas. By limiting the range in which he was willing to see, he could flirt with perfection without presumption. As one critic put it, there results a "breathtaking modesty," finished in patient humility. World Five understands.

Similarly, one is reminded of St. Theresa of Lisieux's doctrine of the "Little Way." Within narrow parameters, she carved out a simple spirituality through a year and a half of teenage suffering. Or Mother Teresa, who exhibits hints of sainthood. It is through the dynamic of World Five that the nameless ones seem "selected by the great Blacksmith of history, heated in the fires of turmoil and trouble and then hammered into usable shape on the hard anvil of conflict and struggle."[25] Scripture understands, for it is a broken and contrite heart that is "not despised." Such is the Spirit valued somehow for its own rare sake.

From this perspective, one can understand why the Synoptic Jesus wants to make it clear that "tax collectors and harlots go into the kingdom of God before you" (Matt. 21:31b). If, as Berdyaev insists, "suffering is the inmost essence of being, the fundamental law of life," then by definition, the dwelling place of God is on the second floor of The Naughty Lady, right down the street at Chestnut and Twelfth, pinpointed by a four-by-six mattress. Much goes on, but little happens. It is a gaping void, *unless* we can "reconcile ourselves to the tragedy of the world because God suffers in it too. God shares [the creature's] destiny."[26] It is not that God's involvement is instrumental to, or for, anything else. God's participation is intrinsic, and that is enough.

This World moves silently past me every Sunday. It has faces and bodies attached to uncertain legs, swaying up the center aisle of Holy Trinity Church. It is painful to look into such eyes, eyes so uncertain about looking back—or forward. Pale mouths open, etched with browned teeth and chapped lips. "The body of Christ." "Amen." What incredible stories buried at soul-depth, covered firmly by glazed eyes. These are the victims, the walking wounded, themselves a crippled crucifix, their heads sometimes bloody and always gently bowed. Again and again I give a flimsy wafer, coated with a thin prayer for a strange resurrection. Here the Eucharist is a movable feast, with each person on Israel's forty-year desert trek, sometimes extended. To these belong the Anaphora of Basil of Caesarea (ca. A.D. 357): "Grant them rest in the bosom of Abraham, Isaac, and Jacob, in green pastures, by waters of comfort, whence pain, sorrow, and sighing have fled away."[27] It is deep within such moments that their Christology takes on scriptural clarity:

Though he was in the form of God, [he] did not count equality with God a thing to be grasped, but emptied himself, taking the form of a servant, being born in the likeness of men. And being found in human form he humbled himself and became obedient unto death, even death on a cross. *Philippians 2:6-8*

If Jesus Christ is the suffering servant, and the Christ Event is the Divine self-disclosure, then Isaiah, in chapter 53, is painting a portrait of *God:* no form, no comeliness, despised, rejected, sorrow, grief, without esteem, ugly, bruised, stricken, afflicted, oppressed, cut off, poured out of soul unto death. This is God involved in our condition—not for us, but *with* us. This is the key. God does not interfere with the way things are, either to reward or to make things come out right. We are in it together, and only in that assumption is there the power of endurance.

Jesus is martyr. This is true not only at the end, but throughout. He was born in a barn, illegitimate, born to die. The ark, the cradle, and the coffin are the same. Thus the supreme act is not the Lord's Supper, but the Last Supper. It is where the *mysterium* is experienced as God broken. To taste this is to be baptized by the blood of God's death, and rebirthed by drowning into God's pain. And it is good—for never again will I be alone.

Though in the blush of Romanticism Keats may have been able to call this earth "the vale of soul-making," inhabitants of World Five will have little truck with any God who designed this World for such ends. Participated in from within, it appears that "thou hast made us like sheep for slaughter" (Ps. 44:11). So the central issue is, where is God *now?* For epiphania, God must be participant, and the disclosure of that fact is, itself, reconciliation.

Bernanos gives additional hints concerning christological possibilities in World Five. Gone is the transactional nature of atonement that is so important for World Four. There is no blame, and thus no condemnation. Just as the human dilemma cannot be explained, neither can that which gives it meaning be understood. The atonement that results is

simple and allusively childlike, standing almost as fairy tale
does to theodicy:

Even from the cross . . . He did not own Himself a victim of
injustice: they know not *what they do.* Words that have meaning for
the youngest child, words some like to call childish, but the spirits
of evil must have been muttering them ever since without
understanding, and with ever growing terror. Instead of the
thunderbolts they awaited, it is as though a Hand of innocence
closed over the claim of their dwelling.[28]

This is an atonement of innocence, naive perseverence,
knowing unknowing, of quiet confidence that outlasts—a
continuing on that is somehow its own answer. This is how
it dawns that "human agony is beyond all an act of love."[29]

The motion picture *Cool Hand Luke* is a powerful
expression of the dynamic involved. In a fight with a bully
he could not possibly defeat, Luke is struck again and again
until he goes down. He rises, and it begins again. The
rhythm goes on, as blood continues and eyes puff closed.
"Stay down," friends yell. But he rises, again . . . and
again. The watchers look away, then walk away. Finally
there are only the two fighters. Luke is hit again. "Stay
down!" But he won't. With tears, the bully leaves. Luke
stands alone, as if with the question: "Where are your
accusers?" A strange turning of the other cheek is not a
strategy, but a way of life—for God too.

One novelistic expression as context for atonement
within World Five is Nathanael West's *Miss Lonelyhearts.* It
is indicative that the central figure has no name, only a
role—a newspaper columnist who answers the letters of
troubled subscribers. The theme is clear: the pathos of
suffering, focused in women. One letter writer was
gang-raped. A paralytic cries to play the violin. A teenager
born with a deformed face yearns for just one date—but her
only friend is her mother, who "cries terrible when she
looks at me." These are the victims of injury, rejection, and
abandonment, writing letters "stamped from the dough of
suffering."[30]

The columnist attempts to respond with what he thinks

would be a Christian answer—that Christ gives suffering in order to bring persons to Him—but he destroys his copy in disgust. There is no sin to be forgiven. There is only the pathos of universal suffering, in a World whose sky "looked as if it had been rubbed with a soiled eraser." Overwhelmed by it all, his mind shapes everything into a giant cross, and he falls asleep in Gethsemane-like exhaustion. But he cannot escape. It is as though a burden of suffering has been placed upon him. What he needs, taunts Shrike, the mocking editor, is Jesus Christ, the "Miss Lonelyhearts of Miss Lonelyhearts."[31] If he could only believe in Christ. He cannot.

He spends three days in bed, as the stone in his stomach, which cannot be rolled away, is identified as "an ancient rock." He is tried in the courtyard of Peter's denial, experiences fever as a refining fire, goes mad in a vision of attempting to heal all suffering with love, and is killed in the embrace of a Judas. Throughout, the violence is unrelenting. Yet it is more than external. It is within as well. He tells of his first feeling of pity, when years ago he accidentally crushed a frog. He felt pity, only to discover that pain turned his pity to rage. He "beat it frantically until it was dead."[32] There is no we or they to condemn. We are in it together.

Yet it is in the midst of such suffering, both from and unto, that he is struck with the thought that underneath it all there may be a "bird called the soul." This too is ridiculed by Shrike, named for a bird with shrill voice and hooked beak who, says the dictionary, thrives on eating insects, small birds, and frogs, which the shrike sometimes impales on thorns. He functions as a Greek chorus, rendered lewd: "The Catholic hunts this bird with bread and wine, the Hebrew with a golden rule, the Protestant on leaden feet with leaden words, the Buddhist with gestures, the Negro with blood."[33]

The word finally emerges—*blood*. The image of sacrifice permeates the text. Central is the image of the lamb slain—as Isaac, as Jesus.[34]

In the midst of it all, the columnist seeks respite from the

cup in a Gethsemane which poses as Eden. With the
Eve-like Betty, he visits her farm birthplace, now abandoned. They eat an apple, and she loses her virginity—on
schedule. Symbolized by the thinness of a later strawberry-
soda interlude, the tempo cannot be halted. It moves
relentlessly forward. There can be no return to "all the
things that went with strawberries and farms in Connecti-
cut."[35] We are irremediably "east of Eden."

"Forget the crucifixion, remember the renaissance"—
Shrike gives the call for World Three. But the obsessio
cannot be focused on the self for long. It slops over, running
down the sides of life. There is no solace, for no one is
untainted. The eye of the needle is for all. "Crowds of
people moving through the street with a dream-like
violence . . . broken hands, and torn mouths." The columnist tries not to identify with them, keeping them away as
"they." Yet in the presence of "Eve," he falls to the
universal level, for "she was like a kitten whose soft
helplessness makes one ache to hurt it."[36] This is a World of
ambiguity, strange ambiguity. But what undoes him is the
perseverence of her smile through the tears. What does one
do with the unhurtable hurt—or is it the hurtable unhurt?

Here the ingredients of World Five take on iridescence as
epiphania aches in the wings. But the Jesus figure remains
only human. The pathos remains unresolved—unrelent-
ingly so. The only Christ entertained within this novel is the
unacceptable One "you preach about," who promises to
take it all away. Yet a Christology fit for World Five could
emerge here. It would mean affirming that the "King of
Kings . . . [is in fact] Miss Lonelyhearts of Miss Lonelyhearts."[37]

What of a Christology built upon such an image, with a
presence like a "sponge drawing the world's suffering"—
not to take it away but to participate in it? This would make
the crucifixion a drowning under the weight of yeses to the
question, "Do you have room in your heart for one more
sufferer?"[38] The epiphania is in hearing the reply, "Ninety
and nine, seventy times seven." If Jesus is a name for the *via
dolorosa*, identifying the human path as the one trod by God

as well, then to take up the cross is no longer a sentence but a strange and renascent friendship. It is to perceive the new Eden as life on Golgotha, lifting a cup to the Friend who looks back with a pained but knowing smile—"It's OK."

In prison, Bonhoeffer drafted a prayer that is a Christology for World Five:

> Lord Jesus Christ
> You were poor
> and in distress, a captive and forsaken as I am.
> You know all [our] troubles;
> You abide with me
> when all [others] fail me;
> You remember and seek me . . . .[39]

Nothing changes, yet everything is different. There is an identity, a companion presence. God has a name—Emmanuel.

With these faceted dimensions in place, we can develop some of the atonement alternatives resident within World Five:

As Radical Incarnation

Atonement here means "withness." Barth identified incarnation as a radical wedding, beyond the point of recall. This means taking the phrase, "We're in it together," and rendering it cosmic. It means looking out on the World from the perspective of Grunewald's Isenheim *Altar Piece*, as the figure pointed to as God writhes in agony. It is then that one cannot help understanding Paul in a new way: Nothing can separate us from the love of God—not tribulation, or distress, or persecution, or famine, or nakedness, or peril, or sword—because in Jesus Christ, God has disallowed every separation. "I am sure that neither death, nor life, nor angels, nor principalities, nor things present, nor things to come, nor powers, nor height, nor depth, nor anything else in all creation, will be able to *separate us* from the love of God in Christ Jesus our Lord" (Rom. 8:35, 38-39, italics added). There is nothing in the human plight that God is not also drinking, gagging, vomiting, bemoaning—nothing.

Moltmann insists upon this affirmation, one the church has often skirted for fear of heresy (Patripassianism):

When God becomes man in Jesus of Nazareth, [God] not only enters into the finitude of [humankind], but . . . death on the cross also enters into the situation of [our] godforsakenness. In Jesus, [God] does not die the natural death of a finite being, but the violent death of complete abandonment by God.[40]

The Godforsaken God is not an experience once had, but a condition deep within very God of very God. Here one need not falter before images of God as powerless, noneffective, soft, halted, languid. What can be said of such a God—one whose cheeks are turned until they are hollow? Only that S/he "is here." It is enough. "The crucified God is near . . . in the forsakenness of every [person]. There is no loneliness and no rejection . . . not taken to [God's self] and assumed in the cross of Jesus."[41]

What the Council of Chalcedon attempted to say christologically, through substance terminology, is stated here in functional terms. It is God's will to be defined essentially by the human condition. God too is fugitive and victim. Thus atonement as epiphania is the disclosure that our obsessio is God's as well. If baptism means being branded by the mark of the cross so that we are no longer our own person, an image from Isaiah provides the Divine counterpart: "I have graven you on the palms of my hands" (49:16). We have been tattooed onto, burned into, etched upon, punctured with nails into the palms of God. Jesus Christ, then, is the baptism of God into the human condition. Never again will God be the same, and never again will we be alone—for the soul of Reality is declared to be participative, assumptive, and suffering.

But the Divine motive is crucial. Such Divine "impotence" is born less out of inability than out of lovesickness—"like a wife forsaken and grieved in spirit" (Isa. 54:6). "How can I give you up, O Ephraim! . . . My heart recoils within me, my compassion grows warm and tender" (Hos.

11:8). Greater love hath no God than the One who lays down One's life for a friend. It follows that the greater the suffering, the greater the love of the Suffering One who shares totally, no matter what. "My soul is very sorrowful, even to death" (Matt. 26:38). God dies with us.

As Primal Scream

Primal-scream therapy insists that there is no health in us until we scream out our hatred, our rage, and our indignities at our biological parents.[42] For World Five, the dis-ease is deeper. The obsessio rests with the primal *ontic* Parent, the One from whom we might assume that all suffering comes. Thus epiphania may appear at the moment of our most intense fist-shaking at what may turn out to be a very empty stratosphere. Here we meet the One who went before, gathering up every shriek; the One who, with bloody abandonment, screamed out for all of us from that spot called the Skull. Here, in a cosmic moment, one may be grasped by the truly *Primal* scream. It is sufficient to halt all of time: My God, my God, why have you forsaken me/us? And with a loud cry, he breathed his last. There was darkness over the land. This is the moment of sheer nothingness. The emptying is total, and at hand.

Yet in that nothingness, if primal-scream therapy gives us any clue, atonement as reversal may come as the uprooting of our fundamental assumptions. Before we can scream against the parameters of our immediate parentage, it is God who, in this figure, curses the total darkness *with* us, *in* us, *as us*. Herein is known the "God who pleads the cause of [God's] people" (Isa. 51:22). With whom does God plead? No one. The railing is to and with and for the way things are. "And behold, the curtain of the temple was torn in two, from top to bottom; and the earth shook" (Matt. 27:51).

As Internalization

To know another, we are told, one must walk a mile in that person's moccasins. And to know who we are, God has walked a lifetime in ours. To live from *within* knows no counterpart in knowing from *without*. "To know," for Scripture, means full bodily intercourse. It is understandable, then, that in Luke's Gospel we have the image of incarnation as Divine interconnection in flesh. As a result, God's act in Jesus becomes epiphania. When God sees our condition from within, through eyes glazed with cruciformed agony, the words tumble out: Father, forgive them.

This is to suffer the pathos known only by going backstage, by learning the name of each dressing-room cockroach, by looking into the worn and aging eyes behind the makeup. Going out the stage-door exit past the garbage cans after the last performance—this is enough to melt even a God who might be tempted to thrash the janitor for arrogance. A hierarchical God can remain so only by remaining an outsider. The God of incarnation, in contrast, is able to embrace us with a sad but knowing smile—we whose makeup is never quite able to cover the bravado of our frightened pretense.

"Pity," says Isaiah. "Compassion," says Hosea. "Love," says Luke. All are part of a common epiphania—the One who aches for, by standing with. Reconciliation, in the end, comes not so much in knowing as in being known, precisely as I am, in all my humanness. Therefore, unlike World Four, here in World Five forgiveness does not issue from our paying anything. It issues almost spontaneously from a God who, in seeing from within, now understands in a new way. This is the reverse of Abelard's World Three—there Jesus is seen as providing us with a new way of seeing God. But in World Five, Psalm 78 can provide a contrasting clue. The compassion which restrains God's anger is tied to God's remembrance of the human condition, "that they were but flesh, a wind that passes and comes not again" (vs. 39).

This distinctive note provides a corresponding image for understanding Eucharist. Humble pie was made from the undesirable inner parts of a deer. It was served to the servants after the hunt, while the royalty partied in festive separation in the Great Hall. In World Five, to eat of this common bread and drink of this daily wine is to empty the Banquet Chamber, for the real festivities are around the kitchen table, where the King/Queen is eating humble pie with us.

As Kippur

Judaism has a powerful image for dealing with reconciliation—the Day of Atonement. Central is a scapegoat upon which all the sins of the people are placed (Lev. 16:7-8). The goat is sent into the desert—out of sight, out of mind. This is Yom Kippur. *Kippur* means to "cover," "hide," "send away," "pass over"—"to mask the eyes."

Near the Trappist abbey at Gethsemani, Kentucky, are two statues in a remote wood, a gift in memory of Jonathan Daniels, a civil-rights martyr. As one ascends the path, one sees the first statue of three sleeping disciples. Continuing toward the summit, one comes unexpectedly upon a startling figure of Jesus. Here is no devout Jesus in hand-folded piety. He is on his knees, staggered, clutching hands *masking his eyes*. His face is upturned toward an unseeing sky. Here is the scapegoat, almost out of sight. Standing in front of the statue, one sees the divinely covered eyes, crying out to see no more. But as one walks behind the silhouette, one looks down upon the crouching disciples below. And suddenly we understand, beyond words. Facing death puts things in perspective. What once seemed so monumental now becomes of no account.

So with God. It is not even a matter of pardoning human foibles. It is simply a writing off of the eternally trivial, a much ado about nothing. The psalmist makes the request well: "Hide thy face from my sins, and blot out all my iniquities" (51:9). Epiphania comes in knowing that it is being done—for no good reason at all. God's understanding from within brings the freedom to blot out. "I will love them freely," says Hosea's God, for "I will have pity" (14:4; 2:23). The sins are covered—commuted, exonerated, mitigated, glossed over, palliated. "Blessed is [the one] . . . whose sin is covered" (Ps. 32:1). Why? Because the sin that once seemed so gross, seen through the eyes of the flesh, now becomes pathos. "I will remember their sins and their misdeeds no more" (Heb. 10:17).

Here lamb and shepherd commingle, for *God leaves the ninety and nine to bring back the scapegoat.* Therefore crucifixion is not a death offered to God, but is, in a real sense, a death of God. God is the shepherd whose life is given for the sheep (John 10:11).

As Reversed Forgiveness

Atonement in World Five can take yet one step more. "Your sin [is] forgiven" means that "your guilt is taken away" (Isa. 6:7). Since, in Jesus Christ, God takes upon God's self the sins of the world, it follows that God takes on the *guilt* as well. It is meaningless for God to assume the sin while regarding the sinner as still guilty. Therefore the amazing love of the cross is that in assuming the guilt, *God confesses responsibility for the condition of the world!* In Jesus Christ, we hear God's plea: "Forgive me for what I have done." Suffering the meaning of humanness brings the reversal, as God cries out, "I'm sorry." Grace as graciousness issues out of compassion pleading for compassion.

In experiencing betrayal by Gomar, Hosea suggested that God might be feeling about Israel what Hosea was feeling. But in World Five, it is proposed that Incarnation pushes us toward a God who sees life through *Gomar's* eyes. What we see depends on where we stand. Correlatively, reality depends upon where God stands to see. Scripture is clear. God chooses to stand with the outcasts, the poor, the prostitutes—with the Gomars. The last shall be the eyes for the First—in this case, God.

Such linking of incarnation and crucifixion through the obsessio of World Five receives strong dramatic expression in Guenter Ruterborn's *Sign of Jonah*. The play is a trial. Some of the accusers are events: "Nineveh, Berlin, Babylon, Rome

. . . tomorrow it might be New York, Moscow . . . who knows?"[43] Other characters are historical. In being careless with their masks, they reveal themselves as also our contemporaries:

Well, is there another more weighted down with guilt and blood, and at the same time filled with excuse and self-justification? The face of [the] twentieth-century . . . . So much cruelty, self-righteousness and emptiness, while at the same time . . . devoid of all religious feelings.[44]

After such confession/accusation characteristic of World Four, the trial takes a curious turn. Where is God in all this? God "changeth the seasons and times [World One]; [God] removes kings and sets up kings [World Two]; [God] gives wisdom to the wise, and knowledge to those endowed with understanding [World Three]." But if this is so, a denouncement follows with deadly logic: For all the suffering of this universe, "God is guilty, God is guilty, God is guilty."[45] And so humanity reads the sentence:

If you can locate the God whom I lost in the course of two wars, condemn [God] as I am condemned, to lead the life of a man on earth. Let [God] wander about, as I must wander about, without a home to rest [my] weary head. Let [God] feel the pain, as I feel the pain, of having lost [my] Son. Let [God] suffer, as I had to suffer, hunger and thirst and fear of death.[46]

The epiphania occurs through irony, when the character Jonah recalls that it is precisely in Durer's woodcut of the birth of Christ and in Grunewald's painting of the crucifixion that not only had this "actual execution of the verdict" already occurred, but it had happened *by God's own choice*. "God condemned God!"[47] The obsessio becomes epiphania:

[God] shall be born to a woman, somewhere along a country road, and the moans of the poor creature shall ring in [God's] ears day and night. [God] shall be surrounded by the feeble, the sick, the filthy, by people bearing the marks of leprosy. Rotting corpses shall bar God's path. [God] shall know what it means to die.[48]

So be it—for atonement means that it has been done in Jesus Christ and that it will continue to be so.

As Outlasting

Some residents of World Four are led to posit hell or some other form of final damnation. Such impatience, however, is foreign to World Five. The love which this World forges, rather than being erratic, stormy, or capricious, is tired, sage, life weary, and longsuffering. In this sense, it is more conative than emotive, evidenced not so much by strong feeling as by tempered resolve. Its power is one of promised determination to outlast through longsuffering. Love is the promise that no matter what, one will be there—to the end.

God's question in Hosea is classic: "How can I give you up?" The answer, "Easily," would result in hell. But for Hosea's God, the implicit reasoning is the bonding that makes many marriages work—"We've been through so much together." The heart of atonement here is a dual hope—that God's ways are not our ways, yet God has chosen our ways as God's own. Life is hell enough. But even if there were a hell, God would outlast that too—waiting at the door. In Jesus Christ, God has taken wedding vows with us unto death: To have and to hold, from this day forward, for better, for worse, for richer, for poorer, in sickness and in health, to love and to cherish.

As Poverty

In World Four, we explored the option of Jesus' sacrifice as token, as a way of establishing grace more centrally in the atoning transaction. Such an effort moves in a direction understandable to World Five. A face emerges: "This poor widow . . . *out of her poverty put in all the living that she had*" (Luke 21:3-4, italics added). This is an incredible phrase. World Four might prefer more serious quantitative factors— being impressed with the "perfect one without sin," for he alone can offer the surplus from which to pay for others. But with the parable of the widow, there enters a qualitative factor. The motive for one who puts in *all her living* is qualitatively different from one who makes only a contribution, no matter how sizable. Here less is more, and the less one becomes, the more one is.

Somehow this links with Barth's insistence that at the time of the incarnation, it was necessary that Jesus be a Jew—one of the hunted outcasts of history. If so, in our time it would be necessary for the incarnate one to be black (Cone), female (Daly), third-world peasant (Miguez-Bonino), outcast (Teresa), aged (Kuhn). In effect, the only Divine event of infinite meaning would be an assumption of the state of finite nothingness. This is atonement—that God "out of her poverty put in all the living that she had."

In World Four, the Holy Spirit comes as announcement that God's lawsuit against the world was decided in God's favor, and thus ours by default. In World Five, the decision has been rendered in our favor, and thus in God's, for God has declared no contest. The issue, rather than being that of humans paying the price, is that of God paying the dues.

In the end, atonement and Eucharist become one. There is a cloaked double meaning in Psalm 80:5: "Thou hast fed them with the bread of tears, and given them tears to drink in full measure." This is the Divine-human Eucharist known by World Five. Thus a hermit friend closed his recent letter to me with these words: "So much of life is a Good Friday sanctuary, waiting for a moment of Easter filling. Let us pray for one another, that we never tire of waiting."

"We rejoice in our sufferings, knowing that suffering produces endurance, and endurance produces character, and character produces hope, and hope does not disappoint us" (Rom. 5:3-5).

CHAPTER FIVE

A Conclusion

*Theological Worlds and the Church as
Variegated Community*

Our concern in this book has been to explore the subjective as foundational ingredient in faith as universal phenomenon. Central has been the image of a theological World as that meaning-space in which each person attempts to domesticate the chaos as home. Such a World, we identified as given birth by an impulsing logic, discernible as one's autobiographic thread. This dynamic is formed by the interplay of one's particularized *obsessio* and *epiphania*.

Obsessio, on the one hand, is the crystallization of deep need around focused imagery so powerful as to become a driving impetus toward satisfaction. *Epiphania*, on the other hand, is the congealing of those events which so function as hints that they give hopeful contours worthy of wager. A theological World, then, is a preconceptual gestalt of meaning-feeling which, in picturing reality, directs behavior, shuns contradiction, and thrives on communal confirmation.

Therefore the difference between the traditional believer and nonbeliever does not concern the facts, but the attitude (blik) toward particular data.[1] All of us are believers, so the issue at stake is not *whether*, but *which* metaphor functions as one's interpreting pattern. Reality provides no check

233

beyond the power of one's convictions, in interplay with
the parameters that shape one internally and externally. In
this sense, we control, or at least permit, ourselves to
perceive and feel in certain ways.[2] Thus Dillard can insist, "I
see what I expect."[3] Seeing the gift of faith functionally in
this way, we have a primal theological paradox: "From a
Christian point of view . . . truth is not something that we
find or by which we are found, but something that we make
true."[4] Faith is a gambling upon the future, a living "as if,"
with such intense commitment that one's life is the foretaste
of making true the not yet. The proof for any faith is one's
willingness to die for it—and thus to live within it.

Illustratively, the proof of the resurrection is "how those
Christians love one another." At the same time, faith's
strength, William James insists, is a determined will that
there shall be a new face on the "half wild universe." Paul
explains it best in insisting upon both as necessary
ingredients, held together as faith's paradox. Faith is both
determination and gift, combining an imperative with an
indicative: "Work out your own salvation with fear and
trembling; for God is at work in you, both to will and to
work for his good pleasure" (Phil. 2:12c-13).

The power of imagery in establishing such contours can
be illustrated. Consider the contrasting modes of seeing
entailed by three images which distinguish types of
spirituality: (1) the World as foreign land, drawing one by
the impulsing logic of faithful traveler; (2) the World
perceived as desert, evoking a call as penitential pilgrim;
(3) the World as mountain, enticing one as religious
quester. Such imagery suggests that the meanings involved
in each theological World are not added, but are implicit
within the eyes that behold, honed to see what otherwise
would be absent or perceived differently.

The five theological Worlds we have identified are best
understood as clusterings around common rhythms,
shaped by what Wittgenstein calls family resemblances.
An analogy is suggested by frequency distribution on a
scale or graph, to determine the modes or peaks where
occurrences maximize. The result is a typology of Weber's

ideal types, which serve as models. Although too pure to be found in practice, they are descriptively useful for identification, analysis, and for understanding the interaction of Worlds.

Weber's method of understanding is similar to the aesthetic method of faceting we have employed. For the sake of imagining oneself into the experiences of others as they act out of their frames of reference, one operates methodologically, with "an empathetic understanding of what people's subjective meanings are."[5] Paul expresses such meanings as a "mind"—to be a Christian is to have the "mind of Christ." The result is a theological World which emerges ongoingly as an exciting work of imagination.[6]

Our commonality as humans, then, is that each of us exists in some sort of story-shaped World. Thus theology is story-shaped autobiography, built upon the recognition that "not to have any story is to experience nothingness: the primal formlessness of human life below the threshold of narrative structuring."[7] It follows that one's lived story is theological, for "the unity of a human life is the unity of the narrative quest,"[8] and that informing unity, discovered performatively, is the home base that forges what we have called a theological World.

Therefore theologizing is the process of identifying, nurturing, forging, or reforging one's impulsing logic as identifiable narrative, whether magnetized by imagery of battlefield or of cottage. And while it is to such narrative Worlds that traditional theology points conceptually, the weakness has been twofold. On one hand is the tendency to portray and defend such a World by methods foreign to the originating process. On the other hand, this is done with an arrogance that treats the theologian's own World as exclusive anatomy for the Whole.

Although no person's theological World is ever pure, since it emerges as autobiography shot through with the Worlds of competing cultural and subcultural myth, the World of each individual is precious and rare. There is no other like it. Behind each set of eyes is profound mystery, a tender, unique, fragile, and special creation which identifies the self as theological artist. And in such artistry, the self is always a social creature.

Theological Worlds so overlap that communities of discourse are as necessary as they are unavoidable. Related imagery, emerging liturgies, common stories, structural inevitabilities, interacting needs—these emerge for the sake of survival, control, growth, security, accountability, and support. Whether they take the form of a coffee klatch or an Anglo-Catholic sacramentalism, communal Worlds impose parameters against which the individual's impulsing logic is permitted to wash and find channeling. The particularly severe socialization forces that operate today make clear the workings of communal disciplining. As promises of reward and acceptability, they operate as lures, while as coercion, they manifest themselves as threats of marginality, failure, deviance, invisibility, or insanity.

Many of these communuities of discourse are informal in their impact on the individual. Their primary power is the threat of isolation, the promise of belonging. Mainline denominations and their constitutive congregations operate in this way, as if they were sects, each composed of a common theological World. The result is ironic. Members receive the expectation, expressed or assumed, that all should be claimed by a defining uniformity. Yet functionally, uniformity no longer exists, other that as peripheral vestiges. As a result, some feel excluded, others unfed, a few guilty, many restless, and most are brought to protective indifference.

In truth, as this book insists, mainline Protestant churches are functionally pluralistic. Unfortunately, by operating as if they were sects, they are driven to establish their commonality in terms of least common denominator. This is the mark of liberalism, grounded in breadth. But in failing to recognize the existence of theological Worlds, this amplitude is incapable of evoking deep and concrete commitment. We need a church capable of grooming these contrasting communities of family resemblance, each capable of inviting into theological allegiance the hosts of spiritually malnutritioned in our contemporary culture.

The recognition of theological Worlds entails the recovery of spiritual direction as the church's central task. This means midwifing the integrity of each individual's theological quest into individual and communal accountability. In so doing, the church can discover that social justice is commitment to the sacredness of such theological intimacy for each and all. The development of family resemblances within church communities of theological pluralism will mean finding new ways to cross-correlate methods of liturgy, preaching, education, administration, and social change. It will entail the creation of subcongregations to distill alternative modes of worship, decision making, faith development, learning styles, support, belonging, and outreach. Each subcongregation will have its own persuasive theological integrity, while cross-feeding with others through an interacting presence that is energizing. The day of uniform ministry within mainline churches is dated.

Correlatively, authentic Christian theology must henceforth be acknowledged as pluralistic. Systematic theology should no longer be taught in seminaries as an objective, monolithic discipline, but should be exhibited functionally and typologically. Thus Tillich's systematic theology must be recognized as precisely that—it is Tillich's. Its value is as evocative example, a viable model of how the correlation of obsessio and epipania provided one person the "courage to be." It is not the universal Christian answer to be mastered as one's own.

Doctrine as Dialogical

No one is without an obsessio. While its forms are diverse, each arises out of the need for things to be more than they appear. Such yearning opens one to the possibility of metaphorical insinuation, since more often than not, epiphania begins as a gamble upon a particular metaphorical stance. God, then, is not so much a name that signals a separate experience, but an overtone that is implied in all of one's experiences.

Such a metaphor, functioning as gestalt, becomes entertainable as vision. In so being, it becomes "set" for the images polarized by one's obsessio. It begins to function as epiphania when that threshold is passed whereby a tentative way of seeing is affirmed as a separate reality. It takes on a life of its own by purporting to disclose the way things are.

From this orienting base, that which is more traditionally identified as theology emerges as content. Such content, identified conceptually, functions as clusters of convictions which evoke responsive obedience.[9] A doctrinal system that organizes the whole may be formulated, to serve as a final stage in seeking conceptual coherence for the metaphorical process we have seen emerging as a theological World.

Yet even if such conceptualization as doctrinal formulation does not occur, doctrine cannot be avoided functionally. Doctrines arise as conceptual distillations of answers to the generic questions unavoidably contained in every obsessio. Unfortunately, Christian doctrines about questions to which they purport to be answers usually are unclearly taught and affirmed. Such questions are by no means restricted to persons with a religious penchant. They are universal:

—*Salvation* is that state promised when an epiphania is powerful enough to incorporate an obsessio rather than be absorbed by it.

—*Sin* is a nonhealing way to deal with obsessio.

—*Redemption* is the process of the ongoing struggle for dominance of obsessio and epiphania, empowered by spiritual disciplines and liturgy as the enacted enfoldment of the two.

—*Human nature* implies the question, "Who are we meant to be?"

—*Human condition* points to what we actually are.

—*Original sin* asks, "Why the contrast between nature and condition?"

—*Christology* queries, "Who (what) can change the situation?"
—*Atonement* inquires, "How?"
—*Justification* wonders, "When?"
—*Sanctification* addresses, "To what effect?"
—*Ecclesiology* questions, "In what context?"
—*Eschatology* points toward promised completion of the whole.

In other words, doctrines are conceptual grids which overlay the answers to life's fundamental questions, indicating the more formal relationship of obsessio and epiphania.

George Lindbeck is helpful in drawing the implications of such an approach. He insists that the content of creedal formulas, in turn, are not ends but guides for right information about the World they reflect. Consequently, doctrines function as "idioms for the constructing of reality and the living of life"—so much so that they shape and constitute experience. This means that "adherents of different religions do not diversely thematize the same experience; rather they have different experiences."[10] The dialogical nature of meaning is true not only of different religions. We are contending that there is a necessary and authentic pluralism within Christianity itself.

Christianity as Pluralistic

If it is true that there are as many theological Worlds as there are persons, it follows that Christianity is not only "one paradigm alongside other paradigms of the divine-human relationship," but that within Christianity itself there have been major "paradigm shifts in emphasis which, while distinctive and significant, do not constitute the creation of a new religion."[11] Rather, the pluralistic nature of truth applies both outside of and within the Christian disposition. In fact, Christianity is really a construct of overlaying configurations, loosely held together by witness to a common overlap as epiphania—the story called Jesus as the Christ. It cannot be otherwise, for at the most basic level of being human, we recognize that the way "we think about reality is internal to who we are, not external," at the same time that communally, "our visions of reality are incorporated into how we are, who we are, what we do."[12] We are who we are in terms of those with whom we make common confession. And when one can do so only with embarrassment to one's self, one is ripe for conversion.

Being a Christian means acknowledging the Christ Event as that root metaphor (logos) by which one's life is ordered as to seeing, and thus measured as for doing. Thus the question, Does God exist? is not really a question. *God* is functional symbol for the universally sought intersection of one's obsessio with epiphania. Understood functionally as a generic term, *God* is given a proper name by the Christian—that of Jesus Christ. What this means becomes clothed functionally as and within contrasting theological Worlds. Since how this epiphania functions depends upon the impulsing logic of one's obsessio, the resulting Worlds, while Christian, exhibit a diversity almost as broad as Christianity.[13] The five alternative rhythms that emerge for the Christian as pure types are held together by a common confession—that in Jesus, one beholds the face of God.

Whether people serve themselves or serve others is not in their power to choose. This is decided wholly in terms of the kind of world that they see ruling the roost. The issue lies at the level of the god they worship and not in the kind of person they might want to be. In New Testament terms, they live according to the king that holds them and the kingdom to which they belong.[14]

One never begins one's pilgrimage afresh. We "begin with a borrowed significance."[15] Thus there is never such a thing as a discrete and isolated theological World, which then seeks some form of interaction with others. From the beginning, each of us functions within intersecting "communities of discourse"—some recognized, most undetected —perhaps months before our birth. These act much like wedge-shaped pieces of pie, laying some claim to a portion of one's space-time. But it is our contention that at one's most functional level, there is a primal, centering rhythm. For each person, this manifests itself in some expression of overlapping community, which functions as either latent or manifest "church." Around this center, dimensions of other theological Worlds radiate as means to an end. Such community is where the impulsing logic that patterns one's World is rehearsed, supported, nurtured, and held accountable. Understood functionally, there is no "salvation" outside a "church."

Within the theological family called Christianity, a final question arises. Are the contrasting obsessios that characterize individual Worlds reducible in the end to one? Or at least, is there a composite human condition for which all five are ingredients in or variations on a primal theme? Or do these obsessios represent, to the end, an irreducible pluralism? While Christian theologians tend to write as if there were a singular obsessio, such descriptions serve as least common denominator only through abstraction. Either that, or the obsessio of a particular theologian is made universal. More illuminating is the approach of redaction criticism to Scripture. Our present biblical writings are the result of editing from contrasting resources, and as a result, Scripture is a composite of contrasting perspectives which reflect the theological Worlds through which various editors perceived an ordering whole. We cannot go beyond this phenomenon.

Protestantism had its originating impetus in the emergence of new denominations, each functioning monolithically as a sect. Had those denominations held together as "orders" within a universal church, they would have been powerful witnesses both to the human situation and to the nature of Christianity. But having failed in witnessing to the common center from which they emerged, and each failing now to preserve the foundation of their originating theological World, the crisis situation today is calling us toward a new understanding and structuring of the local congregation.

An Epilogue

We end with a celebration of dignity. There is something special in knowing that no one else is like me, that I live in a World uniquely my own. Yet it is terrifying if one cannot believe deeply in that World, and thus in one's self as product and fashioner. Yet even if one could, the search is not for isolated meaning. By our natures, we need others with whom to explore and validate that meaning as community, enhancing its fullness through sharing, being driven to conversion if necessary, being held accountable for deepening and broadening our commitment.

But even that is not enough. Surely one must learn to domesticate one's World by living passionately and fully within it. But in addition, one must become an intrigued neighbor with those whose Worlds acknowledge different drummers. For this creative interplay of pluralism and commitment, the church stands to become a unique instrument. Persons today are caught in a loneliness of self-centered individualism, tempted by an appetite for success to narrow their pilgrimages into rigid conformity. In such a society, where tolerance for authentic difference is slim and reward for acquiescence high, the church, rather than wavering on the edge of obsolescence, is touched with rare calling.

The details of such an ecclesiology as mission must wait another time. What is important here is to recognize the grounding for such a calling. The crisis in contemporary theology is leading to a phenomenology of theological Worlds. Christianity, in turn, must come to understand itself as a composite of such alternative rhythms. Thus, in becoming true to its nature, Christianity can make a graphic contribution to religion as the universal dance.

This book, in the end, is a simple one. Wallace Stevens

wrote a poem about it. Once upon a time he placed a jar upon a hill. This jar held the wilderness at bay, taming the edges that sprawled around it. That jar "took dominion everywhere." Even though gray and bare, there was nothing like it in all of Tennessee. Each of us has such a jar, on a hill, somewhere.

NOTES

CHAPTER ONE: Functional Theology and Theological Worlds

1. Paul Tillich, *The Courage to Be* (London: Nisbet & Co., 1952), pp. 30ff.

2. William F. Zuurdeeg, *Man Before Chaos* (Nashville: Abingdon Press, 1965), p. 10.

3. Peter Berger, *The Sacred Canopy* (Garden City, N. J.: Doubleday & Co., 1967), pp. 154, 3-21; Max Black, *Models and Metaphor* (New York: Cornell University Press, 1962); David Tracy, *The Analogical Imagination: Christian Theology and the Cultures of Pluralism* (New York: Crossroad Press, 1981).

4. Tillich, *Courage to Be*, pp. 169ff.

5. Gordon Kaufman, *The Theological Imagination: Constructing the Concept of God* (Philadelphia: Westminster Press, 1981), pp. 154-56.

6. Sallie McFague, "An Epilogue: The Christian Paradigm," *Christian Theology*, ed. Peter Hodgson and Robert King (Philadelphia: Fortress Press, 1982), p. 328.

7. H. Richard Niebuhr, *The Meaning of Revelation* (New York: Macmillan & Co., 1941), pp. 40-41.

8. Ibid., pp. 132-37.

9. Rubem Alves, *What Is Religion?* (Maryknoll: Orbis Books, 1984), p. 90.

10. Sheila Collins, *A Different Heaven and Earth* (Valley Forge: Judson Press, 1974), pp. 34-35.

11. Berger, *Sacred Canopy*, pp. 47-48, 163-64; see Peter Berger and Thomas Luckmann, *The Social Construction of Reality* (Garden City, N. J.: Doubleday & Co.), pp. 92ff.

12. Nikos Kazantzakis, *The Saviors of God* (New York: Simon & Schuster, 1960), p. 26, intro. by Kimon Friar.

13. Carol Christ, *Diving Deep and Surfacing* (Boston: Beacon Press, 1980), pp. 4-7, regarding Stephen Crites and Michael Novak.

14. Traditionally, Sisyphus, because of his misdeeds, was condemned to the endless rolling of a stone. Here I am using Camus's adaptation, *The Myth of Sisyphus* (New York: Vintage Press, 1959), pp. 88-91.

15. Steven Pepper, *World Hypotheses* (Berkeley: University of California Press, 1970), ch. 5; Herbert W. Richardson, *Toward An American Theology* (New York: Harper & Row, 1967), pp. 37-46; Thomas Kuhn, *The Structures of Scientific Revolutions* (Chicago: University of Chicago Press, 1970); cf. Ian Barbour, *Myths, Models, and Paradigms* (New York: Harper & Row, 1974), pp. 104-105.

16. John Steinbeck, *East of Eden* (New York: Viking Press, 1952), intro.

17. Northup Frye, *The Great Code* (New York: Harcourt, Brace, Jovanovich, 1982), p. xviii.

18. For an aesthetic equivalent, see "Siegfried Idyll," *Bruno Walter's Wagner*, Columbia Records M2L 343.

19. Neal F. Fisher, *Context for Discovery* (Nashville: Abingdon Press, 1981), pp. 73-74.

20. Piotr Hoffman, *The Human Self and the Life and Death Struggle* (Gainesville: University Presses of Florida, 1984).

21. Annie Dillard, *Pilgrim at Tinker Creek* (New York: Bantam Books, 1974), p. 71.

22. Annie Dillard, *Teaching a Stone to Talk* (New York: Harper & Brothers, 1982), p. 150.

23. See Dillard, *Pilgrim*, p. 209. I am making use of her basic idea, but in my own way.

24. T. S. Eliot, "Four Quartets," *The Complete Poems and Plays of T. S. Eliot* (New York: Harcourt, Brace, 1952), p. 136.

25. Nicholas Berdyaev, *Dream and Reality* (New York: Macmillan, 1951).

26. Thomas H. Groome, *Christian Religious Education* (San Francisco: Harper & Row, 1980), pp. 165-66, 184-206.

27. Geoffrey Wainwright, *Doxology* (Oxford: Oxford University Press, 1980).

28. Niebuhr, *Meaning of Revelation*, pp. 59-60.

29. Zuurdeeg, *Man Before Chaos*, p. 15.

30. Sören Kierkegaard, *Either/Or* (Princeton: Princeton University Press, 1944), Vol. II, pp. 133-50, 177-84.

31. Elijah Jordan, *Essays in Criticism* (Chicago: University of Chicago Press, 1952), p. 51, cf. pp. 75-77; James Joyce, *Portrait of the Artist as a Young Man* (New York: New American Library, 1954), p. 131; William Temple, *Nature, Man, and God* (New York: Macmillan & Co., 1949), pp. 153, 164.

32. Ernst Cassirer, *Language and Myth* (New York: Dover Publications, 1946), p. 37; cf. Mildred B. Bahan, "American Sociology and Related Disciplines," *Review of Metaphysics*, Vol. VI, 1952-53, pp. 145-46.

33. Temple, *Nature, Man, and God*, p. 153.

34. Rudolf Bultmann, *New Testament and Mythology* (Philadelphia: Fortress, 1984), p. 69.

CHAPTER TWO: *Anatomy of the Theological Question*

1. *Kansas City Times* (March 1, 1985).

2. Fyodor Dostoevsky, *The Brothers Karamazov* (Garden City, N. J.: Literary Guild of America, 1953), p. 127.

3. Albert Camus, *The Rebel* (New York: Alfred A. Knopf, 1956).

4. Archibald MacLeish, "The End of the World," *A Little Treasury of Modern Poetry*, ed. Oscar Williams (New York: Charles Scribner's Sons, 1952), p. 343.

5. Franz Kafka, *The Trial* (New York: Alfred A. Knopf, 1957); *The Castle* (1954).

6. W. Paul Jones, "The Burned of God: Portrait of the Postliberal Pastor," *Quarterly Review* (Summer 1985).

7. Ernest Becker, *The Denial of Death* (New York: The Free Press, 1973), p. 4.

8. Paul Tillich, *The Shaking of the Foundations* (New York: Charles Scribner's Sons, 1948), p. 155.

9. Richard Rubenstein, *After Auschwitz* (New York: Bobbs-Merrill, 1966), pp. 204, 135, 257, 154, 219.

10. T. S. Eliot, "The Four Quartets," *The Complete Poems and Plays of T. S. Eliot* (New York: Harcourt, Brace, 1952), pp. 123, 129, 145.

11. Herman Hesse, *Steppenwolf* (New York: Bantam Books, 1929), pp. 19, 38, 41.

12. Ibid., p. 73.

13. Thomas Wolfe, *Look Homeward Angel* (New York: Charles Scribner's Sons, 1929), p. 1.

14. Ibid., p. 518.

15. Ibid., pp. 519, 520.

16. Ibid., pp. 3, 518.

17. Nicholas Berdyaev, *The Meaning of the Creative Act* (New York: Collier Books, 1962), p. 216.

18. Robert Stevenson, quoted in R. D. Darrell, *Program Guide for Gregorian Chants*, VOX SVBX 5206, pp. 4-5.

19. Thomas A. Dorsey, "Precious Lord, Take My Hand," *Songs of Zion* (Nashville: Abingdon Press, 1981), no. 179.

20. Dietrich Bonhoeffer, *Letters and Papers from Prison: The Enlarged Edition* (New York: Macmillan, 1971), p. 157.

21. Miguez de Unamuno, *Abel Sanchez and Other Stories* (Chicago: Henry Regnery, 1956), p. xvii, quoted by Anthony Kerregan.

22. Dylan Thomas, "Do Not Go Gentle," *The Collected Poems of Dylan Thomas* (New York: New Directions, 1939), p. 128.

23. Dylan Thomas, "And Death Shall Have No Dominion," *A Little Treasury*, ed. Williams, p. 517.

24. Becker, *Denial of Death*, p. 5.

25. Ibid., p. 285.

26. Bonhoeffer, *Letters and Papers*, pp. 286, 336.

27. Jose Miguez-Bonino, *Toward a Christian Political Ethic* (Philadelphia: Fortress Press, 1983), p. 84.

28. Bonhoeffer, *Letters and Papers*, p. 146.

29. Reinhold Niebuhr, *The Nature and Destiny of Man* (New York: Charles Scribner's Sons, 1949).

30. Phaedo, *The Dialogues of Plato*, ed. B. Jowett (New York: Random House, 1937), Vol. I.

31. Dostoevsky, *Brothers*.

32. Arthur C. McGill, *Suffering: A Test of Theological Method* (Philadelphia: Westminster Press, 1982).

33. Beverly Harrison, *Making the Connections* (Boston: Beacon Press, 1985), p. 14.

34. Ibid., p. 19.

35. Edna St. Vincent Millay, "Conscientious Objector," *Collected Lyrics* (New York: Harper & Row, 1969), p. 216.

36. Eugene O'Neill, *The Great God Brown*, produced by Macgowan, Jones and O'Neill, The Greenwich Village Theatre, New York, January 23, 1926; see *Selected Plays of Eugene O'Neill* (New York: Random House, 1940), pp. 217-80.

37. T. S. Eliot, "The Hollow Men," "The Waste Land," *Complete Poems and Plays*, pp. 56, 39.

38. Ralph Ellison, *The Invisible Man* (New York: New American Library, 1947), p. 7.

39. Erik H. Erikson, *Childhood and Society* (New York: W. W. Norton, 1950), quoted in Carol Gilligan, *In a Different Voice* (Cambridge: Harvard University Press, 1982), p. 12.

40. Anders Nygren, *Agape and Eros* (Philadelphia: Westminster Press, 1953).

41. Peter Homans, *Theology After Freud* (Indianapolis: Bobbs-Merrill, 1970), pp. 162-63, 231.

42. Sam Keen, *Voices and Visions*, (New York: Harper & Row, 1974), pp. 21, 27.

43. Norman O. Brown, *Life Against Death* (Middletown, Conn.: Wesleyan University Press, 1959), esp. chap. xvi, pp. 307-22.

44. e. e. cummings, *Collected Poems* (New York: Harcourt, Brace, 1963), intro.

45. Leo Tolstoy, *The Death of Ivan Ilych and Other Stories* (New York: Signet, 1960), pp. 104, 119, 127, 134.

46. Ibid., pp. 146, 137.

47. Ibid., pp. 150, 152.

48. Ibid., p. 155.

49. James Joyce, *A Portrait of the Artist as a Young Man* (New York: New American Library, 1954), pp. 193, 197, 133.

50. Ibid.

51. Matthew Fox, *Breakthrough: Meister Eckhart's Creation Spirituality* (Garden City, N. J.: Doubleday & Co., 1980), intro.

52. Sam Keen, *To a Dancing God* (New York: Harper & Row, 1970), p. 144.

53. Charles N. Cochrane, *Christianity and Classical Culture* (Oxford: Oxford University Press, 1944), pp. 399ff.

54. Niebuhr, *Nature of Man*, Vol. 1, pp. 203-204.

55. John Milton, *Paradise Lost* (New York: Odyssey Press, 1935), bk. 9, lines 811-77.

56. Quoted in Daniel Maguire, *The Moral Choice* (Garden City, N. J.: Doubleday & Co., 1978), p. 402.

57. William Saroyan, *The Time of Your Life* (New York: Harcourt, Brace, 1939), intro.

58. Sören Kierkegaard, *Stages on Life's Way* (Princeton, N. J.: Princeton University Press, 1940).

59. Immanuel Kant, *Critique of Practical Reason* (New York: Liberal Arts Press, 1956), pp. 64ff.

60. Fyoder Dostoevsky, *Crime and Punishment* (New York: Dell Publishing Co., 1959), p. 445.

61. Albert Camus, *The Plague* (New York: Alfred A. Knopf, 1957), pp. 230-31

62. Eliot, "Waste Land," p. 50.

63. T. S. Eliot, "The Cocktail Party," *Complete Poems and Plays*, p. 362.

64. David Stendle-Rast, "Man of Prayer," *Thomas Merton, Monk*, ed. Patrick Hart (New York: Sheed & Ward, 1974), p. 81.

65. Karl Barth, *Prayer* (Philadelphia: Westminster Press, 1985), p. 75.

66. Dostoevksy, *Brothers*, p. 127.

67. Matthew Kelty, *Sermons in a Monastery* (Kalamazoo: Cistercian Publications, 1983), p. 92.

68. Niebuhr, *Nature of Man*, Vol. 1, p. 181.

69. Joseph Conrad, *The Heart of Darkness* (New York: W. W. Norton & Co., 1963), p. 61.

70. Bernanos, *Diary of a Country Priest* (New York: Image, 1954), pp. 112, 131, 38, 15, 76, 80, 48, 18, 149, 127, 129.

71. Ibid., pp. 126, 124, 85, 83, 226, 232.

72. Nathaniel Hawthorne, *Selected Tales and Sketches* (New York: Rhinehart, 1957), p. 299.

73. Ibid., p. 306.

74. Anita Marie Caspary, ed., *François Mauriac* (St. Louis: Herder Book Co., n.d.), pp. 91, 93.

75. François Mauriac, *The Desert of Love* (New York: Bantam Books, 1951), p. 182.

76. William Faulkner, *The Sound and the Fury* (New York: Modern Library, 1946), pp. 313, 122, 313.

77. William Faulkner, *Light in August* (New York: Modern Library, 1950), p. 221.

78. Irving Howe, *William Faulkner: A Critical Study* (New York: Vintage Press, 1962).

79. Faulkner, *Light in August*, p. 407.

80. H. Richard Niebuhr, *The Kingdom of God in America* (Chicago: Willett, Clark & Co., 1937).

81. Gustavo Gutierrez, *A Theology of Liberation* (Maryknoll: Orbis Books, 1971), pp. 287-302.

82. Edward S. Curtis, *In a Sacred Manner We Live* (New York: Weathervane, 1972).

83. Bonhoeffer, *Letters and Papers*, p. 282.

84. Rubenstein, *After Auschwitz*, pp. 257, 264.

85. Reinhold Niebuhr, "Must We Do Nothing?" *The Christian Century* (March 30, 1932), pp. 415-17.

86. Niebuhr, *Nature of Man*, Vol. 2, pp. 88, 97, 302, 308, 114.

87. Ibid., pp. 320, 321.

88. Elie Wiesel, *Night* (New York: Avon Books, 1969), p. 104.

89. Elie Wiesel, *A Jew Today* (New York: Random House, 1978), p. 163.

90. Elie Wiesel, *Ani Maamin: A Song Lost and Found Again* (New York: Random House, 1973), p. 105.

91. Ibid., p. 187.

92. Elie Wiesel, *The Accident* (New York: Avon Books, 1961), p. 96.

93. Wiesel, *Ani Maamin*, p. 87.

94. See Heyward Carter, *The Redemption of God* (Washington, D. C.: University Press of America, 1982). I am indebted to Heyward for insights into Elie Wiesel.

95 Elie Wiesel, *The Town Beyond the Wall* (New York: Avon Books, 1964), p. 123.

96. Camus, *Plague*, p. 277.

97. Sören Kierkegaard, *Purity of Heart* (New York: Harper & Brothers, 1948).

98. Hart Crane, *The Collected Poems of Hart Crane* (New York: Liveright Publishing, 1946), p. viii.

99. Tennessee Williams, *Camino Real* (New York: New Directions, 1953), p. viii.

100. Ibid., pp. 45, 55, 68.

101. Ibid., pp. 111, 115, 132, 73, 111, 96, 72.

102. Ibid., pp. 133, 156, 159.

103. Archibald MacLeish, *"Immortal Autumn," Collected Poems, 1917–1952* (Boston: Houghton Mifflin Co., 1953), p. 53.

104. Samuel Beckett, *Waiting for Godot* (New York: Grove Press, 1954), p. 22.

105. Donald Evans, *Religious Studies Review* (January 1979), p. 25.

CHAPTER THREE: *Anatomy of the Theological Answer*

1. Thomas Merton, *New Seeds of Contemplation* (New York: New Directions, 1972), p. 3.

2. Rufus Jones, *The Double Search* (Richmond: Friendship Press, 1906), p. 10.

3. Thomas R. Kelly, *A Testament of Devotion* (New York: Harper & Row, 1941), pp. 96, 111.

4. Friedrich Schleiermacher, *The Christian Faith* (Edinburgh: T. & T. Clark, 1928), pp. 131-41.

5. Robert Jastrow, *God and the Astronomers* (New York: W. W. Norton & Co., 1978), pp. 11-22.

6. Nikos Kazantzakis, *Odyssey: A Modern Sequel* (New York: Simon & Schuster, 1969), bk. 19, pp. 257-59.

7. *The Collected Works of St. Teresa of Avila* (Washington, D. C.: Institute of Carmelite Studies, 1976).

8. The quotations in this paragraph and in the two following paragraphs are taken from a typical collection of Merton writings to illustrate how apparent this thread is, even under severe abridgement. Thomas Merton, *The True Solitude* (Kansas City: Hallmark, 1969), pp. 19, 30, 27.

9. Ibid., pp. 54, 11, 22, 32.

10. Merton, *New Seeds of Contemplation*, pp. 33-34.

11. Merton, *The New Man* (New York: Farrar, Straus & Giroux, 1961), pp. 117-18.

12. Merton, *Zen and the Birds of Appetite* (New York: New Directions, 1968), pp. 23-24.

13. James Finley, *Merton's Palace of Nowhere* (Notre Dame: Ave Maria Press, 1978), p. 91.

14. Carol P. Christ, *Diving Deep and Surfacing* (Boston: Beacon Press, 1980), p. 10.

15. Annie Dillard, *Pilgrim at Tinker Creek* (New York: Bantam Books, 1974), p. 279.

16. August Strindberg, *Six Plays of Strindberg*, trans. Elizabeth Sprigge (Garden City, N. J.: Doubleday, 1955), p. 303.

17. Ibid., p. 304.

18. Ibid.

19. Eugene O'Neill, *Long Day's Journey into Night* (New Haven: Yale University Press, 1956), pp. 153-54.

20. Ibid.

21. James Joyce, *Ulysses* (New York: Modern Library, 1914), p. 768.

22. Hart Crane, "White Buildings," *The Collected Poems of Hart Crane* (New York: Liveright Publishing, 1946), p. 61.

23. Crane, *Collected Poems*, intro., p. x.

24. Crane, "White Buildings," p. 61.

25. Ibid., pp. 102, xvii, 108.

26. Hart Crane, "The Bridge," *Collected Poems*, p. 39.

27. Ibid., p. 58.

28. Deryck Cooke, "Notes," Gustav Mahler's Symphony No. 2 in C-Minor, "Resurrection," London Records CSA2217.

29. Paul Tillich, *Systematic Theology* (Chicago: University of Chicago Press, 1957), Vol. II, pp. 29ff.

30. *Augustine: Confessions and Enchiridion*, trans. Albert C. Outler (Philadelphia: Westminster Press, 1955), bk. 1, ch. 1, p. 31.

31. Paul Tillich, *The Courage to Be* (London: Nisbet & Co.), pp. 60ff., 110ff.

32. Paul Tillich, *The Protestant Era* (Chicago: University of Chicago Press, 1948), pp. 206ff.

33. Tillich, *Systematic Theology* (1951), Vol. I, pp. 235ff.

34. Tillich, *Protestant Era*, pp. 44ff., 55ff.

35. Tillich, *Systematic Theology*, Vol. II, pp. 102, 115-18.

36. Ernst Bloch, *Atheism in Christianity* (New York: Herder & Herder, 1972), p. 271.

37. Nicholas Berdyaev, *Dream and Reality* (New York: Macmillan, 1951), pp. 1, 9, 45.

38. T. H. Huxley, *Selections from the Essays of T. H. Huxley* (New York: Appleton-Century-Crofts, 1948), p. 109.

39. Herbert Butterfield, *Christianity and History* (London: G. Bell & Sons, 1950), p. 95.

40. Austin Farrer, *Finite and Infinite* (Glasgow: Dacre Press, 1943), p. 300.

41. This is climaxed for Berdyaev in his *The Beginning and the End*, published posthumously (New York: Harper Torchbooks, 1952), esp. ch. 9.

42. Karl Barth, *Epistle to the Romans* (London: Oxford University Press, 1933), pp. 38-39, 60.

43. G. Ernest Wright, *God Who Acts* (London: SCM Press, 1952).

44. Stanley Haverwas and William H. Willimon, "Embarrassed by God's Presence," *Christian Century* (January 30, 1985), p. 100.

45. Martin Marty and Dean Peerman, eds., *New Theology No. 6* (New York: Macmillan, 1969), pp. 131-34.

46. Arthur Cohen, *The Natural and the Supernatural Jew* (New York: Pantheon Press, 1963), p. 298.

47. Teilhard de Chardin, *The Future of Man* (New York: Harper & Row, 1964), pp. 11-12.

48. Teilhard de Chardin, "The Divinization of the Possible," *The Divine Milieu* (New York: Harper & Brothers, 1960), pp. 65-66, et passim.

49. Dietrich Bonhoeffer, *Letters and Papers from Prison: Enlarged Edition* (New York: Macmillan, 1971), p. 170.

50. "NCBC Statement on Black Theology," 1976, quoted in Allan Boesak, *Farewell to Innocence* (Maryknoll: Orbis Books, 1977), p. 45.

51. Ibid., p. 13.

52. Rosemary Radford Ruether, *To Change the World* (New York: Crossroad Press, 1983), p. 49.

53. Nikos Kazantzakis, *The Saviors of God* (New York: Simon & Schuster, 1960), pp. 130-31.

54. John Steinbeck, *The Grapes of Wrath* (New York: Modern Library, 1939), pp. 477, 592, 521, 577, 383, 523, 570.

55. Ignazio Silone, *A Handful of Blackberries* (New York: Harper & Brothers, 1953), p. 75.

56. Ibid., p. 311.

57. William Fleming, *Acts and Ideas* (New York: Holt, Rinehart & Winston, 1963), p. 624.

58. Rosino Gibelli, ed., *Frontiers of Theology in Latin America* (Maryknoll: Orbis Books, 1979), p. 301.

59. T. S. Eliot, "The Love Song of J. Alfred Prufrock," *The Complete Poems and Plays of T. S. Eliot* (New York: Harcourt, Brace & Co., 1952), pp. 5-7.

60. Adolf Harnack, *What is Christianity?* (New York: Harper Torchbooks, 1957), pp. 63-69.

61. Carl R. Rogers, *Client-centered Therapy* (Boston: Houghton Mifflin, 1965), pp., 34, 40.

62. Horace Bushnell, *Christian Nurture* (New Haven: Yale University Press, 1988), pp. 3-4.

63. Robert Graves, *The White Goddess* (New York: Farrar, Straus, Giroux, 1948), p. 481.

64. See particularly James Fowler and Sam Keen, *Life Maps: Conversations on the Journey of Faith* (Waco: Word Books, 1978); Sam Keen, *Beginnings Without End* (New York: Harper & Row, 1975).

65. Rudolf Bultmann, *Essays: Philosophical and Theological* (New York: Macmillan, 1955), p. 85 et passim; *Theology of the New Testament* (New York: Charles Scribner's Sons, 1951), pp. 330-31.

66. Daniel Day Williams, *The Spirit and the Forms of Love* (New York: Harper & Row, 1968), pp. 146ff.

67. Williams, *Spirit and Forms of Love*, ch. 7; Marjorie Hewitt Suchocki, *God-Christ-Church* (New York: Crossroad Press, 1982), pp. 58, 101, 107, 121, 133.

68. John B. Cobb, *A Christian Natural Theology* (Philadelphia: Westminster Press, 1965), esp. ch. 7.

69. Charles Hartshorne, *The Divine Relativity* (New Haven: Yale University Press, 1948), e.g., pp. vii-xvi.

70. Paul A. Schilpp, ed., *The Philosophy of Alfred North Whitehead* (New York: Tudor, 1951), "Immortality," sec. 14, p. 694.

71. Eugene Peters, *The Creative Advance* (St. Louis: Bethany Press, 1966), p. 117.

72. Christopher Marlowe, *Doctor Faustus* (New York: Appleton-Century-Crofts, 1950), pp. 4, 15, 19, 12.

73. Martin Luther, "The Fourteen Consolations," *Works*, Vol. 1, p. 148.

74. Francis Thompson, "The Hound of Heaven," *A Little Treasury of Modern Poetry*, ed. Oscar Williams (New York: Charles Scribner's Sons, 1952), pp. 598-603.

75. H. Richard Niebuhr, *Christ and Culture* (New York: Harper & Brothers, 1951), pp. 149-89.

76. H. Richard Niebuhr, "The Center of Value," *Radical Monotheism and Western Culture* (New York: Harper & Brothers, 1943), pp. 100-113.

77. Joachim Jeremias, *The Prayers of Jesus* (Philadelphia: Fortress Press, 1967), pp. 57, 63.

78. Summarized by Niebuhr, *Christ and Culture*, p. 157.

79. Barth, *Epistle to the Romans*, e.g., pp. 273, 275.

80. Ibid., pp. 380-81, 142, 347, 144.

81. Ibid., p. 110.

82. *The Heidelberg Catechism* (Philadelphia: Reformed Church Publication Board, n.d.), p. 4.

83. Georges Bernanos, *The Diary of a Country Priest* (Garden City, N. J.: Image, 1954), pp. 182-83.

84. Fyodor Dostoevsky, *The Brothers Karamazov* (Garden City, N. J.: Literary Guild, 1953), pp. 370, 384.

85. Ibid., p. 387.

86. Ibid., p. 436.

87. Ibid., pp. 676, 937-40.

88. John Wesley, "Watch Night Service," *The Book of Worship for Church and Home* (Nashville: United Methodist Publishing House, 1965), p. 387.

89. William Faulkner, *The Faulkner Reader* (New York: Modern Library, 1959), speech delivered in Stockholm, December 10, 1950.

90. Bonhoeffer, *Letters and Papers*, p. 10.

91. "Showbill," Chelsea Playhouse production, pp. 28-29.

92. Ibid.

93. Samuel Beckett, *Waiting for Godot* (New York: Grove Press, 1954), p. 35.

94. John Phillips, *Eve: The History of an Idea* (New York: Harper & Row, 1984), ch. "Redemption."

95. James W. Fowler, *Stages of Faith* (San Francisco: Harper & Row, 1981), p. 198

96. Albert Camus, *The Myth of Sisyphus* (New York: Vintage Press, 1959), p. 91.

97. Joseph Krutch, *The Best Nature Writings of Joseph Wood Krutch* (New York: William Morrow & Co., 1969), p. 41, quoted in Jerald H. Jackson, "Wilderness and Pastoral Care," *Circuit Rider* (May 1985), p. 7.

98. Jackson, "Wilderness and Pastoral Care," p. 7.

99. J.R.R. Tolkien, *The Return of the King* (Boston: Houghton Mifflin Co., 1965), pp. 38-39.

100. Josiah Royce, *Sources of Religious Insight* (New York: Charles Scribner & Sons, 1912), pp. 166ff; Royce, *Philosophy of Loyalty* (New York: MacMillan, 1916), pp. 99ff.

101. David Knight, "Desert Spirituality: An Answer to Massah and Merbah," *Studies in Formative Spirituality* (May 1980), p. 189.

102. William Faulkner, *The Sound and the Fury* (New York: Modern Library, 1946), p. 22.

103. Ibid., pp. 310, 313.

104. Ibid., p. 105.

105. Bernanos, *Diary of a Country Priest*, pp. 48, 155, 148.

106. Ibid., pp. 212, 218.

107. Bonhoeffer, *Letters and Papers*, p. 22.

108. Bernanos, *Diary of a Country Priest*, pp. 223-24.

109. Ibid., p. 225.

110. Bonhoeffer, *Letters and Papers*, pp. 361, 360.

111. Ibid., pp. 369-70.

112. Leonard Bernstein, *Mass*, piano-vocal score (New York: G. Schermer, 1971); Columbia Records M2-31008.

113. R.D.C. Jasper and G. J. Cuming, eds., *Prayers of the Eucharist* (New York: Oxford University Press, 1980), p. 49.

114. Sören Kierkegaard, *Concluding Unscientific Postscript* (Princeton, N. J.: Princeton University Press, 1941), pp. 523, 527.

115. Sören Kierkegaard, *Stages Along Life's Way* (Princeton, N. J.: Princeton University Press, 1940).

116. Sören Kierkegaard, *Either/Or* (Princeton, N. J.: Princeton University Press, 1944), Vol. I, pp. 15-31.

117. Ibid., Vol. II, pp. 133ff.

118. Kierkegaard, *Concluding Unscientific Postscript*, pp. 350-65.

119. Ibid., p. 387.

120. Sören Kierkegaard, *The Journals of Sören Kierkegaard* (Oxford: Oxford University Press, 1938), pp. 173-74.

121. Ibid., p. 367.

122. Kierkegaard, *Concluding Unscientific Postscript*, p. 182.

123. Sören Kierkegaard, *Philosophical Fragments* (Princeton, N. J.: Princeton University Press, 1936), p. 31.

124. Sören Kierkegaard, *The Concept of Dread* (Princeton, N. J.: Princeton University Press, 1944), pp. 174, 197.

125. Sören Kierkegaard, *Training in Christianity* (Princeton, N. J.: Princeton University Press, 1944), p. 232.

126. Ibid., p. 218.

127. Sören Kierkegaard, *Fear and Trembling* (Princeton, N. J.: Princeton University Press, 1941), pp. 54-55.

128. Ibid., pp. 55-56.

129. Kierkegaard, *Journals*, p. 367.

CHAPTER FOUR: Anatomy of the Theological Dialectic

1. F. J. Taylor, *Theological Word Book of the Bible* (New York: Macmillan, 1960), "Save."

2. See Allan Richardson, ed., *Theological Word Book of the Bible* (London: SCM Press, 1950), p. 220.

3. Basil Moore, ed., *The Challenge of Black Theology in Africa* (Atlanta: John Knox Press, 1973), p. 53.

4. Jose Arguello, "Cardenal's Theo-Poetry," *Christianity and Crisis* (April 15, 1985), p. 143.

5. Cf. Dorothy Sayers, *The Mind of the Maker* (New York: Meridian Books, 1956).

6. See Henry Mitchell, *Black Belief: Folk Beliefs of Blacks in America and West Africa* (New York: Harper & Row, 1975), p. 9, et passim.

7. Karl Barth, *Dogmatics in Outline* (London: SCM Press, 1949), p. 69.

8. Arguello, "Cardenal's Theo-Poetry," p. 142.

9. Michael Swanton, ed., *The Dream of the Rood* (New York: Barnes & Noble, 1970), p. 71.

10. Gustaf Aulen, *Christus Victor* (New York: Macmillan, 1951), p. 159.

11. J.A.T. Robinson, *The Human Face of God* (Philadelphia: Westminster Press, 1973), p. 243.

12. Ogden, *Christ Without Myth* (New York: Harper & Row, 1961), pp. 111-26.

13. Whatever its historical accuracy, this is the evocative power of the motion picture *Brother Sun, Sister Moon.*

14. Irenaeus, *Heresies: 5,* preface.

15. Quoted in Aulen, *Christus Victor,* p. 18.

16. D. D. Williams, *The Spirit and the Forms of Love* (New York: Harper & Brothers, 1968), pp. 160-72.

17. Robinson, *Human Face of God,* pp. 241, 242, 241.

18. Marjorie Suchocki, *God-Christ-Church* (New York: Crossroad Press, 1982), p. 101.

19. Louis Evely, *The Church and the Sacraments* (Denville, N. J.: Dimension Books, 1971), p. 39.

20. John Wesley, "Watch Night Service," *The Book of Worship for Church and Home* (Nashville: United Methodist Publishing House, 1965), p. 387.

21. *The Sacramentary* (New York: Catholic Book Publishing Co., 1974), p. 1011.

22. Paul Tillich, *Systematic Theology* (Chicago: University of Chicago Press, 1957), Vol. II, p. 176.

23. Roy Sano, "Bright Rainbows and Dark Clouds," *Occasional Papers* (United Methodist Board of Higher Education and Ministry, September 1, 1982), p. 6.

24. C. S. Song, *Third Eye Theology* (Maryknoll: Orbis Books, 1979), p. 67.

25. James Fowler, *Stages of Faith* (San Francisco: Harper & Row, 1981), p. 202.

26. Nicholas Berdyaev, *Destiny of Man* (London: Geoffrey Bles, 1948), pp. 118, 30.

27. R.D.C. Jasper and G. J. Cuming, eds., *Prayers of the Eucharist* (New York: Oxford University Press, 1980), pp. 22-25.

28. Georges Bernanos, *Diary of a Country Priest* (New York: Image Press, 1954), p. 227.

29. Ibid., p. 228.

30. Nathanael West, *Miss Lonelyhearts* (New York: Avon Books, 1955), pp. 7, 6.

31. Ibid., pp. 12, 14.

32. Ibid., p. 33.

33. Ibid., p. 16.

34. Ibid., p. 19.

35. Ibid., p. 100.

36. Ibid., pp. 69, 26.

37. Ibid., p. 14.

38. Ibid., p. 94.

39. Dietrich Bonhoeffer, *Letters and Papers from Prison: Enlarged Edition* (New York: Macmillan, 1971), p. 140.

40. Jurgen Moltmann, *The Crucified God* (New York: Harper & Row, 1974), p. 276.

41. Ibid., p. 277.

42. Arthur Janov, *The Primal Scream* (New York: Putnam Publishing Group, 1981).

43. Guenter Ruterborn, *The Sign of Jonah* (New York: Thomas Nelson & Sons, 1960), p. 22; see also pp. 27-28.

44. Ibid., p. 33.

45. Ibid., pp. 67, 71.

46. Ibid., p. 78.

47. Ibid., p. 90.

48. Ibid., pp. 78-80.

CHAPTER FIVE: A Conclusion

1. See also Paul M. Van Buren, *The Secular Meaning of the Gospel* (New York: Macmillan, 1963), pp. 198-200; R. B. Braithwaite, *An Empiricist's View of the Nature of Religious Belief* (Cambridge: Cambridge University Press, 1955).

2. Sam Keen, *To a Dancing God* (New York: Harper & Row, 1970), p. 122.

3. Annie Dillard, *Pilgrim at Tinker Creek* (New York: Bantam Books, 1974), p. 19.

4. Dorothee Soelle, *Political Theology* (Philadelphia: Fortress Press, 1974), p. 77.

5. Randall Collins and Michael Makowski, *The Discovery of Society* (New York: Random House, 1972), p. 125.

6. David Kelsey, *The Uses of Scripture in Recent Theology* (Philadelphia: Fortress Press, 1974), p. 9.

7. Michael Novak, *Ascent of the Mountain, Flight of the Dove* (New York: Harper & Row, 1971), p. 52.

8. Alasdair MacIntyre, *After Virtue* (Notre Dame: University of Notre Dame Press, 1981), p. 203.

9. Julian Hartt, *Theological Method and Imagination* (New York: Seabury Press, 1977), pp., 13, 75.

10. George Lindbeck, *The Nature of Doctrine* (Philadelphia: Westminster Press, 1984), p. 40.

11. Sallie McFague, "An Epilogue: The Christian Paradigm," *Christian Theology*, ed. Peter Hodgson and Robert King (Philadelphia: Fortress Press, 1982), p. 326.

12. Marjorie Suchocki, *God-Christ-Church* (New York: Crossroad Press, 1982), p. 120.

13. Gordon Kaufman, *An Essay on Theological Method* (Missoula: Scholars Press, 1975), p. 59.

14. Arthur McGill, *Suffering* (Philadelphia: Geneva, 1968), p. 120.

15. Suchocki, *God-Christ-Church*, p. 6.

the life of wanting to be
loved; to be included; to
belong.

By saying 'no' what then
is my 'yes'?